Reprint

The Proverb

An Index to "The Proverb"

An Introductory Bibliography for the Study of Proverbs

Archer Taylor

Fathom Publishing Company

The Proverb was first published by Harvard University Press, Cambridge,
Mass., U.S.A., 1931.

An Index to "The Proverb" was first published by FF Communications,
No. 113, Helsinki, 1934.

An Introductory Bibliography for the Study of Proverbs was first published
in Modern Philology, Vol. XXX, No. 2, November, 1932.

ISBN: 978-1-888215-71-7
Library of Congress Control Number: 2017906523

Fathom Publishing Company
PO Box 200448
Anchorage, AK 99520-0448
www.fathompublishing.com
www.archertaylor.com

Archer Taylor

Archer Taylor (center) on an Atlantic cattle boat during a summer trip to Europe during his Swarthmore years.

Archer Taylor (left) with a friend and his sisters.

Introduction to Taylor Reprints

Archer Taylor was born August 1, 1890 and died September 30, 1973. He was called Archer because the family had difficulty agreeing on a name, and his uncle began calling him Sagittarius, symbolized in Greek mythology by the archer—half-man, half-horse in the ninth astrological sign.

Taylor wrote many books and a vast number of articles, some extended studies of the subject at hand and others short notes or queries. He grew up in a world in which academic-minded students learned Latin and Greek in grammar school, and he learned. In the years that followed, he continued to learn. Ultimately he read and spoke thirteen languages, with varying degrees of proficiency to be sure. In high school and early college years at Swarthmore, he worked on a cattle boat to Europe at the start of the summer. Once there, he traveled to the various countries in Europe learning the languages and meeting the people before returning to port to sign on a boat for the trip home. These experiences left him with a love of language and languages (and a life-long dislike for marmalade, pumpernickel and salt pork, the only foods for the crew on the voyage once the fresh things had been eaten). These experiences ended with World War I when he was caught in Europe at the start of the war and had to make his way home. His family sought news of his location and condition in the flyer shown on the next page.

After finishing Swarthmore in three years, Taylor taught and studied, earning his M.A. at the University of Pennsylvania and his PhD at Harvard and publishing his dissertation on the Wolfdietrich epics in 1915. He taught at Washington University in St. Louis starting in 1915, moving to the University of Chicago for the years

Mr. ARCHER TAYLOR, born August 1st, 1890, West Chester, Pennsylvania, U. S. of America, Father, American born Citizen, Lowndes Taylor, West Chester, Pennsylvania.

Instructor and Assistant Professor for two years at "State College" Pennsylvania.

Specialty, German Language and literature.

He went to Europe in June 1914, to persue special studies toward his Ph. D degree.

He was last heard from by postal mailed Wilhemlshohe, (Bz. Cassel) Germany.

In that postal he announced his intention to go at once to Gottingen.

He gave his address as "Archer Taylor, Dresden, Poste Restante. Germany.

But he has acknowledged no mail so addressed to him.

He has visited Germany several times on summer tours, and is somewhat familiar with the people and their language.

He speaks also a little French.

He is a graduate of Swarthmore College, a Quaker Institution, and also of the University of Pennsylvania.

He was studying at Harvard University for his Doctor's Degree, and went to Germany sssisted by Swarthmore College.

He had sufficient Credits for ordinary purposes and usual expenses in times of peace.

Please assist him in any way possible, also give any information of him to the German Police, and inform the local American Representatives, (Consul &c.)

Also kindly send information pegarding him to his uncle, Ervine D. York, Flushing, New York.

Or to his father,

Lowndes Taylor, West Chester, Pennsylvania,
U. S. of America.

1925 into 1939. He ended his teaching career at the University of California, Berkeley, where he served from 1939 to 1958 and was chairman of the Department of German from 1940 to 1945. Taylor published *The Proverb* in 1931, followed by *Index to the Proverb* in 1934. His *Bibliography of Riddles* was published in 1939, and a number of other riddle books followed. Archer Taylor and Bartlett Jere Whiting published *A Dictionary of American Proverbs and Proverbial Phrases, 1820-1880* (Cambridge, Massachusetts: Harvard University Press 1958). Although much of his writing concerned folklore, he also wrote *A History of Bibliographies of Bibliographies* in 1955 and *General Subject-Indexes Since 1548* was published in 1966. Other books and an extraordinary number of articles flowed from his ongoing research, and these were the years before computers and word processing. My sister and I remember alphabetizing yellow 2x3 slips he prepared, one for each proverb or riddle.

Taylor married Alice Jones in 1915, and she bore him three children, Margaret, Richard and Cynthia. Alice sadly died early in 1930, and he married Hasseltine Byrd in 1932 and fathered two more children, Mary Constance and Ann.

A collateral benefit of his teaching position at the University of California was that Taylor could send his professional mail through the University. He carried on a prodigious correspondence with individuals and journals of similar interests around the world. When these individuals came to California, they often stopped to visit and to discuss their scholarship. Former students became close friends, illustrated by the friendship between Wayland Hand and Taylor that lasted the rest of Taylor's life. Many of Taylor's letters are collected at universities and some of the collections are available online.

His large library is now with the University of Georgia in Athens, except his ballad collection which is with the University of California, Berkeley. In addition to collecting books himself, Taylor watched for books and collections that he knew were sought by universities around the world. He might buy and send the desired books or notify the university so it could buy them. He was honored after World War II for his extended efforts to rebuild the university library in Dresden.

Wolfgang Meider published one of the reprints of *The Proverb* and posted a Biographical Sketch that included the following:

> In 1960 Archer Taylor was rightfully and deservedly honored by a most impressive "Festschrift" which his two friends Wayland D. Hand and Gustave O. Arlt edited with the befitting title *Humaniora, Essays in Literature, Folklore, Bibliography, Honoring Archer Taylor on His Seventieth Birthday* (Locust Valley/New York 1960). The subtitle summarizes Taylor's three major areas of expertise and such internationally renowned contributors as Bartlett Jere Whiting, L. L. Hammerich, Dag Strömbeck, Stith Thompson, Walter Anderson, Taylor Starck, Kurt Ranke, Lutz Röhrich, Matti Kuusi, Georgios A. Megas, Robert Wildhaber, Francis Lee Utley, Anna Brigitta Rooth, Will-Erich Peuckert, Wolfram Eberhard, Julian Krzyzanowski, etc. acknowledge Taylor's worldwide influence.

Influenced by Wayland Hand, the Western States Folklore Society (formerly California Folklore Society) holds annual meetings to encourage professional and amateur folklorists to meet each other, present papers, and engage in discussions of all aspects of folklore and folklife. Since Taylor's 1973 death, the annual meeting has included the Archer Taylor Memorial Lecture. These lectures often reappear as scholarly articles, something that would have pleased Taylor.

Archer Taylor lived and died with friends around the world. He never passed up opportunities to explain and teach—the difference between anecdote and antidote, for example, when a teenage daughter got it wrong. He generously shared his knowledge and curiosity with all.

Ann Taylor Schwing

February 2018

Table of Contents

Note on page numbering:
Page numbers at the top of pages are from the original printing. Numbers centered at the bottom of this reprint apply to this publication only. These numbers are used in the Table of Contents.

THE PROVERB

LONDON : HUMPHREY MILFORD
OXFORD UNIVERSITY PRESS

THE PROVERB

BY

ARCHER TAYLOR

HARVARD·UNIVERSITY·PRESS

CAMBRIDGE·MASSACHUSETTS

1931

PRINTED AT THE HARVARD UNIVERSITY PRESS

CAMBRIDGE, MASS., U. S. A.

To

MY MOTHER

PREFACE

THE proverb and related forms have long been objects of general interest and the occasion for many books, but they have attracted little serious and thorough study. As a result, fundamental problems are neglected and even their existence is not clearly realized. After all, we know little or nothing of the origin, dissemination, and literary style of proverbs. Books give us curious and often unreliable information on these matters, although rarely systematically or in such a fashion as to permit or encourage the reader to look farther. Proverbs attract people interested in the didactic or in the quaint and strange, and neither group is noted for thoroughness or accuracy. To be sure, diligent scholars have spent lifetimes of labor in making storehouses of materials for the use of future generations, but as yet this wealth has profited us little. Its utilization requires constant attention to detail and a clear perception of aims and methods.

In the following pages I have endeavored to describe briefly and systematically the ways in which proverbs arise, the kinds of proverbs, and the details of proverbial style. It has seemed inadvisable to seek examples outside the ordinary European languages, where we have a fairly distinct cultural tradition and clearly marked proverbial types. What is true of the English proverb is, in the main, true of the German or the French proverb. Oriental, African, Malay,

Japanese, or Chinese proverbs involve such widely differing cultural spheres and have in general so little connection with European proverbs that I have not hesitated to leave them out.

For the scholar's convenience I have compiled an index of the English, German, and Latin proverbs cited, and in it I have given what seemed to me the most useful references from works on the comparative study of proverbs. So far as possible, I have listed all proverbs under English forms with cross-references from German and Latin. For proverbs from other languages, when no parallel English, German, or Latin form appears in this book, I give sources and references in foot-notes. Proverbs which do not appear in the index and which are not supported by a reference are cited from oral tradition. I have profited by the opportunity offered by the index to cite additional proverbs and the literature on them. Such additional proverbs set interesting and important problems for future study, problems which I have discussed at sufficient length and which do not call for further illustration. This index will appear in *FF Communications* (Helsinki).

Suggestions and encouragement from Margaret Hardie and Richard Jente, who read this book in manuscript, have added to its usefulness and value. The scholarship of my teacher, George Lyman Kittredge, has enriched this book as it has enriched and enlarged my life and ideals.

CHICAGO, June 8, 1931.

CONTENTS

THE PROVERB

I

THE ORIGINS OF THE PROVERB

THE definition of a proverb is too difficult to repay the undertaking; and should we fortunately combine in a single definition all the essential elements and give each the proper emphasis, we should not even then have a touchstone. An incommunicable quality tells us this sentence is proverbial and that one is not. Hence no definition will enable us to identify positively a sentence as proverbial. Those who do not speak a language can never recognize all its proverbs, and similarly much that is truly proverbial escapes us in Elizabethan and older English. Let us be content with recognizing that a proverb is a saying current among the folk. At least so much of a definition is indisputable, and we shall see and weigh the significance of other elements later.

The origins of the proverb have been little studied. We can only rarely see a proverb actually in the making, and any beliefs we have regarding origins must justify themselves as evident or at least plausible. Proverbs are invented in several ways: some are simple apothegms and platitudes elevated to proverbial dignity, others arise from the symbolic or metaphoric use of an incident, still others imitate already existing proverbs, and some owe their existence to the condensing of a story or fable. It is convenient to distinguish as "learned" proverbs those with a long literary history. This literary history may begin in some apt Biblical or classical phrase, or it may go back to a more recent source. Such "learned" proverbs differ, however, in only this regard from other proverbs. Whatever the later history may be, the manner of ultimate invention of all proverbs, "learned" or "popular," falls under one or another of the preceding heads.

It is not proper to make any distinction in the treatment of "learned" and "popular" proverbs. The same problems exist for all proverbs with the obvious limitation that, in certain cases, historical studies are greatly restricted by the accidents of preservation. We can ordinarily trace the "learned" proverb down a long line of literary tradition, from the classics or the Bible through the Middle Ages to the present, while we may not be so fortunate with every "popular" proverb. For example, *Know thyself* may very well have been a proverb long before it was attributed to any of the seven wise men or was inscribed on the walls of the temple of Delphic Apollo. Juvenal was nearer the truth when he said it came from Heaven: "E caelo descendit γνῶθι σεαυτόν" (*Sat.*, xi, 27). Yet so far as modern life is concerned, the phrase owes its vitality to centuries of bookish tradition. St. Jerome termed *Don't look a gift horse in the mouth* a common proverb, when he used it to refer to certain writings which he had regarded as free-will offerings and which critics had found fault with: "Noli (ut vulgare est proverbium) equi dentes inspicere donati." We cannot hope to discover whether the modern proverb owes its vitality to St. Jerome or to the vernacular tradition on which he was drawing. St. Jerome also took *The wearer best knows where the shoe wrings him* from Plutarch, but we may conjecture that this proverb, too, was first current on the lips of the folk. Obviously the distinction between "learned" and "popular" is meaningless and is concerned merely with the accidents of history.

PROVERBIAL APOTHEGMS

Often some simple apothegm is repeated so many times that it gains proverbial currency: *Live and learn*; *Mistakes will happen*; *Them as has gets*; *Enough is enough*; *No fool like an old fool*; *Haste makes waste*; *Business is business*; *What's done's done*. Characteristic of such proverbs is the absence of metaphor. They consist merely of a bald assertion which is recognized as proverbial only because we have heard it often and because it can be applied to many different situations. It is ordinarily difficult, if not impossible, to determine the age of such proverbial truisms. The simple truths of life have been noted in every age, and it must not surprise us that one such truth has a long recorded history while another has none. It is only chance, for example, that *There is a time for every-thing* has a long history in English, — Shakespere used it in the *Comedy of Errors*, ii, 2: "There's a time for all things," — and it is even in the Bible: "To every thing there is a season, and a time to every purpose under the heaven" (Omnia tempus habent, et suis spatiis transeunt universa sub caelo, *Eccles*. iii, 1), while *Mistakes will happen* or *If you want a thing well done, do it yourself* have, on the contrary, no history at all.

Just such proverbs as these simple apothegms are perhaps the most difficult of all to recognize in a later age when they have ceased to circulate and when our ears are deaf to their value as oft-repeated sayings. We shall never know, for example, which of the Exeter Gnomes in Old English poetry are proverbial and which are the collector's moralizing in the same pattern. In the ears of the Anglo-Saxon author there may have been a proverbial ring to such truisms as

The frost shall freeze, fire consume wood, the earth sprout, ice shall form a bridge. . . . The sea shall be restless. The solemn way of the dead is longest secret. Holly shall go to the fire. The property of a dead man shall be divided. Fame is best.

Even so, the possibility of demonstrating proverbial usage in such cases hardly exists in the scanty poetic remains at our disposal. In a dead language the means which are available are various, but not always effective or easily applied. A passage, when it varies grammatically or syntactically from ordinary usage or from the usage of the context, can be safely declared to be proverbial. The test of proverbial style may be invoked: *At home everything is easy* (Dælt er heima hvat)[1] has the terseness of a proverb and so has *Better blind than burned*, i. e. 'dead' (Blindr er betri, en brendr sé).[2] In an alliterative poem, that is to say, in almost all old Germanic poetry, a defect in the alliteration warns us that the poet was using materials which he could not rephrase to suit his immediate metrical needs and calls our attention to the presence of a proverb, e. g. *Bú er betra, þótt lítit sé* ('[One's own] home is better, though it be small').[3] Here we observe that alliteration is absent in the second half-line, although it is demanded by the rules of Old Norse versification. The most convincing evidence is, of course, the actual proverbial use elsewhere of the doubtful passage, and, above all, its use in contexts where it cannot easily be a quotation from the passage under examination. The Icelandic *Two are an army against one* (Tveir ro eins heriar) is clearly a proverb, for we have the same phrase in Middle High German (Zwêne sint eines her, *Iwein*, l. 5350) and in mediaeval Latin (Duo sunt exercitus uni, *Ysengrimus*, ii, 311). Two Old High German expressions *When it rains, the trees become wet* (So iz regenôt, sô nazscênt tê

1 Heusler, *Zeitschrift des Vereins für Volkskunde*, XXV (1915), 110, No. 1.
2 The same, 113, No. 27.
3 The same, 111, No. 4.

bouma) and *When it blows, the trees shake* (So iz uuât, sô uuagônt tê bouma) are certainly proverbs, for the first is found again in a manuscript collection of the fourteenth century, and the second is in a modern collection of Low German proverbs. In such instances as these last proverbs the metaphorical application of the situation has lost all meaning for us.

Proverbs originating in apothegms contain a moral or ethical truth, although often in a form which utterly lacks dignity, e. g. *One should keep old roads and old friends* (Alt weg und alt freundt soll man behalten). *God is above all* (God es boven al) is a proverb frequently used in Elizabethan England, and before that in Holland; but it seems to us no more than a platitude. Such wholly commonplace phrases are still found in proverbial use: *A place for everything and everything in its place*; *You never can tell till you've tried*; *A man can die but once*; *All men must die*; *Seeing is believing*; *If you want a thing well done, do it yourself*.

Such truisms and platitudes gain proverbial significance from implication and use, that is, from vague emotional and connotational values which can mean little to another age and give these homely sentences a meaning beyond the simple and obvious uses of the words involved. A similar change has occurred in every proverb, and ordinarily takes the form of a metaphor; but in these simple platitudes the change does not attain metaphorical dignity.

Simple maxims find a ready response in naïve minds. Such admonitions as *Everything comes to him who waits*; *Steady and slow go far in a day*; *Set a thief to catch a thief*; *If you can't be good, be careful*;[1] *A young man married is a young man marred* have provided many with standards of conduct and guiding principles for life. The stock broker couches warning counsel in similar terms: *Cut your losses and let your profits run*; *You never lost money taking a profit*; *Don't sell America short*. Some maxims have only a brief life. *Let George do it*, which is perhaps a vaudeville phrase, is now less frequently heard than formerly and is perhaps on its way to extinction.[2]

In some maxims the age or the circumstances of origin are more or less distinctly suggested, but ordinarily we cannot even guess when or how they came into being. *Money talks* may be a saying of the stock market or the poker game.[3] *Dead men tell no tales* arose in a ruthless, quarrelsome society. Although we are perhaps inclined to associate it with the moral code of a pirate, it must be older than Captain Kidd and belong to a somewhat higher social level, for it is already an established proverb in Elizabethan times. *The*

1 An old maxim. Compare *Caute, si non caste*. In France, our soldiers paraphrased it as *If you can't be good, be sanitary*.
2 Possibly we can see a connection with *Laissez faire à George, il est homme d'âge*, a historical proverb. We are told that Louis XII expressed his confidence in his minister, George d'Amboise, in these words. The traditional explanation in America is based on "George" as a name used in addressing Pullman porters.
3 Cf. "Argens fait le jeu" (*Baudoin de Sebourc*, xxiv, 443).

only good Indian is a dead Indian breathes the air of our own western frontier. The warning *Watch your step* employs a metaphor from the New York subway or the Pullman sleeping car.

METAPHORICAL PROVERBS

The most interesting and artistic proverbs arise from the metaphorical use of a simple act or event: *Fish or cut bait*; *Chickens come home to roost*; *Vinegar catches no flies*; *Soft fire makes sweet malt*; *Barking dogs never bite*; *You can lead a horse to water, but you can't make him drink.* A novel application of a familiar scene arrests our attention, imprints itself on our minds, and drives home the lesson. Of all the ways in which proverbs develop, the most important is illustrated by such extensions of the meaning of a simple phrase. By this process a sentence comes to mean far more than the sum of the words composing it. *New brooms sweep clean* is a housewife's observation of fact, but as a proverb it may find use in any field. An important corollary to this is the fact that no single application of a proverb exhausts its meaning. Except in a vague paraphrase there is no defining a proverb.

Some metaphorical proverbs are as old as any that we know. Others have no history: they appear for the first time in recent collections or are perhaps even yet unrecorded. The temptation to reprint older sources without real effort to enlarge them or to verify them by reference to oral tradition, a temptation which besets all collectors, makes even the best modern collections unreliable guides to the stock of current proverbs. In English the situation is particularly serious: hardly any of the available collections is entirely trustworthy.

Dateless as such recent or unrecorded proverbs necessarily are, they are nevertheless of great interest. As we shall see later, internal evidence or comparison with proverbs in other languages often gives us a hint of their age and history. A few instances will show how erroneous is Tylor's notion [1] that the age of proverb-making is past. "We can collect and use the old proverbs," he says, "but making new ones has become a feeble, spiritless imitation, like our attempts to invent new myths or new nursery rhymes." Certainly *Put up or shut up!* possesses as much vitality as can be demanded of a proverb, and from the metaphor we can safely conclude that it is not many generations old. *No tickee, no washee,* i. e. 'without the essential prerequisite, a desired object cannot be obtained,' with its evident allusion to the Chinese laundryman, bespeaks for itself a still more recent origin. *Three generations from shirtsleeves to shirtsleeves* is an invention of yesterday, but there are English parallels, e. g. *There is nobbut three generations atween clogs and clogs,* which carry its ultimate beginnings back to England. For the origin of such proverbs as *Every*

1 *Primitive Culture,* I, ch. iii, 89–90.

man must skin his own skunk; *It pays to advertise*; *Paddle your own canoe*; *Read 'em and weep*; *Don't take any wooden nickels*; *One boy's a boy, two boys is half a boy, three boys is no boy at all*, we need not look outside of America. It would be more correct to say that proverb-making, as well as the interest in proverbs, exhibits remarkable fluctuations from age to age. To this subject we must return later.

Proverbs which smack of the soil and the folk, and yet have no long history so far as our records go, exist in great numbers. The naïve metaphor involved in them has struck popular fancy, and the proverb lingers in tradition. Examples of such proverbs are: *A short horse is soon curried*; *A shady lane breeds mud*, i. e. 'secrecy creates wrong-doing or scandal'; *You never miss a slice from a cut loaf*; *Politics makes strange bedfellows*; *Don't bite the hand that feeds you*; *Money makes the mare go*; *The grey mare is the better horse*, i. e. 'the wife is more competent than the husband,' which is as old as 1546; *Don't bite off more than you can chew*; *Don't cut off your nose to spite your face*; *You can't get blood out of a turnip*; *Dog eat dog*; *You can't spoil a rotten egg.*

Naturally such tradition draws its materials from the interests and the world of the common man. There is little or no question here of "gesunkenes Kulturgut," intellectual materials which were shaped in higher social circles and have descended from them to lower ones. Possibly the very fashion of proverbs as a manner of expression has descended in this way; but certainly most proverbs actually current in oral tradition have been coined by the folk, whatever the ultimate models may have been. The metaphors are chosen from the household and the simple events of life: *A burnt child dreads the fire*; *You must learn to creep before you can go* (i. e. 'walk'); *There's many a slip between cup and lip*; *When the cat's away, the mice will play*; *Half a loaf is better than no bread*; *The pot calls the kettle black*; *Every tub must stand on its own bottom*; *The proof of the pudding is in the eating*; *An ill weed spoils a whole pot of pottage*; *A drowning man will catch at a straw*; *There is no smoke without fire*; *It's ill halting before a cripple*. The peasant's world, the farmstead and the countryside, yields many an observation which lends itself to metaphorical use in a proverb: *Don't count your chickens before they are hatched*; *A ragged colt may make a good horse*; *A cock is mighty on his own dunghill*; *Curst cows have short horns*; *A cur will bite before he will bark*; *Make hay while the sun shines*; *Look before you leap*; *It's a long road that has no turning*; *Steady and slow go far in a day*; *The master's eye makes the horse fat*; *The still sow eats up all the draff.*

As we might expect, hunting and fishing provide us with a goodly share of proverbs: *All fish are not caught with flies*; *It is good fishing in troubled waters*; *It is ill fishing before the net*; *A bird in the hand is worth two in the bush*; *A miss is as good as a mile.* So far as my ob-

servation goes, proverbs alluding to fishing are somewhat more numerous than those alluding to hunting.[1]

Proverbs which show themselves to be the invention of sailors are not abundant.[2] *A stern chase is a
long chase* is a familiar saying, and a few others might
be collected; but Apperson's large dictionary of English proverbs does not include many sea proverbs.

Proverbs which clearly reflect village life, e.g. *Sweep
in front of your own door*, or which imply any form
of society more highly organized than the single
household complete within itself, are comparatively
rare. Such sayings as *A stitch in time saves nine* or
The shoe will hold with the sole need have of course no

1 See the bibliography in Bonser, *Proverb Literature* (London, 1930),
   p. 434, Nos. 3791–3797.
2 Sea proverbs have been collected for their own sake. Perhaps the first
   work which makes special mention of such proverbs is a Dutch dictionary of sea terms (W. A. Winschoten, *Seeman* [Leiden, 1681]).
   F. A. Stoett extracts some curious superstitions and words from this
   work; see "W. A. Winschoten's Seeman," *De Nieuwe Taalgids*, XIII
   (1919), 97–106. For Dutch sea proverbs see van Dam van Isselt,
   Nederlandsche Muzen-Almanak (1838), pp. 135–139, and particularly
   Sprenger van Eijk (*Handleiding tot de Kennis van onze Vaderlandsche
   Spreekwoorden . . . van de Scheepvaart en het Scheepsleven Ontleend*
   [Rotterdam 1835–36]). D. H. van der Meer (*Verzameling van Stukken
   betreffende de Friesche Geschiedenis*, etc. [Franeker, n.d.], I, 121–133)
   notes some Frisian sea proverbs. Sébillot (*Légendes, Croyances, et
   Superstitions de la Mer* [Paris, 1886–87]) and Corbière ("Des Proverbes
   Nautiques," *Revue de Rouen et de la Normandie*, Vol. XIII [1845])
   collect French examples. English and German collections have been
   made by Cowan (*A Dictionary of the Proverbs and Proverbial Expressions Relating to the Sea* [Greenesburgh, Pennsylvania, 1894]), Lypkes
   (*Seemannssprüche* [Berlin, 1900]), and in the anonymous *Sea Words
   and Phrases along the Suffolk Coast* (Lowestoft, 1869–70), a reprinting
   of articles from the *East Anglian Notes and Queries*, January, 1869 and
   January, 1870.

larger background than the household, while on the other hand *The cobbler's wife is always ill shod* and *Cobbler, stick to your last!* are metaphors based on a trade. In general, proverbs reflect the peasant's or common man's attitude toward a particular calling: the miller and the tailor are objects of suspicion. If we disregard proverbs of this class, to which such a book as Rudolf Eckart's *Stand und Beruf im Volksmunde* (1900) is primarily devoted, we shall have very few left.

The trades and mercantile pursuits have coined almost no proverbs.[1] *A cunning knave needs no broker* is a peasant's observation of the course of the world and involves some notion of its organization, but the proverb is not the invention of a broker. A few sayings from the stock market have been accepted as proverbial. Such a book as F. López Toral's *El Evangelio de los Comerciantes ó Explicación de los Refranes . . . para Todos se dedican á la Práctica del Comercio* (The Merchant's Bible or the Interpretation of Proverbs . . . for All who occupy Themselves with Business),[2] which I have been unable to obtain, would be very interesting. The clerk, the miner, the mason, the butcher, the printer, the painter, the smith (*Strike while the iron is hot*), the weaver, the carpenter (*A carpenter is known by his chips*), and the merchant are almost silent in the world of proverbs.

1 See the bibliography in Bonser, *Proverb Literature* (London, 1930), pp. 447–448, Nos. 3914–3927.
2 Zaragoza, 1899.

PROVERBIAL TYPES

New proverbs have often been made on old models. Certain frames lend themselves readily to the insertion of entirely new ideas. Thus the contrast in *Young . . ., old . . .* in such a proverb as *Young saint, old devil* yields a model for *Junge Bettschwester, alte Betschwester.* A methodical comparison would probably reveal the proverb which gave the original impulse to the formation of the others; but no one has ever undertaken a study of this sort. Martha Lenschau conceives the development as follows: *Young angel, old devil* (Jung Engel, alt Teufel, thirteenth century); *Young knights, old beggars* (Junge Ritter, alte Bettler, sixteenth century); *Young soldiers, old beggars* (Junge Soldaten, alte Bettler, seventeenth century). The first form made no distinction for sex. When the substitution of "knight" or "soldier" made the distinction, a by-form for women was invented on the same model: *Junge Hure, alt Kupplerin* appears to have been the first of such by-forms, although *Jung Hure, alt Wettermacherin* must also be ancient, since the notion involved in "Wettermacherin" reaches far back. The most recent development is probably the Low German *Young gamblers, old beggars* (Junge Späler, ole Bedler), and the corruption *Young musicians, old beggars* (Junge Musikanten, alde Beddellüde), which arises from the misunderstanding of "Späler," 'players' (i. e. gamblers), as 'players of music' and the later substitution of a synonym.

It is not always easy to recognize or identify the earliest form which provided the model for later developments; and until several proverbs have been minutely examined from this point of view and our methods of study have been improved, it is hard to say which arguments are safe to use and which are unsafe. In all probability, we may trust to the general principles which have been worked out for märchen, i. e. those employed in the so-called Finnish or historico-geographical method. The relative age and distribution of the various forms of a proverb will throw much light on the development. In the present instance, for example, we might regard the old and widely known *Jung gewohnt, alt getan* ('What one is accustomed to in youth, one does in old age') as a possible model, even of the whole group. Certainly it has given us *Jung gefreut, alt gereut* ('Rejoiced in youth, repented in age') and as a secondary development: *Jung gefreit, alt gereut* ('Married in youth, repented in age'). Since, however, *Young saint, old devil* is even older and more widely known, I am inclined to consider it the parent of all later forms. Often other arguments than age and wide currency may be brought into court. Usually, a dialectal variation which is essential to a particular form and which limits it to a narrow area is secondary in origin, e. g. *Jung gefreit, alt geklait* ('Wed in youth, bewailed in old age') can have arisen only in a region where "geklagt" is pronounced "geklait." So, too, *Jung gefreit, alt gereut* originated in a region — somewhat larger, to be sure, than the one just mentioned — where the dialectal pronounciation of "gereut" made the rhyme tolerable.

A few more illustrations of the creation of new proverbs on the model of old ones will suffice. A familiar German proverbial type employs the notion that the essential qualities of an object show themselves from the very beginning, e. g. *Was ein Häkchen werden soll, krümmt sich beizeiten* ('Whatever is to be a hook, bends early'). English representatives of this type are rare, but we may cite *Timely crooks that tree that will be a cammock* (i. e. 'gambrel,' a bent piece of wood used by butchers to hang carcasses on) and *It pricketh betimes that shall be a sharp thorn*. A German derivative of the type is *Was ein Nessel werden soll, brennt beizeiten* ('Whatever is to be a nettle, burns early'). This proverb has found rather wide currency. Although the evidence is not all in, the type or at least its ready employment in new proverbs is German. The form characteristic of *Es sind nicht alle Jäger, die das Horn blasen* ('They are not all hunters who blow horns'), a form which appears to have been first recorded by Varro ('Non omnes, qui habent citharam, sunt citharoedi'), enjoyed a remarkable popularity in mediaeval Germany and gave rise to many new proverbs, e. g. *They are not all cooks who carry long knives* (Es sind nicht alle Köche, die lange Messer tragen); *They are not all friends who laugh with you* (Zijn niet alle vrienden, die hem toelachen). Outside of Germany and countries allied culturally, the form appears to have had no notable success, except in *All is not gold that glitters*, which refers to a thing and not a person. Seiler thinks that "Many are called, but few are chosen" (Multi enim sunt vocati, pauci vero electi, *Matt.* xx, 16; xxii, 14) was the ultimate model for these proverbs, but the similarity is one of thought and not of form. Possibly one could imagine a class based on simple balance and contrast, of which the *young-old* type and the *called-chosen* type might both be derivatives, but the fundamental differences in syntactical structure speak strongly against a development of this sort. *Young saint, old devil* is an old proverbial form which has no verb; *Many are called, but few are chosen* consists of balanced, antithetical sentences; *All is not gold that glitters* uses a subordinate clause. The syntactical differences are so great that an influence from one of these types on another does not seem likely.

Not all proverbial types have been equally success-ful in propagating themselves. *One swallow does not make a summer* gives us *One man does not make a dance* (Unus homo non facit choream) and *One man does not make a team*, but it has not been very produc-tive otherwise. *After the calm comes a storm* appears to have preceded *After joy comes annoy*; and *Quem ode-*

rint dii, hunc pedagogem fecerunt ('Whom the gods hate, they make a teacher') is a derivative of the anonymous *Quem Deus perdere vult, dementat prius* ('Whom God wishes to destroy, he first drives mad'), a Christian version of *Quem Iuppiter perdere vult, dementat prius* (a maxim of obscure origin which may have been invented in Cambridge about 1640) and of such other phrases as the Plautine and Menandrian "Whom the Gods love, die young" (Quem di diligunt Adulescens moritur, *Bacch.*, ll. 816–817). *The tree falls not at the first blow* (Der Baum fällt nicht vom ersten Streiche) gave some butcher a model for *The ox does not fall at the first blow* (Der Ochse fällt nicht vom ersten Streiche). *Politics makes strange bedfellows* is evidently a derivative of *Misery acquaints a man with strange bedfellows* and *Poverty makes strange bedfellows*. Such recently invented proverbs as *Politics makes strange bedfellows* and *One man does not make a team* show that new formations on old models are still possible in tradition; but forces which are not easy to name or estimate determine whether a proverbial type becomes widely creative. Clearly the first and most important requirement is familiarity with the formula. A single proverb is often widely enough known to supply a model for many nonce-formations. A second requirement is the applicability of the formula. Not all formulae can give rise to new proverbs.

Occasionally the history of a proverbial type is difficult to decipher. The saying *The nearer the church*, *the farther from God* is old and widely known: the English tradition, which is often scanty, dates from 1300 and the proverb is also found in German, Dutch, Swedish (Finland), French, Italian, and no doubt other languages. In the more easterly portions of Europe (Bohemia, Poland, Hungary, Croatia; but also Denmark) a similar proverb declares *The nearer to church, the later in* (Jo nærmere kirken, jo senere dertil). Another related form is *The nearer Rome, the worse Christian* (Quo Romae propiores, tanto christiani tepidiores), which is first found in the early years of the sixteenth century in Germany and countries culturally allied to Germany, and although it breathes the hostile spirit of the German Reformation, a still more violent and personal expression of the same mood is found a generation earlier: *The nearer the Pope, the worse Christian* (Zo nader den paeus, so quader kersten). The eleventh-century *Fecunda Ratis* of Egbert of Liège has "The nearer the fire, the hotter" (Tanto plus calidum, quanto vicinius igni) and Chaucer says "The ner the fire, the hatter is" (*Troilus*, i, 449). Perhaps the latest invention on this model, although it goes back to 1559 and, in Dutch, to an even earlier time, is *The nearer the bone, the sweeter the meat.* Clearly we have a single type according to which all these proverbs have been made; but the age and distribution of the different forms do not seem to offer much assistance in arriving at the archetype. The proverbs involving Rome and the Pope we may discard as later inventions, since neither their age nor their restriction to Germanic territory marks them as suitable models for later development. In this case we have almost at the very beginning of our history of the type a sharp division into certain clearly marked forms which show no obvious interrelations. To be sure, these difficulties may be more apparent than real; a minute examination might after all disclose new clues.

Variations of Proverbs in Tradition

Oral transmission creates minor variations in proverbs. These variations are produced by changes of the same general kinds as we find in märchen, ballads, and other popular materials: one specific detail is replaced by another; a general trait is replaced by a specific one, and vice versa; details suggested by similarity or contrast enter the proverb; expansions are brought about by the addition of duplicate or parallel traits; obsolete or misunderstood details are removed, and so on. The familiar proverb *A bird in the hand is worth two in the bush* illustrates many of the changes produced by oral transmission. The characteristic changes in the following examples concern first, the number of birds referred to; second, the place where the birds are seen; third, the kind of bird described. In 1562 John Heywood included *A birde in the hand is worth ten in the wood* in his epigrams, and still older is the form *A birde in hond is better than thre in the wode.* The Roumanians say *Better a bird in the hand than a thousand on the house*; the Italians, *Better one bird in the cage than four in the arbor*; and the Frisians, *A bird in the pan is better than many in the air.* The Latin forms *Una avis in laqueo plus valet octo vagis* ('A bird in the snare is worth more than eight flying'); *Plus valet in dextra passer, quam quatuor extra* ('One sparrow in the right hand is worth more than four out of it'); *Plus valet in manibus passer, quam sub dubio grus* ('A sparrow in the hands is worth more than a crane in doubt') have no parallels in the texts at hand. In such forms as these we have chiefly variations in number, although the reader will have already noticed some other incidental variations. A variation in regard to the location of either member of the comparison is very frequent: *Better a sparrow in the hand than two flying* (Portuguese); *Better one bird in the pot than ten in the wood* (Swedes in Finland); *Better a bird in the fist than ten in the wood* (Swedes in Finland); and *Better one bird in the cage than seven in the bush* (Swedes in Finland). We have already noted in the preceding examples the variation which replaces the general term "bird" by "sparrow." The simplest form of such characterization is *Better a little bird in the hand than a big bird in the wood* (Swedes in Finland). More interesting are the variations which deal with the species of the birds: *Better a sparrow in the hand than a crane on the roof* (German); *A sparrow in the hand is worth a vulture flying* (Spanish); *A finch in*

the hand is better than a thrush afar off (North Italian);
Better a bird in the hand than ten doves on the roof (Low
German); *Better a hawk in the hand than two in flight*
(Icelandic). The extent to which such alterations
can go is seen in the North Italian variants: *Better a
feather in the hand than a bird in the air*; *Better a sparrow in the pan than a hundred chickens in the pastor's
yard*; or the Finnish *Better a wood-grouse in the fist
than nine or two on the branch.*

A specific detail is replaced by a general one or vice
versa: *Where the Devil can't go, he sends an old woman*
(Wo der Teufel nicht hinkommen kann, schickt er ein
altes Weib), and the variant *Where the Devil can't go,
he sends his grandmother.* In the old proverb *The pot
goes so often to the well that it comes home broken* the
place is often named as "water" or "stream." Occasionally a reason can be found for the change. Thus
the old rhyme which the followers of John Ball sang
in 1381:

> When Adam delved and Eve span,
> Where was then the gentleman?

sets in parallel the words "delved" and "span,"
which belong to entirely different spheres of activity.
The Swedes in Finland have simplified the proverb by
referring to a single activity:

> Då Adam vävde och Eva spann,
> Var fanns då en adelsman?
> ('When Adam wove and Eve span,
> Where was there then the nobleman?')

The change was made easier by the similarity of "grävde" ('delved') and "vävde" ('wove'). In the variants of *Rome was not built in a day* the replacement of "Rome" by the names of other cities occurs frequently. Along the lower Rhine and westward we find Cologne and Aix-la-Chapelle, occasionally both together, in this proverb. In Brabant and Limburg they are replaced by Ghent and Bruges, e. g. *Gent en Brugge zijn op eenen dag niet gebouwd*, or Brussels and Ghent. The French name either Paris or Rome. Such substitutions are efforts to bring the proverb up to date or to accommodate it to a new country.

Another class of substitutions appears in the replacement of an object by its opposite; e. g. *A hasty bitch bears blind puppies* (Cagna frettolosa fa catellini ciechi) circulates in Italy also in the form *A hasty cat bears immature kittens* (Gatta frettolosa fa i gattini acerbi). It is not easy to find a general head under which to put such substitutions as *Much noise and little milk* (Viel Geschrei und wenig Milch) and *Much noise and few eggs* (Viel Geschrei und wenig Ei), which have developed from *Much noise and little wool* (Viel Geschrei und wenig Wolle).

A very characteristic way of making new forms consists in expansion by introducing new parallel or contrasting elements. Pope's verse "To err is human, to forgive, divine" (*Essay on Criticism*, l. 525), which has almost, if not entirely, established itself as a proverb, arises from *Errare est humanum* by employing the logical contrast of "human" and "divine." The second part of *Pride goes before and shame comes after* has developed in the same way. *Each man for himself* seems to have been the first form, to which is later added *and God for us all* or *and the Devil for all*. Now the proverb runs *Every man for himself and the Devil take the hindmost*. At the present moment the fact that *Each man for himself and the Devil for all* is found only in Florio's *First Fruits* (1578) does not concern us. It is sufficient to note that we have two forms of the proverb, one with "God" and one with "Devil." We need not now inquire which came first, but it is obvious that one produced the other by contrast.

Often the expansion is quite whimsical. Some wit, I conjecture, has enlarged *I have other fish to fry* into *I have other fish to fry and their tails to butter*. So, too, arose *Neither fish, flesh, nor good red herring*. The old proverb *Praise the fair day at even* has suffered many an expansion of this sort, e. g. *Vespere laudatur lux, hospes mane probatur* ('The day is praised in the evening, the host in the morning'); *Schöne Tage soll man abends loben, schöne Frauen morgens* ('One should praise beautiful days in the evening, beautiful women in the morning'). So also *Clothes make the man* becomes in German *Kleider machen Leute und Lumpen machen Leuss* ('Clothes make the man and rags make lice'), a form which apparently enjoyed some currency in the sixteenth century. More casual modifications are *Clothes make people, priests make brides* (Kleider machen Leute, Pfaffen machen Bräute) and *Clothes make people, shoes the soldier* (Kleider machen Leute, Schuhe den Soldaten). In Essex they say *Every dog has his day, and a cat has two Sundays.* The addition *and a pudding has two* frequently occurs with the proverb *All things have an end.*

PROVERBS BASED ON NARRATIVES

In addition to making proverbs from other proverbs, tradition creates them from materials which seem at first sight more refractory. The relation of the fable and the proverb is particularly close, and not all nations have regarded them as distinct forms: the Greek αἶνος means both 'fable' and 'proverb.' So also the Aramaic-Syriac *mathla* and the related Hebrew *maschal* as well as the Old English *gied.* We are not well informed about the process of making fables into proverbs.[1] In general, it seems to be a characteristic of Oriental and savage proverbs. Many sayings of African and Asiatic peoples are entirely

1 See Otto, *Die Sprichwörter und Sprichwörtlichen Redensarten der Römer* (Leipzig, 1890), p. xxv; Bolte and Polívka, *Anmerkungun zu den Kinder- und Hausmärchen,* IV (1930), 116 n. 11, 365; "Fabel" in Pauly-Wissowa, *Realencyclopädie;* Crusius, "Märchenreminszenzen im Antiken Sprichwort," *Verhandlungen d. 40. Philologenversammlung zu Görlitz* (1890); L. Friedländer, *Bilder aus der Römischen Sittengeschichte,* I (5th ed., 1881), 469 ff., I (6th ed., 1888), 522 ff.; Büchmann, *Geflügelte Worte* (Berlin, 1920), pp. 71–86; Seiler, *Lehnsprichwort,* I, 22 f., 83 f.; Jente, "Märchen im Sprichwort," *Handbuch des Deutschen Märchens* (forthcoming). The article by Kasumović (*Rad* of the Jugoslav Academy, CXCI, 195), which is cited in *Zeitschrift des Vereins für Volkskunde,* XXIII (1913), 317, has not been accessible to me.

unintelligible to us because we do not know the story behind the allusion. There may perhaps be certain classes of stories which yield proverbs more readily than others. The Aesopic fable, for example, stands godfather to many a proverb: *Sour grapes*; *A dog in the manger*; *Don't kill the goose that lays the golden eggs*; *Don't count your chickens before they are hatched* (which belongs in the modern Aesopic tradition, although it is not part of the original stock of fables). I am not sure that the Latin proverb *We lose the certain things, while we seek the uncertain ones* (Certa amittimus, dum incerta petimus) alludes to the fable of the dog which lost its meat by snapping at the reflection in the water. Possibly we have two independent expressions of the same idea, the proverb in literal and the fable in figurative form. The beast epic gives us *When the fox preaches, beware your geese* and the traditional descriptions of the Land of Cockaigne, *Roast doves fly into no one's mouth* (Gebratene Tauben fliegen niemand in den Mund). Possibly we may see a parallel in "All thy strongholds shall be like fig trees with the first ripe figs: if they be shaken, they shall even fall into the mouth of the eater,"[1] but more probably the Biblical passage serves merely to illustrate how obvious the figure is. In a similar way, the ass playing the lute or, as in Boethius and Chaucer, the harp, was a proverbial symbol for impossibilities

---

[1] *Nahum* iii, 12. Quitard regards this passage as source; see p. 37. Compare Büchmann as above, p. 84.

and is perhaps derived from some comparison involving or implying an impossibility rather than from a specific narrative. There are other allusions which cannot be referred to a definite fable and which can perhaps be better interpreted as allusions to such vividly conceived scenes as we have been describing: the Roman proverbial exclamation "Asinus de Aesopi puteo!" was used on seeing an unexpected person whose outcry disturbs everyone, and Petronius says "The ass on the roof" (Asinus in tegulis) of an unheard-of, ominous event; but in neither case do we fully understand the allusion.

Perhaps *One swallow does not make a summer* is associated with a story, but the suggested relationship is different from that exemplified by the proverbs already mentioned. A youth squandered his inheritance and, when he saw the first swallow, sold his cloak. But it turned cold and the swallow died, whereupon the youth, who was suffering from the cold, cried, "One swallow does not make a summer." Possibly the longest and most curious history of a proverb arising from a narrative is that of Αἴξ (var. Οἶς) τὴν μάχαιραν ('The goat [var. the sheep], the knife').[1] When a goat was about to be sacrificed, no knife could be found. But the pawing of the animal revealed a knife in the ground and the sacrifice was carried out. The story has Arabic and even Hindu

1 Wesselski, *Erlesenes* (Gesellschaft Deutscher Bücherfreunde in Böhmen, VIII, Prague, 1928), p. 98.

parallels. In a curious Italian form of the proverb a hen replaces the goat or sheep. We might regard this as merely a casual substitution, but Wesselski, who studies the history of the fable and the proverb exhaustively, shows that it arises from the misunderstanding of a Spanish word.

In several instances we can suppose that a story lies behind a proverb, although we can no longer identify it: *A fool would take the song of the cuckoo for the music of the harp* (Ein tore næme des gouches sanc für den süezen harpfen klanc); *Those who eat cherries with great lords shall have their eyes sprinted out with the stones.* Possibly a connection with the fairy-tale of the Frog-Prince (Grimm, No. 1; Aarne-Thompson, No. 440) may be seen in *He who was a frog is now king* (Qui fuit rana, nunc est rex) and *If one loves a frog, one thinks the frog to be Diana* (Si quis amat ranam, ranam putat esse Dianam); but it is at best doubtful.

There are, we may note in passing, examples of reverse process: a proverb is turned into a tale. Odo of Cheriton, who versified Latin fables in twelfth-century England, turned *Do not throw pearls before swine* (Neque mittatis margaritas vestras ante porcos, *Matt.* vii, 6) into a dull story, and also *The cat would eat fish but will not wet her feet.*[1] According to Otto, the author of the standard collection of Latin proverbs, the proverb *The mountains give birth, a ridiculous*

[1] For these and other examples see Voigt, *Zeitschrift für Deutsches Altertum*, XXIII (1879), 294 (No. 30*a*), 305 (No. 11), 287 (No. 14), 301 (No. 58), 304 (No. 8).

mouse is born (Parturiunt montes, ridiculus mus nascetur) preceded the story. The proverb is definitely Greek in origin, if we may trust the allusions in Latin writers; and it is referred to as a proverb, not a fable. The fable, which is first found in Phaedrus, is never mentioned in Greek. Under the circumstances the precedence of the proverb over the fable seems reasonably clear. In the same connection [1] Otto contradicts himself in regard to the proverbial phrase "to nurse a viper in one's breast," which is, he maintains on one occasion, older than the fable in Phaedrus and, on another, younger. Perhaps the best example is the old saying *For the want of a nail the shoe was lost; for the want of a shoe the horse was lost; for the want of a horse the rider was lost; for the want of a rider the battle was lost; and all for the want of a horseshoe nail.* Expanded into a narrative, this saying has found a place in the *Household Tales* of the Brothers Grimm.

The development of fables from proverbs is readily understood when we stop to think how easily a story could spring from *A bull in a china shop*. Yet in many cases it is difficult to determine which came first. Whenever the scanty narrative content of the fable is summed up in the proverb, we are justified in suspecting that the fable is secondary in origin. Thus,

---

1 *Sprichwörter*, p. xxv, where additional examples are given. He also believes that *They have put a saddle on the ox; it is no task for me* (Clitellae bovi sunt impositae plane, non est nostrum onus) is an allusion to a fable; cf. p. 262 and *Archiv für Lateinische Lexikographie*, VI (1889), 9 n. 1.

the Italian *I am not the lamb Pecorella which loses a mouthful because it says "Baa!"* (Io non son Pecorella che perde il buccone per dire Umbè) has so little narrative substance that we need hardly invent a fable as a source. Similarly, *"Look at his hands and not at his eyes," said the bird* ("Pongli mente alli mani, e non a gli occhi," disse l'uccellino) contains all that is essential in the fable of the bird-catcher whose eyes fill with tears from the cold while he wrings the necks of the birds. The fable which can be positively recognized as the source of a proverb appears in its proverbial dress as an allusion, intelligible to those familiar with the story, and not as a summary, e. g. *Sour grapes*; *Dog in the manger*; *Ass in a lion's skin*.

Proverbs and Folk-verse

The very curious and interesting relations of certain proverbs to some simple and primitive forms of verse have never been cleared up satisfactorily.[1] Obviously such a proverb as *Auch rote Äpfel sind wurmstichig* ('Even red apples are wormy') stands in some intimate connection with a widely sung quatrain, which is reported as early as 1613:

1 See K. Euling, *Das Priamel bis Hans Rosenplüt* (Germanistische Abhandlungen, No. 25), p. 179 n. 3; Strack, *Hessische Blätter für Volkskunde*, II (1903), 69, 174; *Die Österreich-Ungarische Monarchie in Wort und Bild* (Vienna, 1891), VIII (Kärnten und Krain), 151; A. Kopp, *Ein Sträusschen Liebesblüten im Garten Deutscher Volksdichtung Gepflückt* (Leipzig, 1902), No. 19. See also the interesting remarks in the preface to D. Hyde, *Songs of Connacht* (Dublin, n. d.). Apparently a literary tradition lies behind the metrical form of certain Irish proverbs.

Es ist kein Apfel so rosenrot,
es steckt ein Kernlein drin;
es war keine Jungfrau nie so schön,
sie trägt einen falschen Sinn.[1]

Some have maintained that the proverb came before the quatrain; others, who declare that the germ of all poetry is the strophe and not the line, have zealously defended the contrary opinion. Certainly such matters are not to be decided on the basis of doctrinaire notions of primitive poetry. The old proverb *When it rains, it becomes wet* (Wenn es regnet, wird es nass), which is known in Old High German, is found in *Schnaderhüpfel*, the quatrains sung so widely in southern Germany and the Tyrol, and in the first stanza of a children's song, but no one has suggested that the songs are older than the proverb. Machado y Alvarez collects a few examples of proverbs occurring in similar Spanish quatrains ("coplas") and offers some general comment without reaching a decision.[2] Further discussion of the evidence is not very likely to bring us closer to the origins of poetry, but we may learn to understand better the interrelations of certain proverbs and traditional verses. The situation is perhaps a little different where improvisation in verse is extremely easy. A distinction between proverbs,

1 Wander, *Deutsches Sprichwörter-Lexikon* (Leipzig, 1867–80), *s. v.* Apfel, 6; Kopp, as above; Strack, as above, II, 174.
2 *Estudios sobre Literatura Popular* (Biblioteca de las Tradiciones Populares, Vol. V [Sevilla, 1884]), pp. 67–71, "Coplas sentenciosas," pp. 75–79, "Antinomia entre un refrán y una copla."

short lyrics, and charms is not always readily made, and the forms flow into one another.[1]

Proverbs and Individual Authors [2]

Of course an individual creates a proverb and sets it in circulation. The inventor's title to his property may be recognized by all who use it or his title may be so obscured by the passage of time that only investigation will determine the source of the saying. No one disputes Shakespere's claim to *To be or not to be*, but Sir Francis Bacon has not maintained his hold on *Knowledge is power* with equal success. We must also consider the many instances of faulty or erroneous ascription. The works of ready reference which deal with all these problems in "familiar quotations" or, as the Germans say, "winged words" (geflügelte Worte) are invaluable in proverb study.

1 See, for example, Krohn, "Die Entwicklung eines Sprichwortes zum Lyrischen Liede," *Mélanges en l'Honneur de Vaclav Tille* (Prague, 1929), pp. 109–112.

2 See the bibliography of collections of familiar quotations in Büchmann, *Geflügelte Worte* (Leipzig, 1912), p. xxvi. The more important collections are Arlaud, *Bevingede Ord* (Copenhagen, 1878); Bartlett, *Familiar Quotations* (Boston, 1924); Benham, *Book of Quotations, Proverbs, and Household Words* (London, 1924); Alexandre, *Musée de la Conversation* (Paris, 1902); Büchmann, *Geflügelte Worte; der Citatenschatz des Deutschen Volkes* (Leipzig, 1864, 1920); Nehry, *Citatenschatz, Geflügelte Worte, Sprichwörter und Sentenzen* (Leipzig, 1889); Winter, *Unbeflügelte Worte* (Augsburg, 1888); Fumagalli, *Chi l'ha detto? Reportorio Metodico e Ragionato di 1575 Citazioni e Frasi di Origine Letteraria* (Milan, 1895); Otto, *Die Sprichwörter und Sprichwörtlichen Redensarten der Römer* (Leipzig, 1890); Curti, *Schweizer Geflügelte Worte* (Zurich, 1896); Ahnfelt, *Bevingade Ord* (Stockholm, 1879).

At the very beginning of a proverb's history there is obviously no question of "communal composition," although the acceptance or rejection by tradition which follows immediately upon the creation of the proverb is a factor in its making quite as important as the first act of invention. Oliver Wendell Holmes, if I am not mistaken, expresses the idea more simply thus: "Next the originator of a good saying is the first quoter of it." In Germanic proverbs Heusler [1] recognizes two strata of different ages. The older proverbs reflect the mood and literary style of the Viking Age; the younger proverbs deal with household life and show a resignation and whimsical humor which are entirely new. The differences arise not solely from the passing of the viking but also from the fact that the genre has fallen into the hands of the peasant and the common man. This explanation, if it is correct, involves a descent of literary and intellectual goods and fashions from one social level to another on a large scale. Of course we cannot hope to reach back to individual authors in contemplating this process, but the process does imply clearly a person and not a group as the starting point. We may perhaps see something analogous to the development which Heusler describes in *Faint heart ne'er won fair lady*. Although this is an old proverb, it was never, I suppose, vulgar and colloquial. Neither the language nor the

---

[1] *Altgermanische Dichtung* (Handbuch der Literaturwissenschaft, Wildpark-Potsdam, 1923), p. 68, § 61.

figure suggests the peasant. *Love 'em and leave 'em* is more in the vulgar mood, although it smells of the vaudeville stage and thus bespeaks a sophisticated origin.

A few proverbs can be assigned to definite authors with a reasonable degree of confidence. Naturally our assurance becomes less and less, the farther back we must go to find the source or the inventor. Many such proverbs are of course Biblical or classical and will be taken up later. Here we need cite only a few instances of proverbs which can be traced to particular persons. According to his saga, Ragnar Loðbrókr said, "Gnyðia mundu nu grisir, ef þeir visse, hvat enn gamle þyldi" ('The pigs would grunt now, if they knew what the old one suffers'), when he was in the snake-pit. The sentence, which implies an allusion to a particular situation and cannot be a metaphor from daily life, has become proverbial in the Scandinavian languages: the Swedish *Grisarna skulle grymta om de visste vad galten lider* ('The little pigs would grunt, if they knew what the boar was suffering') may serve as an example.[1] Petrarch created the apothegm *A good death does honor to a whole life* (Un bel morir tutta la vita onora, *Canz.*, xvi, st. 5, ll. 12–13), which was widely used in later Italian literature.[2] It was in the nature of things that Petrarch's apothegm should call

---

1 *Ragnarssaga Loðbroka*, 15; Kock and Petersen, *Ostnordiska och Latinska Medeltidsordspråk* (Copenhagen, 1889–94), II, 194; Bugge, *Arkiv för Nordisk Filologi*, X (1894), 96.

2 Wesselski, *Angelo Polizianos Tagebuch* (Leipzig, 1929), p. 45, No. 96.

forth a burlesque version: *A good flight saves life again* (Un bel fuggir salva la vita ancora).[1] We are indebted to Francis Bacon for *Knowledge is power*. *God tempers the wind to the shorn lamb* is ordinarily credited to Sterne, but before him it had a long history in France. Perhaps the proverb was introduced into England by George Herbert in the *Jacula Prudentum*. *To err is human; to forgive divine* is a literary proverb invented by Pope. *Three removes are worse than a fire* may be Benjamin Franklin's. Possibly Robespierre fathered *Omelets are not made without breaking eggs*. Lincoln said, *Don't swap horses in the middle of a stream*. It is generally believed that he was inventing the proverb, although it is possible that he was merely using one that was already current. *Verify your references* is a scholar's maxim which tradition assigns to Routh, Jowett, and Skeat. *The bigger they come, the harder they fall* is the property of James J. Corbett. The warning *Don't sell America short*, which is often said to have been uttered by J. Pierpont Morgan, was probably, according to the belief of those associated with the firm, first voiced by his father, Junius Spencer Morgan, when in business in London. It was couched in the technical language of the time as *Do not sell a bear on the United States*. J. Pierpont Morgan adapted it to the idiom of Wall Street. A new proverb took form when he rejected the proposal to dissolve the trusts with *You can't unscramble eggs*.

1 Wesselski, *Angelo Polizianos Tagebuch* (Leipzig, 1929), p. 45, No. 96.

Conceivably a proverb may for a time be associated with the inventor's name, although all ascriptions to definite persons must be looked upon with suspicion. So old a proverb as *Know thyself* is variously assigned to Thales, Chilon, Solon, Bias, Phemonoe, "through whom the Pythian God is said to have first distributed favors to men," Phanothea, the priestess of Delphi, and the Delphic oracle. It no doubt owes much of its wide circulation to its use as an inscription in the temple of Delphic Apollo. Certainly a significant indication of its proverbial nature lies in the fact that it is credited to so many sources; furthermore, we must hesitate in assigning it to any one of them. Erasmus can scarcely be right in finding the source of *What is bred in the bone will not out of the flesh* in Horace. He is, of course, referring to "Drive out nature with a fork,[1] it will come back nevertheless" (Naturam expellas furca, tamen usque recurret, *Ep.*, i, 10, 24); but in this we have the idea and not the form of the modern proverb. The illustration shows how much care must be exercised in ascribing proverbs to definite persons and sources. *Verify your references* is perhaps nowhere more in place than in such matters.

A few more examples will show the nature of such ascriptions of proverbs.[2] When St. Jerome quotes the

1 This may mean a pitchfork or a fork used to punish slaves.
2 Compare the examples of Latin quotations which verge on proverbs: Otto, *Sprichwörter*, p. xxii; Otto, *Die Geflügelten Worte bei den Römern*

remark of Epicharmus (or Pittacus), "When they do not know how to talk, they cannot keep silence" (Cum loqui nesciant, tacere non possunt), and characterizes it as an old saw (vetus proverbium), we need not for a moment hesitate to accept his characterization, although the uncertainty as to the author casts doubt on the correctness of any ascription. *Like a fish out of water* (Sicut piscis sine aqua caret vita, ita sine monasterio monachus) is attributed to a Pope Eugenius, but it is found in Sozomen's *Ecclesiastical History* and still earlier in a life (not later than A.D. 373) of St. Anthony ascribed to St. Athanasius. The Irish *Better old debts than old grudges* is declared to belong to Prince Aldfrid, son of Oswy, King of Northumbria, and, with a slight variation, to Fíthal, lawgiver to King Cormac macAirt. Probably the most interesting of all such ascriptions is that of

> Wer nicht liebt Wein, Weib und Gesang,
> Der bleibt ein Narr sein Lebelang.

> ('He who does not love wine, women, and song
> Is a fool all his life long.')

This saying is generally credited to Martin Luther, but except for one of his remarks at table — and it is not directly parallel — there is no ascription to him before 1775. Nor is there any good reason for believing that Louis XIV ever said "L'état c'est moi

(Breslau, 1890). See in general the many handbooks of familiar quotations, of which the most useful and most accurate is Büchmann, *Geflügelte Worte* (Berlin, 1920).

(I am the state)," even though it is often assigned to
a speech before the French parliament on April 13,
1655.[1] The international proverb *Sunt tria damna
domus: imber, mala femina, fumus* ('There are three
accursed things in a house: dripping, an evil woman,
smoke'), which Pope Innocent III recast, is assigned
with some show of justice to Solomon, but Aristotle
cannot rightfully claim it. Nor did Plato ever say
Homo proponit, Deus disponit or anything similar,
although the *Vision of Piers Plowman* gives him that
honor. Figures about whom traditions of wisdom
have gathered attract proverbs to themselves in the
same way that jests collect about Eulenspiegel and
Joe Miller.

The incidents narrated to explain the origins of
proverbs are often curious, and, so far as authenticity
is concerned, must be classed with the ascriptions of
proverbs to definite persons. In some instances, the
story, like the ascription, may rest on fact; in others,
the narrative has been made *ad hoc.* Generally speaking, we cannot hope to control the truth of either
story or ascription. The explanation, for example,
that *When in Rome, do as the Romans do* takes its rise
in a conversation of St. Ambrose with St. Augustine
may be correct, but we cannot be sure. St. Augustine,
the story goes, had found that the Romans did not
fast on the day to which he had been accustomed at
Milan. He asked St. Ambrose on what day he should

1 Büchmann, *Geflügelte Worte* (Leipzig, 1920), p. 456.

fast, and received as answer, "When I am here, I do not fast on the Sabbath; when I am at Rome, I fast on the Sabbath. To whatever church you come, observe its practice, if you do not wish to suffer or to create a scandal." It is important to note that the actual words of the proverb are not used by either saint; hence the proverb is not a direct quotation. Yet it sums up the situation and the moral in pregnant words. A similar condensation is probably seen in *Vox populi, vox Dei* ('The voice of the people, the voice of God'), for which no exactly corresponding source exists. The famous maxim *The end justifies the means* is, I suspect, open to a similar explanation, for the Jesuit motto *Exitus actus probat* will scarcely suffice as a source. And I cannot refrain from mentioning here the famous phrase *Das Volk dichtet* (The folk composes poetry), which bears within itself the Romantic doctrines of poetic origins. Although it is usually fathered on Jacob Grimm, no one has found a source for it nearer than "das dichtende Volk." The very creation of the direct, effective form *Das Volk dichtet* out of an inferior form is an illustration of the process of poetic origins.

But to return to our muttons: the stories told to explain the origin of proverbs are often not worthy of credence. Possibly Pliny is narrating an actual occurrence when he explains the origin of *Shoemaker, stick to your last!* When Apelles had painted a picture, he displayed it for public criticism and hid where he might hear the comments. The remarks made by a cobbler were too sharp for the painter to bear and he burst forth, saying, "Shoemaker, stick to your last!" Perhaps Apelles was using a familiar proverb; perhaps he coined it for this occasion. A famous Greek story and myth is told to explain the origin of *There's many a slip 'twixt cup and lip*: a slave whom his master had treated with great cruelty prophesied that the master should never live to drink wine from the vineyard in which he was working. When the wine was ready, the master taunted the slave and forced him to hold the cup. But before the cup was tasted word came that a boar was laying waste the vineyard; the master hastened to kill the boar and was killed in the encounter. Hence the Greek proverb, *Many things find place between the cup and lip*. Since this story is none other than the widely told tale of Attis,[1] it is altogether probable that the story originally had nothing to do with the proverb, but was linked with it by some chance. In the same way, the notion is quite erroneous that *A cat may look at a king* or its variant German form, *A cat may look at an emperor* (Darf doch die Katze den Kaiser ansehen), takes rise in a visit (in 1517) of Maximilian I to the shop of Hieronymus Resch, the maker of wood-cuts. The cat which lay on the work-table looked at the emperor suspiciously, but did not move. Hence, it is

[1] See Taylor, "The Death of Orvar Oddr," *Modern Philology*, XIX (1921), 93–106.

said, came the proverb. The date of the emperor's visit is definitely fixed, and consequently the fact that the proverb was printed in northern Germany in 1514 makes the traditional explanation impossible. A French parallel, *A dog may look at a bishop* (Un chien regarde bien un évêque), is explained as an allusion to a prohibition formulated by the second council of Mâcon in A.D. 585. Bishops might not keep dogs, for if they did those who sought aid might be bitten. The absence of any direct historical connection between the prohibition and the proverb makes it hard to accept the explanation at its face value. We can probably consider the French proverb a traditional variation of the English and German forms. Instances in which the explanation turns on old or supposedly old manners and customs, and not on stories, will be mentioned later.

TRANSLATED PROVERBS

Throughout the history of proverbs an abundant source of new sayings has been translation from one language into another. We can often recognize what has happened by the presence of stylistic or metrical irregularities: the translator has failed to reproduce the symmetry and polish of the original. As regards ultimate origins, such proverbs fall into two classes: sayings which are actually proverbs from the beginning and therefore have come into being in one or another of the ways already described, and sayings, or-

dinarily Biblical or classical, which owe their wide
currency to literary and religious associations, but
have in the course of time lost connection with their
origins and are recognized as proverbs like any others.
Such proverbs we may call "learned," as contrasted
with "popular," although the term refers only to our
own more extensive knowledge and not to an essential difference in origin or kind.

Translation of proverbs from one language into another has always occurred when two languages have
stood in intimate cultural relations for some length of
time. For example, Latin proverbs of Greek origin
are not infrequent.[1] Even *The die is cast* (Alea jacta
est) is probably Greek: Pompey tells us that Caesar
spoke the Greek words on crossing the Rubicon.[2]
Love cures the very wound it makes (Amoris vulnus
idem sanat) is Greek, too, and Tertullian's *Nihil
enim ad Andromachen* ('That has nothing to do with
the case' [an English proverb, ultimately a quotation
from Gilbert and Sullivan's operetta, *The Mikado*]).
A rolling stone gathers no moss is said to be a Greek
proverb recorded by Lucian, which is the source of a
mediaeval Latin proverb, *Saxum volutum non obdu-
citur musco.*

No one has attempted, so far as I am aware, to define the extent and nature of Latin borrowings of

1 See in general Otto, p. xxii.
2 Since the Greek proverb employs the imperative, Erasmus is very
likely justified in correcting the Latin to read "Let the die be cast"
(Alea jacta estò).

Greek proverbs.[1] Obviously the incompleteness of the
record and the inconvenience of bringing together the
Greek sources make such a study difficult, but the
situation is no more discouraging than in many another investigation in classical philology. Among the
possible foreign influences of Latin proverbs we need
consider only the Greek, for the two Punic proverbs,
one from classical Latin and one preserved for us by
St. Augustine, will scarcely provide a basis for specu-
lation. In Latin proverbs of Greek origin we perceive
more or less clearly three degrees of adaptation to the
new surroundings: (1) complete acceptance by the
folk, (2) deliberate employment of a foreign proverb,
(3) casual and fumbling translation. Among these we
cannot always distinguish with ease and confidence.
The retention of a proverb by the Romance peoples,
if we could always recognize it as retention and distinguish it from later learned borrowing from the classics, could be used to identify and define classical
Latin proverbs which had fully established themselves in oral tradition. The existence of Greek proverbs of Latin origin is doubtful.[2] An exhaustive study
of the problems involved in these relations of Latin
and Greek culture would apparently be profitable.
Only experience will show what obstacles lie in the
way of solving this and similar problems which turn

1 Crusius makes some helpful remarks on this problem in his review of
 Otto, *Wochenschrift für Klassische Philologie*, VIII (1891), coll. 428–
 429. See also Otto, pp. xviii–xix.
2 See Otto, pp. xviii–xix; Crusius, as above, col. 426.

on the borrowing and translating of proverbs. The
bravest effort in this direction is Altenkirch's comparison [1] of Greek and Slavic proverbs, but in the
choice of subject we cannot limit ourselves so strictly
as he thinks necessary. He demands that one of the
two proverbial stocks compared should have been
recorded before cultural contacts had begun. Of
course such a limitation facilitates the comparison,
but it is rarely present. As he points out, we must
also be on our guard lest we compare analogous proverbs which are nevertheless of entirely independent
origin. He does not consider the possibility of stylistic criteria as standards in determining the nature
and direction of these cultural currents.

A particularly interesting question presents itself
in connection with certain medieval Latin proverbs
associated with vernacular proverbs. In collections
from widely separated places we find the same Latin
versions; e. g. *Passere sub tecto remanente recedit
yrundo* ('While the sparrow remains under the eaves,
the swallow departs') appears in a thirteenth-century
Vienna manuscript, a fifteenth-century Basel manuscript of probably Low Franconian (Dutch) proveni-
ence, and, for the first time with the vernacular original, in the Dutch and Latin *Proverbia communia sive
seriosa* of the end of the fifteenth century, and no
doubt in many other places. *Qui tenet anguillam per*

1 " Die Beziehungen zwischen Slaven und Griechen in ihren Sprichwörtern," *Archiv für Slavische Philologie*, XXX (1909), 1–47, 321–364.

caudam, non habet illam ('He who holds an eel by the tail does not have it') occurs in the same Vienna and Basel manuscripts and persists in several printed collections of the end of the sixteenth century, so tenacious is the tradition when once established. *Sub nive quod tegitur, dum nix perit, omne videtur* ('All is seen that is hidden under the snow, when the snow melts') is in the Basel manuscript and the *Proverbia communia*. Probably we have enough instances to discover the history of some important mediaeval manuscript collections. Voigt believes, for example, that the rather large collection which he prints under the title *Florilegium Gottingense* contains traces of earlier (perhaps lost) alphabetical collections. Careful comparisons might disclose the history and interrelations of proverb collections just as such comparisons have already clarified the history of glosses.

But to return to the subject of the translation of proverbs. In the flood tide after the Middle Ages, with the Renaissance and the publication in 1500 of Erasmus' *Veterum Maximeque Insignium Paroemiarum, id est Adagiorum Collectanea*, although it was only a thin book of 152 pages, the translation of proverbs from one language into another becomes rampant and everywhere enriches the national stocks of proverbs. Translation has always been an important means of enlarging a nation's proverbial stores, but the systematic manner in which such translations were made in the period following the

Renaissance creates new problems. In the countries where several collections were printed in the course of the sixteenth century, notably in Germany, it is possible to see and study the gradual acclimatization of a proverb. One translation after another is tried and rejected, until finally some form gains general acceptance.

We have a clear and satisfactory description of this process in Jente's history of *Morgenstunde hat Gold im Munde* ('The morning hour has gold in its mouth').[1] In the sixteenth century, collectors struggled with the translation of the humanistic proverb *Aurora Musis amica* ('The dawn a friend to the Muses'), which is first used by Erasmus in a letter of 1497 to Christian Northoff of Lübeck and first printed in his *Colloquies* of 1518. Apparently the need for a translation did not arise before the end of the century, since neither Johannes Agricola (1529) nor Sebastian Frank (1541) in their large collections, which give much space to classical and humanistic materials, mentions either original or translation. At first, we have a clumsy paraphrase, which by its ineptitude suggests the probability that no briefer and better form existed. A translation of 1576, the oldest of all known translations, is to the following effect:

1 "'Morgenstunde hat Gold im Munde,'" *Publications Modern Language Association*, XLII (1927), 865–872; see some additional material in Stoett, *Nederlandsche Spreekwoorden* (Zutphen, 1924–25), *s. v.* Morgenstond.

Aurora amica Musis.
Surgere non cesses, cum Phoebus surgit ab ortu:
Mane bonis studijs quilibet aptus erit.
Welcher begert zstudieren wol,
An morgen er frü auffstehen soll.

A few years later a better form appeared, *Die Mor-genstundt hat die Arbeyt im Mundt* (1582), and at almost the same time *Die Morgenstunde hat Gold im Munde* (1585) entered the lists. The variant *Die Morgenstund hat das Brod im Mund* is found sporadically after 1605. The collections of the seventeenth century contain one or more of these variant forms. It is nearly a century before the competition is definitely settled in favor of *Morgenstunde hat Gold im Munde*. This explanation of the development is supported by the late appearance of the proverb in the Netherlands and Scandinavia. It is striking that the unsuccessful forms had difficulty in crossing the borders of Germany: *Morgenstund har Brød i Mund* is found once in Danish. But even the accepted form never firmly established itself in these adjoining countries, so closely bound to Germany by cultural and linguistic ties. In view of this history we cannot any longer give ear to those explanations which see traces of Germanic myth in the proverb. Nor need we linger over the explanation that an etymological pun, *Aurora quia habet aurum in ore*, is involved. The pun was invented long after *Morgenstunde hat Gold im Munde* had come into being. The situation we have just described exists in other proverbs. In *Inter os et offam* and *Inter manus et mentum*, classical Latin possessed two competing translations of the Greek proverb analogous to *There's many a slip 'twixt cup and lip*.

In later periods the problems of translation from one language into another and of borrowing from one culture by another are of course far more complex than in classical antiquity. True enough, the apparent simplicity of these problems in Latin and Greek tradition may arise from our ignorance of many factors. However this may be, it is certain that problems involving the dissemination of proverbs by translation are very complex after the Renaissance. Yet it is worth while pointing out that they are not necessarily insoluble. There are, for example, two readily distinguishable proverbs comparing the dangers of fire, water, and woman. Each has its own history. One form, *Sunt tria damna domus: imber, mala femina, fumus* ('There are three accursed things in the house: leaking, an evil woman, smoke'), which is ultimately Biblical in origin, has spread over the part of the world directly under the influence of the Latin church. Another form, *The sea, fire, woman: three evils*, is Greek in its beginnings and is disseminated by humanistic means. Only in Italy do we find the slightest signs of confusion and contamination between the two forms.

In studying the dissemination of proverbs during

the Middle Ages and later, we shall have to pay particular attention to a large and important group of
proverbs which Seiler calls "international mediaeval"
(gemeinmittelalterlich). Although they are very
widely known and form indeed a significant part of
our everyday stock, we cannot assign their origin to
one country or language; and it is doubtful whether
we shall ever know more than we do now about the
place, time, and circumstances of their invention.
Often they are found first in Latin, and evidently owe
their wide currency to this international language of
the Middle Ages. Occasionally, but much less frequently, their first appearance is in one of the mediaeval vernacular collections of maxims and sententious
observations, such as Freidank's *Bescheidenheit.* We
know little or nothing about the origin of such proverbs as *What the eye sees not, the heart rues not*; *All is
not gold that glitters*; *Give him an inch and he'll take an
ell*; *New brooms sweep clean*; *Rome was not built in a
day*; *It's an ill bird that fouls its own nest*; *Strike while
the iron is hot.* To the same class of materials belongs
the distich

> When the Devil was sick, the Devil a monk would be;
> When the Devil was well, the Devil a monk was he.

The rhyme has circulated since the early Middle Ages
in Latin, French, English, German, and no doubt
other languages as well. Luther and Melanchthon did
not disdain to cite it, and *Joe Miller's Complete Jest
Book* preserves it for us. The more exact definition of

what constitutes the stock of international mediaeval proverbs is perhaps the most important and extensive task in the whole field. Only when the stock of such proverbs is known and their history written, can we progress to the more special examination of individual national stocks.

BIBLICAL PROVERBS [1]

Two classes of materials, the Biblical and the classical, have quite naturally contributed a far larger share of translated proverbs than any other source. In all the centuries of the Christian Era the Bible, in which were included the Apocrypha and, notably, the book of Ecclesiasticus or Sirach, was an obvious and inexhaustible source. The Church Fathers quoted

1 The special character of Biblical proverbs makes it possible to use collections and studies in any language. The more important reference works for such proverbs are found in Dutch and German: Kat, *Bijbelsche Uitdrukkingen en Spreekwijzen in onze Taal* (Zutphen, 1926); Laurillard, *Bijbel en Volkstaal* (Amsterdam, 1875; 2d ed., Rotterdam, 1901), with the comments by Harrebomée, *Bedenkingen op het Prijsschrift van Dr. E. Laurillard* (Gorinchem, 1877); Sprenger van Eijk, *Handleiding tot de Kennis van onze Vaderlandsche Spreekwoorden* (Rotterdam, 1835–41); Zeeman, *Nederlandsche Spreekwoorden . . . aan den Bijbel Ontleend* (Dordrecht, 1877, 1888); and Schulze, *Die Biblischen Sprichwörter der Deutschen Sprache* (Göttingen, 1860); Büchmann, *Geflügelte Worte* (Berlin, 1920), pp. 1–70. Biblical quotations and allusions in Old and Middle English literature are collected by A. S. Cook (*Biblical Quotations in Old English Prose Writers* [New York, 1898–1903]) and Mary W. Smyth (*Biblical Quotations in Old English before 1350* [New York, 1911]); although these books are not primarily concerned with proverbial materials, they give an idea of the way in which the Bible was used and how Biblical proverbs may have arisen. Marvin (*Curiosities in Proverbs* [New York, 1916]) gives some miscellaneous and unsystematic notes on English Biblical proverbs.

and reshaped in more pregnant form the words of
Biblical wisdom. A little later the efforts to provide
translations of the Bible or of individual books in the
different modern languages poured out a steady
stream of material which was either proverbial or
capable of being made proverbial by slight adaptation. Classical sources did not flow so abundantly,
although from the very beginning of Christian history
classical admonitions united with Christian maxims
in colloquial and formal discourse. A new and
stronger current of classical influence sets in with
Humanism and the Renaissance.

Although proverbs of Biblical origin have often
been collected, they have never been studied as examples of the history and development of oral tradition. The books which deal with them indicate, although unfortunately not always with accuracy, the
Biblical passages which have become current among
the folk. The author, often swayed by his didactic
desires, includes an apothegm which he thinks ought
to be a proverb. These books do not usually discuss
what kinds of Biblical passages succeed in establish-
ing themselves, what changes occur in these quotations during their lives on the lips of the folk, or what
quotations are most exposed to changes. Such books
do not often seek to identify the exact source of the
quotation. A slight variation from the Biblical phrase
— a variation to which, however, the proverb often
clings tenaciously — may tell us that it is derived

from one of the Church Fathers, a mediaeval preacher,
or an obsolete translation of the Bible rather than the
so-called King James Version or some other received
text.

In proverbs of Biblical origin we see all stages of
the disintegration of a phrase: the Biblical quotation
gradually becomes a vague, inaccurate reminiscence.
The Biblical "A living dog is better than a dead lion"
(Melior est canis vivus leone mortuo, *Eccles.* ix, 4) has,
for example, suffered little alteration. Indeed, the
lack of freedom in its use and the bookish atmosphere
in which it seems most at home makes one inclined to
regard it as a learned or semi-learned phrase which
has never quite become a popular proverb. A characteristic alteration is seen in the popular forms of the
Biblical "Every one that doeth evil hateth the light"
(Omnis enim, qui male agit, odit lucem, *John* iii, 20).
It exists as a simple quotation from the Bible in the
Elizabethan *He that doeth evil, hateth the light.* Earlier
than this, about the end of the fifteenth century we
find on the continent *The evil one avoids the light as the
Devil the Cross* (Die quade schuwet dat licht als die
duvel dat cruce), with a Latin translation, *Demon
ipse crucem fugit ut malus undique lucem.* The comparison with the Devil, which is apparently a mediaeval invention and addition, is a typical modification
of a Biblical proverb: the maxim is made more effective by a picturesque and vividly conceived scene.
No particular form of this proverb seems to have definitely established itself in the European proverbial

stock. Another characteristic development is seen in *Money is the root of all evil*, which has sprung from "The love of money is the root of all evil" (Radix enim omnium malorum est cupiditas, *I Tim.* vi, 10). The shift from the abstract to the concrete adapts the sententious apothegm into the direct and suggestive proverb. We have the same sort of thing in *Pride goes before a fall*, which derives immediately from "Pride goeth before destruction, and an haughty spirit before a fall" (Contritionem praecedit superbia et ante ruinam exaltatur superbus, *Prov.* xvi, 18). Once the substitution of "fall" for "destruction" had occurred, the forces of parallelism and contrast could create *Pride goes before and shame comes after.* The scene is conceived still more vividly in the Swedish *Where sin drives, shame sits in the back seat* (Där odygd åker fram, sitter i baksätet skam).

There are many proverbs which do not show such obvious and unmistakable relations to the Biblical sources as those mentioned thus far. *Man proposes, but God disposes* has a long history which probably begins with "A man's heart deviseth his way: but the Lord directeth his steps" (Cor hominis disponit viam suam: sed Domini est dirigere gressus eius, *Prov.* xvi, 9). In the eighth century Alcuin knew "Homo cogitat, Deus iudicat" and in the twelfth, Ordericus Vitalis, the chronicler, has "Homo cogitat, Deus ordinat." The characteristic rhyming form we find in the *Imitatio Christi*, i, 19: "Homo proponit, Deus disponit." It is interesting to see that German, although un-

able to use the rhyming Latin form or its derivatives, has nevertheless invented a rhyming form of its
own: *Der Mensch denkt, Gott lenkt.* The most recent
development seems to be the insertion of the word
but, in this way implying the plans of God and man
are at cross-purposes. The implication, although
vaguely present in the older forms, is not directly
expressed. A proverb which diverges far from its
Biblical source is *The more he has, the more he wants*,
which may conceivably arise from "He that loveth
silver shall not be satisfied with silver; nor he that
loveth abundance with increase: this is also vanity,"
(Avarus non implebitur pecunia: et qui amat divitias,
fructum non capiet ex eis: et hos ergo vanitas, *Eccles.*
v, 9). The old proverb gives us a modern advertising
slogan: "The more you eat, the more you want"
(motto of Cracker Jack).

Occasionally we trace the origin of a Biblical proverb to a single version. Thus Luther translated "Ex
abundantia cordis os loquitur" ('Of the abundance
of the heart his mouth speaketh,' *Lk.* vi, 45; *Matt.*
xii, 34) as 'Wes das Herz voll ist, des geht der Mund
über' and defended it emphatically: "If I should follow the asses who will lay the literal words before me
and translate thus: 'From the superfluity of the heart
the mouth speaks,' tell me, is that talking German?" [1]

[1] "Ex abundantia . . . loquitur. Wenn ich den Eseln sol folgen, die
werden mir die buchstaben furlegen, und also dolmetzschen: Auss dem
überflus des hertzen redet der mund. Sage mir, Ist das deutsch gere-
det?"— *Vom Dolmetschen* (Weimar ed., XXX, ii, 637).

Luther's form drove out the others like "Ex habitu cordis sonitus depromitur oris" ('The sound of the mouth is derived from the habit of the heart') and "Quod in cordi, hoc est in ore," which were struggling to establish themselves. Schiller, it is interesting to remember, attempted a different translation in *Wallensteins Tod*, i, 173–174:

> was der frohe Mut
> Mich sprechen liess im Überfluss des Herzens.

There is of course no question that Luther's version has fixed itself in tradition. If proof were needed, we might find it in a Swabian proverb: *Wes der Magen voll ist, läuft das Maul über* ('Whatever the stomach is full of, with that the mouth runs over'), which is made on the same model.

As a contrast, we may study the history of *Narren soll man mit Kolben lausen* ('One should louse fools with clubs'). This proverb is evidently derived from such Biblical passages as "A rod is for the back of him that is void of understanding" (Et virga in dorso eius qui indiget corde, *Prov.* x, 13); "And stripes for the backs of fools" (Et mallei percutientes stultorum corporibus, *Prov.* xix, 29); and "And a rod for the fool's back" (Et virga in dorso imprudentium, *Prov.* xxvi, 3). It established itself in its present form before the appearance of Luther's translation and persists in tradition, notwithstanding the enormous influence which so widely accepted a version must have. Luther translates the first of these passages more literally and less idiomatically as "Auf den Rücken des Narren gehört eine Rute," and, in his version, the remaining passages contain equally little suggestion of the proverb.

Direct contact with the Biblical text has not been the sole source of tradition. Where it is possible to identify the channel through which the phrase reached the folk, we can often trace it back to some compend. Quotation in preaching and in ecclesiastical writing was abundant and careless, and favored the rise of minor variations. We can at times catch a church writer in the very act of reshaping a Biblical phrase: Pope Innocent III we know to have arranged the climax "Tria sunt quae non sinunt hominem in domo permanere: fumus, stillicidium, et mala uxor" ('There are three things which do not let a man stay at home: smoke, dripping, and an evil wife'). We are not able to identify positively the inventor of *Homo proponit, Deus disponit,* but, as we have seen, its inventor, a man active in ecclesiastical life and writings, lived somewhere north of the Alps between the time of Alcuin and that of Thomas à Kempis. The limits within which the invention of *The tongue breaketh bone, though itself have none* occurred cannot be drawn so closely. Obviously it is derived from "A soft tongue breaketh the bone" (Lingua mollis confringit duritiam, *Prov.* xxv, 15) or "A blow of the tongue breaks bones" (Plaga linguae comminuet ossa, *Ecclus.* xxviii, 21) but since characteristic proverbial modifications are found both in Greek and in the languages culturally associated with Greek, like Bulgarian and Serbian, and in Latin and the vernacular languages of Western Europe, we must conclude that the transformation took place at an early time.

Biblical proverbs, and among them perhaps even those which we have discussed, may have been proverbs before their incorporation into Holy Writ. Ordinarily we are reduced to conjecture in such matters, but there are proverbs which are known to have circulated in oral tradition before their appearance in the Bible. When Our Saviour said "It is hard for thee to kick against the goad" (Durum est tibi contra stimulum calcitrare, *Acts* xxvi, 14) he was using a proverbial phrase which Pindar, Aeschylus, and Euripides knew. "Physician, heal thyself" (Medice cura teipsum, *Lk.* iv, 23) seems to have been a current proverb when the Nazarenes quoted it against Jesus as a rebuke for His having performed miracles in Capernaum and not in Nazareth. "To strain at a gnat and swallow a camel" (Caeci,excolantes culicem, camelum autem glutientes, *Matt.* xxiii, 24) we may conjecture to have been taken from popular speech, and "to eat salt with," i. e. 'to associate with,' an idiom which is still preserved in the Greek συναλιζό-μενος but is obscured in the Vulgate "convescens" (*Acts* i, 4), was an old phrase in Greek long before St. Luke used it. Nor need our illustrations be limited to the New Testament: Hosea probably did not invent the phrase "To sow the wind and reap the whirl-wind," (Quia ventum seminabunt, et turbinem metent, *Hosea* viii, 7). *A soft answer turneth away wrath* was known to Aeschylus as well as Solomon, and Homer used *Like will to like* before it found a place in the Book of Sirach.

Such parallel lines of tradition, the one Biblical and the other classical, are frequently found: *A friend in need is a friend indeed* goes back to Ecclesiasticus and to Ennius. Under these circumstances confusion and contamination of the two traditions is to be expected, although the differences between the two forms may not always be sufficiently marked to permit us to differentiate them. Martha Lenschau sees a joining of Biblical and classical tradition in *Many a one falls in the snare which he has set for others* (Mancher in den Strick selbst fellt, den er andern hat gestellt). The fundamental metaphor is based on "He made a pit, and digged it, and is fallen into the ditch which he made" (Lacum aperuit, et effodit eum: et incidit in foveam, quam fecit, *Ps.* vii, 16; cf. *Prov.* xxvi, 27). She assigns the metaphor of the noose to Ovid's "They fall into the snares which they have set" (In laqueos, quos posuere, cadant, *Art. amat.*, i, 646) and other similar passages in classical authors. Martin Luther, she concludes, established the expression with "pit"; the texts with "snare," "noose," "rope," and the like are either independent inventions or derived from Latin sources. In principle, this explanation is correct, although we cannot accept it in this particular instance. The confusion of "snare" and "pit" versions must rest, at least in some measure, on "The heathen are sunk down in the pit that they made: in the net which they hid is their own foot taken. . . . The wicked is snared in the work of his own hands" (Infixae sunt Gentes in interitu, quem fecerunt. In laqueo isto, quem absconderunt, comprehensus est pes eorum. . . . In operibus manuum suarum comprehensus est peccator, *Ps.* ix, 15–16). St. Jerome alludes to this passage when he says: "While you do not know, you are caught with your own snare" (Dum nescis, proprio captus es laqueo). Such authorities, the Bible, the classical poet, and the Church Father, contributed to the success of the proverb and he would be brave indeed who would endeavor to assign to each his proper share.

CLASSICAL PROVERBS

From classical authors tradition derives many proverbs: *Love is blind*; *Many men, many minds*; *To err is human*; *Easy come, easy go*; *Well begun is half done*; *Better late than never*; *Don't spur a willing horse*; *No sooner said than done*; *Of two evils choose the least*; *Two heads are better than one*; *The master's eye makes the horse fat*; *While there's life, there's hope*; *One swallow does not make a summer*. No particular class of proverbs goes back to Latin and Greek literature, although metaphorical proverbs are perhaps somewhat less frequent than purely sententious observations on the conduct of life. Even a proverb so difficult to translate as a play on words is turned into a different language: *Onus, honos* ('Burden, honor') becomes the German *Würden, Bürden*.

Not infrequently a proverb of classical origin runs parallel with a proverb which seems to have developed independently. Thus the German proverb *They hang the little thieves; the big ones are allowed to run* (Die kleinen Diebe hängt man, grosse lässt man laufen) is found in many collections of popular origin and is clearly a proverb belonging to the folk. There is no definite evidence connecting it with an analogous proverb displaying a thoroughly Roman spirit of law and reverence for sacred objects: "Small sacrileges are punished; great ones are celebrated by triumphs" (Sacrilegia minuta puniuntur, magna in triumphis aguntur, Seneca, *Ep.*, lxxxvii, 23), or with a proverb in Aulus Gellius about the different treatment accorded to thieves of public and private property, or with "The big thieves bear off the little one" [to be hanged?] (Οἱ μεγάλοι κλέπται τὸν μικρὸν ἀπάγουσι, Diogenes Laertius, vi, 2, 6, 45). The classical proverbs, as we see, either refer to social relations of a political or religious nature or accuse the executioners of the same crime as the criminals. Although similar to the classical parallels, the German proverb is quite distinct. The classical examples have a respectable history of their own in German collections, but are not confused with the German parallel and are characteristically associated with authors possessing a learned background. We must conclude that the German proverb is independent satiric comment on the course of the world. Its interest and significance in the eyes of a former generation are shown by the fact that it provided the subject for a legal dissertation: *Dissertatio de trito sermone proverbio: Parvi fures suspenduntur, magni dimittuntur vel in crumena puniuntur sive marsupio reconduntur* (Altdorf, 1726).[1]

Alteration by the forces of tradition occurs quite as frequently in proverbs of classical origin as in those of Biblical origin and it need not be illustrated at great length. Plautus writes "From whatever direction the wind is, the sail is turned accordingly" (Utcumque est ventus, exim velum vortitur, *Poen.*, 754), but mediaeval and modern tradition has generally preferred to say "cloak" or "mantle" instead of "sail": *One should turn his coat according to the weather* (Man soll den Mantel kehren, als das Wetter geht). Possibly the Horatian "They change their climate, not their disposition, who run beyond the sea" (Caelum, non animam mutant, qui trans mare currunt, *Ep.*, i, 11, 27) yields *If a goose flies across the sea, there comes back a quack-quack* (Fleugt ein ganss

1 Cited by D. Murray, *Lawyers' Merriments* (Glasgow, 1912), p. 49; C. C. Nopitsch, *Die Literatur der Sprichwörter* (Nuremberg, 1833), p. 58; Wander, *Deutsches Sprichwörter-Lexicon, s. v.* Dieb, 170.

vber mer, so kompt ein gagag wieder her), and in variant forms we have ass, cat, crow, jackdaw, and fool.

Of course there have been serious accidents occasionally in the passage from Latin into the modern languages, and, furthermore, various modern proverbs have been regarded as descendants of Latin phrases, although the context shows clearly enough that the similarity is merely verbal and does not involve the transmission of ideas. Virgil's "A chill snake, lads, lurks in the grass" (Frigidus, o pueri, latet anguis in herba, *Ecl.*, iii, 93) is not the source of the idea in our proverb *A snake in the grass*. The saying *When the horse is stolen, lock the barn door* cannot rest on a misunderstanding of Juvenal's words: "If in all the world you cannot show me so abominable a crime, I hold my peace; I will not forbid you to smite your breast with your fists, or to pummel your face with open palm, seeing that after so great a loss you must close your doors, and that a household bewails the loss of money with louder lamentations than death" (*Sat.*, xiii, 126 ff.). The reference concerns the Roman custom of closing doors as a sign of mourning. It is wisest not to think of any connection between Juvenal and the proverb and to regard the proverb as a peasant's invention and as comparable to such sayings as *To cover the well after the child is drowned*. We may observe in passing that the substitutions which occur in the variants are quite in the manner of oral tradition: for "horse" we have "cow" or "cattle" and for "lock" we have "repair." But further illustration of such substitutions is unnecessary: proverbs live the same sort of life in tradition, whatever their past history.

II

THE CONTENT OF PROVERBS

UP to this point we have been chiefly concerned with questions of origin and historical accidents of transmission and preservation; now we turn our attention to content and style. The content of proverbs affords a more suitable means of classification and more profitable subjects of study than does the distinction between "learned" and "popular," which we have rejected. Of course not all classifications according to subject are fruitful. Those which are based upon specific objects, such as collections of proverbs concerning dogs,[1] or women,[2] or God, do not form suggestive groups of material. But classifications which involve ideas or which bring together proverbs belonging to a particular cultural sphere, such as those of proverbs dealing with legal notions, the weather, health, agriculture, shipping, and so on, supply us with materials which reward the labor of collecting them. Even the bull ring has its collection of proverbs: Miguel Moliné y Roca, *Paremiografía*

[1] See, e. g., A. Koskenjaakko, *Koira Suomalaisissa ynnä Virolaisissa Sananlaskuissa* (Helsinki, 1909).
[2] See the bibliography in Bonser, *Proverb Literature* (London, 1930), pp. 430–432, Nos. 3750–3777, and C. Benzon, *Kvinden i Ordsproget* (Copenhagen, 1907).

66

Taurina (Barcelona, 1888). Collections devoted to ir-
religious and harmful proverbs, such as E. Meisner's
Ein hundert Drey- und dreyssig Gotteslästerliche, Gott-
lose, Schändliche und Schädliche, auch Unanständige,
und theils Falsche Teutsche Sprüch-Wörter, Höchst-
sträffliche Eingeschlichene Redens-Arten, Ungeziemende
Reime und Grobe Gewohnheiten (Jena, 1705); E[ric]
P[ontoppidan]'s *Onde Ordsprog, som Fordoerver Gode*
Hoeder, Igiendrevne af Guds ord (Bad Proverbs which
ruin Good Morals, Refuted from the Word of God
[Copenhagen, 1739]), which was translated and enlarged in Swedish (Stockholm, 1777); and J. G.
Schöner's *Sprichwörter, womit sich Laue Christen Be-*
helfen (Nuremberg, 1802),[1] might seem likely at first
sight to contain curious and interesting materials, but
the authors' purpose is so exclusively didactic that
they lose themselves in moralizing and quote only an
occasional proverb as text.

CUSTOMS AND SUPERSTITIONS

Quite naturally especial interest attaches to proverbs which contain evidences of manners and customs. Several such proverbs have been already commented upon in other connections. We may here
draw attention to a few more instances in which an
old trait has been preserved. *Good wine needs no bush*
alludes to the fact that wine shops were formerly

1 See *Catalogue des Livres Parémiologiques composant la Bibliothèque de*
Ignace Bernstein (Warsaw, 1900), Nos. 2144, 2412, 3271.

marked by a bush in the same way that the barber still displays a barber's pole. The proverb occurs in two forms, one with "bush" and one with "ivy." The latter, *The best wine needeth no ivie-bush*, appears to have the closer connections with a tradition which begins in Renaissance Latin sources. It has often been said that this proverb reaches back to classical Latin, but the evidence is flimsy. *If the cap fits, put it on* alludes to the fool's cap. The mediaeval attitude toward saints' relics — an attitude which was of fundamental importance in architecture, literature, and life — is briefly summed up in *Every priest praises his own relics* (Ein jeder Pfaff lobt sein Heiligtum). Glass rings were gifts among poor folk in the Middle Ages. The minnesinger Walther von der Vogelweide declares that the glass ring of his sweetheart is dearer to him than the gold of a queen:

> Swaz si sagen, ich bin dir holt,
> und nim din glesin vingerlin für einer küneginne golt.[1]

Long before the twelfth century the fragility of a glass ring was a proverbial comparison for the fragility of certain friendships: as Bishop Salomon of Constance said at the beginning of the tenth century, "Give glass to friends of glass" (Vitrei amici vitro sunt donandi). The proverb *A man is a man still, if he hath a hose on his head* is found as late as 1732 and

---

[1] Ed. K. Lachmann, 50, 12; see the notes in W. Wilmanns, *Walther von der Vogelweide* (4th ed. by V. Michels, Halle, 1924 [Germanistische Handbibliothek, I, 2]), p. 211; Simrock, *Gedichte Walthers*, I, 201.

may allude to some mediaeval custom or game. It may refer to a man who has no cap and wears an old stocking in its place; in other words, a man is not to be judged by his apparel, however grotesque it may be.

Proverbs do not often contain traces of superstitions, myths, or formal religion, and most instances which have been cited fail on closer examination to bear out the correctness of the interpretation. The mythological element in the eighty-odd proverbs which L. de Baecker quotes in *De la Religion du Nord de la France avant le Christianisme* (1854) reduces to almost nothing; H. Lessmann's *Der deutsche Volksmund im Lichte der Sage* (1922), which makes an even more determined effort to find traces of myths, yields as little. A typical illustration is the proverb *Morgenstunde hat Gold im Munde* (The morning hour has gold in its mouth), which has already been mentioned in other connections. It has nothing to do with a possible mythical notion that gold pieces fall from the mouth of the dawn. Proverbs occasionally mention figures of myth and tradition, but it is extremely doubtful how much reliance can be placed on such allusions as sources of mythological information. Classical Greek proverbs are supposed to mention the gods with relative frequency, while Roman proverbs avoid such figures.[1] The proverbs of primitive

1 Otto, "Die Götter und Halbgötter im [Lateinischen] Sprichwört," *Archiv für lateinische Lexikographie*, III (1886), 207–229, 384–387.

peoples rarely mention divine personages or significant religious matters. The notion that red-headed
people are not to be trusted is a firmly established
proverb, *Rotbart nie gut ward*; but we dare not put
much trust in the explanation that it involves an
allusion to the red beard of Thor. Similarly, modern
European proverbs give us little or no idea of the
Christian God or Christian cosmology. A few proverbs show a definite Catholic tinge and are presumably older than the Reformation, e. g. *Where God does
not help, no saint avails* (Wo Gott nicht hilft, da hilft
kein Heiliger).

The Devil is the most frequently mentioned figure
from Christian cosmology, but the allusions are not
abundant or specific enough to build up a picture.
He must have a long spoon that will sup with the Devil
and *Needs must when the Devil drives* tell us very little
about popular notions of the Devil. The German
proverb *Where the Devil can't go he sends an old
woman* (var. *his grandmother*) (Wo der Teufel nicht
hinkommen kann, schickt er ein altes Weib [*var.*
seine Grossmutter]) is equally uncommunicative.
When it rains and the sun shines at the same time, the
folk say *The Devil is beating his grandmother* (var.
wife), but the mythological allusion is obscure. Its
presence, however, is hardly to be questioned, for we
have analogous expressions in many languages of
Western Europe: the French say *The Devil is marry-
ing his daughter* (Le diable marie sa fille), the Dutch,

When it rains and the sun shines, then there is a fair in Hell (Als 't regent en de zon schijnt, dan is het kermis in de hel); and in the province of Groningen, *When it rains and the sun shines, the witches are baking pancakes* (Als het regent en de zon schint, bakken de heksen pannekoeken). The German and English versions are essentially the same. The similarities and dissimilarities of these various forms do not suggest a recent borrowing from one language by another. What the fundamental form from which the versions spring may have been and what its meaning was we cannot even conjecture. It is worth remarking that these mythological allusions, and, I suspect, mythological allusions in general, occur in proverbs which contain no metaphor.

It is easier to find proverbial illustrations of superstitions than of myths and mythical figures other than the Devil. The notion that red-headed men are not to be trusted is a firmly established proverb: *A red beard was never good* (Rotbart nie gut ward), and it is frequently joined with a like warning against bearded women: *Greet a redbeard and a bearded woman from afar* (Ein roth bart vnd bärtig weib grüez von weiten). The situation is somewhat different in a sixteenth-century German proverb which warns us against certain abnormalities: *Beware of a red Italian, a white Frenchman, and a black German* (Hüt dich vor eim roten Walhen, weissen Frantzosen, und schwartzen Teutschen). *A Sunday journey is not good* appears to be Irish superstition as well as proverb. The belief that *A whistling girl and a crowing hen will come to no good end,* which also occurs in the form

> Whistling girls and crowing hens
> Will all (*var.* surely) come to some bad ends,

as well as in the more cheerful, contradictory version:

> Girls that whistle and hens that crow
> Will always have fun, wherever they go,

involves a superstition of international currency. *An unlicked cub* preserves the old belief that bears give birth to a mass of flesh which must be *licked into shape.* The latter phrase, which is of course to be understood quite literally, has found an altogether different interpretation on the lips of the folk. Few such phrases enjoy the metaphorical use so typical of the proverb with ethical or moral content, e. g. *Rats desert a sinking ship,* i. e. 'followers leave a man of wealth and influence when his power wanes.' Of course the danger of seeing an explanation in myth or superstition when it does not really exist is ever present. *The rain falls in the lap of the happy bride* (Felici sponsae pluit in gremium) has naught to do with the golden rain of Danaë but uses an obvious symbolism.[1] The Italian *A woman of good family always bears a girl as her first child* (La donna di buona razza fa sempre la prima figliata femina)[2] and the

[1] There is another and better known proverb: *Happy is the bride the sun shines on, and happy the corpse the rain rains on.*
[2] Wesselski, *Poliziano,* p. 214.

similar Spanish *To the lucky man a daughter is first born* (Al hombre venturero la hija le nasce primero) are probably words of comfort and not proverbial superstitions.

Some superstitions circulate in a form which may be called proverbial, but we do not clearly understand why the folk preserves these particular superstitions in an unvarying form. According to Ovid, honest women did not marry in the month of May. The manner in which he says it makes it probable that the superstition was current in a rigid, proverbial form: "Mense malas Maio nubere vulgus ait" (*Fasti*, v, 490). The belief persists in similar form in German: *Im Maien gehen Huren und Buben zur Kirche*, and in English, *Marry in May, you'll rue it for aye*. Christian modifications are *Twischen Paschen* (Easter) *un Pingsten* (Pentecost) *fryen die Unseligen*, and *Marry in Lent; you'll live to repent*. The superstition that the oil or ashes of a scorpion cure its sting yields an Italian proverb: *Non mi morse mai scorpione, che io non mi medicassi col suo olio*,[1] but it can scarcely be regarded as other than a bit of traditional medical lore. *The more camomile is trodden on, the faster it grows*, which is perhaps part of the euphuistic tradition, is a stock Elizabethan comparison of unknown origin. *A woman, a dog, and a walnut tree, the more they are beaten the better they be* enjoys, on the

---

1 Wesselski, *Erlesenes* (Gesellschaft Deutscher Bücherfreunde in Böhmen, VIII, Prague, 1928), p. 10, n. 1; Skeat, *Early English Proverbs* (Oxford, 1910), No. 117.

contrary, frequent use as a proverb, although there is no apparent reason why the walnut should be particularly favored except as a characteristic northern nut-bearing tree. There is a Spanish variant with the almond.

Allusions which are no longer understood offer extremely interesting problems and very often resist successfully all attempts at their solution. Occasionally the unexplained proverb has an international circulation, and the resulting abundance of materials, often illuminating the difficulty from various angles, ought to make solution easier. Although there are many references in various languages after the late Middle Ages to *Those who eat cherries with great lords shall have their eyes dashed out with the stones* and *If the sky falls, we shall have larks*, the proverbs are obscure. I am reminded that the European lark and the American lark are very different birds and that the European lark flies to great heights. Possibly an explanation can be found in this way. The proverb belongs, of course, to the type of "never-never" sayings.

It has been said that *Those who live in glass houses should not throw stones* rests upon a Spanish idiom according to which a "glass house" is a house with windows. If this is true, — I have not been able to find the idiom in question, — the proverb is ultimately Spanish in origin. *The game is not worth the candle* involves an unexplained allusion, perhaps to some game in which a candle was the stake or forfeit, or, as is more plausibly suggested, it refers to the fact that gamblers were required to pay for the candles to light the gambling rooms, and obviously the game was no longer worth the candle when the stakes became small. The variant *The flame is not worth the candle* illustrates a change arising in oral transmission; it cannot serve to explain the origin. *Tace is Latin for candle*, a proverbial admonition to silence, must contain a pun or allusion. *Lovers live by love as larks live by leeks* is utterly obscure, but it is hardly explicable as mere alliterative nonsense. Possibly *Every dog has his day* has some reference to dog-days, but this is more than doubtful.

The temptation to read the manners of earlier days into a proverb is one which besets every annotator, but not all explanations of the sort can be correct. Perhaps Lean, who collected a huge mass of English proverbs, is right in explaining *The weakest goes to the wall* by supposing that in households of former days the beds of the children were placed next the wall, while the father, as the strongest member of the family, slept next the door, but I am unconvinced. More probably the metaphor implies only a single bed: the child sleeps next the wall so that it will not roll out during the night. The variant explanation quoted as the words of a verger in Salisbury Cathedral may stand on its own merits: "And so, because in the old days there were no seats or pews in the nave, the cripples and old people who could not stand through the service sat on the stone bench [along the wall]: which gave rise to the saying, 'The weak went to the wall.'" Finnur Jónsson declares that the Icelandic proverb *One must honor the oak beneath which one dwells* (Verðr eik at fága, er undir skal búa, *Egilssaga*, 68, 4) alludes to the ancient custom of building houses beneath or around a large tree. If this explanation is correct, he might also have observed that the proverb can scarcely have been native to Iceland, where trees large enough to shade a house, whatever its size, would be difficult to find. In view of the parallels to the proverb, we must not think of "oak" as referring to the roof-tree. All explanations which concern themselves with cultural matters are of course greatly complicated by the familiar tendency of tradition to modernize its materials or to adapt them to local conditions. Thus the proverb which has just been discussed is found in Dutch as *Honor the tree which gives one shade* (Men nighet den boom, daer man die bate af hevet),[1] which does not necessarily allude to a tree shading a house, and consequently throws no light on the early meaning of the proverb. An extensive study of the distribution of the variant forms might determine the facts.

Like words, folk-songs, and cultural objects generally, proverbs may become old-fashioned and pass

---

1 Hoffmann von Fallersleben, *Altniederländische Sprichwörter* (*Proverbia communia*), Horae Belgicae, IX (Hannover, 1854), 31, No. 486; Seiler, *Zeitschrift für Deutsche Philologie*, XLVII (1916–18), 243.

out of use. The reasons for obsolescence necessarily vary from case to case and cannot be brought under a single head: the moral lesson involved in the proverb may not seem so significant as it once did, the symbol employed may have lost its force, the essential elements of the metaphor may have ceased to be part of common experience, the language may have discarded an essential word. A systematic examination of obsolete proverbs might yield interesting results.[1] Typical proverbs that have passed out of use are *The black ox hath not trod on her foot*, i. e. 'She has not known care'; *Out of God's blessing into the warm sun*, i. e. 'from the best into something less good,' a figure which is taken, I suspect, from the scene of the congregation leaving the church. We may, and perhaps with more reason, call to mind the many and very familiar Biblical passages[2] in which shade is called desirable and regard the proverb as meaning 'from the shade into the sun.' *The hasty bitch brings forth blind whelps* and *If the sky falls, we shall have larks*, on which we have already commented, find no echo today. The oft-used Elizabethan proverb *The blind man eats many a fly* throws a flash of light on a dark corner of sixteenth-century culinary manners, and has since that time dropped out of existence. So far as the evidence goes, the proverb is English in origin and currency. A proverb which is limited in its circulation to Germany

1 See the chapter "Obscure Proverbs" in Marvin, *Curiosities*, pp. 52–66.
2 E. g. *Job* vii, 2; *Ps.* cxxi, 5; *Song* ii, 3; *Isa.* xxv, 4, xxxii, 2; *Jonah* iv, 6.

at the time of the Reformation is *Where the abbot provides the dice, the monastery may play* (Wo der Abt die Würfel auslegt, ist's dem Konvent erlaubt zu spielen).

Just as proverbs keep memories of older manners, they may preserve words and forms which are obsolete or are becoming obsolete, and words in meanings which are no longer used. Perhaps the most familiar illustration is *The exception proves the rule*, which is now ordinarily understood to mean 'the exception demonstrates [supports] the rule.' On the contrary, it should mean 'the exception tests the rule' (Exceptio probat regulam). We have the same meaning in the word "proof" in the saying *The proof of the pudding is in the eating.* The retention of old or obsolescent words is no doubt found in the proverbs of every language. The Romans said *Qui semel scurra, numquam pater familias* ('He who was once a man about town, is never a man of settled life') and used "scurra" in a meaning which apparently had become obsolete in classical Latin. The proverbial contrasting of "hostis" and "civis" in *Impransus non qui civem dinosceret hoste* ('He who has not had breakfast will not distinguish a citizen from a stranger') turns on the original meaning of "hostis," 'stranger.' English examples in addition to those already given are *The hailer* (receiver) *is as bad as the stailer* (thief); *When the pig is proffered, hold up the poke.* "Poke," which is now used only in English dialects, means 'bag,' and is the word from which "pocket" was formed as a diminutive.

Some explanations of old or strange words in proverbs are more ingenious than convincing. *First catch your hare* has been declared to be a misquotation from an eighteenth-century cook-book. The directions for preparing a certain dish began: "Take your hare when it is cased ('skinned') and make a pudding." Tradition, it is said, corrupted "case" to "catch" and thus altered a literal command into a metaphor from hunting. In principle, such an explanation is possible, but in this case the whole matter is set straight by a thirteenth-century proverb: *And the common folk say that it is first necessary to catch the stag and then, when it has been caught, to skin it* (Et vulgariter dicitur quod primo oportet cervum capere, et postea, cum captus fuerit, illum excoriare).[1] *A miss is as good as a mile* can scarcely find explanation in the names, Amis and Amile, of two faithful friends in mediaeval romance. The current explanation of an old and obscure German proverb *Nothing is good for the eyes* (Nichts ist gut für [*var.* ynn] die Augen) is a masterpiece of ingenuity. "Nichts" is, we are told, a synonym for the vulgar form "Nix"; but this "Nix" is not what it seems to be, for it involves a pun. On the one hand, "Nix" means 'nothing,' and on the other, 'Nihilum album,' a salve for the eyes made of zinc oxide. Only in certain special circumstances, moreover, does the proverb find application. If one receives "Nichts" as answer to a question, one may

1 Bracton, *De legibus et consuetudinibus Angliae*, IV, xxi, § 4 (Rolls ed., III, 234).

say as repartee, "Nix ist gut für die Augen" ('Nothing is good for the eyes' [but not for me]). This explanation is an old one: Luther must have understood the proverb in somewhat similar fashion, for he says of it, "Minutissima festuca in oculo offendit oculum. Hinc Germani dicunt de remediis oculorum: Nichts ist in die augen gut." In a book devoted to the elucidation rather than the collection of proverbs, *De Oorsprong en Uitlegging van Dagelyks Gebruikte Nederduitsche* (i. e. Dutch) *Spreekwoorden* (Middelburg, 1720), Carolus Tuinman explains *Niet is voor de oogen goed; maar quaad voor de tanden* ('Niet is good for the eyes, but bad for the teeth') by the remark that "niet" is a plant used as a remedy for the eyes. Several signs warn us that this explanation cannot be correct. It disregards the two forms in which the proverb is found: the older with "in die Augen" and the younger with "für die Augen." More than this, it disregards completely the variants, both in German and related languages. The forms *Nothing is good in the eyes, but bad in the stomach* (*purse, mouth*) are well established in German, Danish, Dutch, Swedish, and no doubt elsewhere. Obviously the proverb is to be understood literally; when its dry humor was no longer effective, the second half of the proverb disappeared and the proverb was used as an empty witticism in repartee without knowledge of its earlier history.

No one of the three explanations of *That's the cheese* commends itself. "One authority suggests that cheese is really the French word 'chose,' and would bid us accept 'C'est la chose' as the true rendering. Another informs us that 'chiz' is Bengalee for 'thing,' and that the expression has been imported from the East; while a third, and he is the man that we [i. e. Hulme] would personally pin our faith on, reminds us that 'choice' was in Anglo-Saxon times 'chese.'"[1] The associations of the phrase link it with colloquial and vulgar speech and give no reason to believe it came from French or Bengalee. Nor are there any signs which suggest that it derives from Old or Middle English: old instances are entirely lacking and there is no such Anglo-Saxon word as Hulme supposes to exist. It is entirely probable that we are dealing with a bit of modern slang.

It is often somewhat difficult to find proverbs which exemplify the retention of archaic forms. Language keeps an old or obsolete word more easily than an old grammatical form. The proverb *When the bale is hest, thenne the bote is nest* contains both words ("bale," 'evil, harm'; "bote," 'remedy') and forms ("hest" for 'highest,' "nest" for 'nearest') which have passed out of use. It is a little difficult to say how long this proverb actually circulated. Perhaps the Elizabethan form *Whan bale is greetest, than is bote a nye-bore* ('neighbor'), which Skeat quotes, may show that the old superlatives had been given up. A more famous example involves changes in the conjugation of the

1 Hulme, *Proverb Lore*, p. 125.

verb; it is the traditional German rhyme

> Wie die Alten sungen,
> So zwitschern die Jungen
> ('As the old sang,
> So the young twitter'),

which keeps the obsolete verbal form *sungen*. We have similarly an obsolete declensional form in

> Es ist nichts so fein gesponnen,
> Es kommt doch endlich an die Sonnen.

Thus far we have examined chiefly proverbs expressing an ethical truth, in either aphoristic or metaphoric form. There are many sayings which can find no place among such proverbs. Yet the rigid form in which tradition preserves such sayings entitles them to the name proverb. These sayings deal with historical events, legal rights and procedure, the characterization of social or linguistic groups, the weather, health, and certain oft-recurring social situations. Although a metaphor may be used incidentally, it is not of fundamental importance to the saying. These sayings are understood literally.

HISTORICAL PROVERBS [1]

Proverbs which turn on historical allusions are necessarily rare and short-lived. Since all proverbs make a general application of a particular incident,

---

1 Ordinarily collections make no distinction between historical and other proverbs. There are special German collections by Wick (*Geographische Ortsnamen, Beinamen und Sprichwörter* [Leipzig, 1896]) and Wurzbach (*Historische Wörter, Sprichwörter und Redensarten* [2] [Leipzig, 1866]) and

it is clear that the meaning and implications of the incident must be obvious to speaker and hearer. The handbooks, as well as Heinrich Heine, tell us that *Divide and rule* (Divide et impera) was a maxim of Philip of Macedonia. Polybius, Bossuet, and Montesquieu used it. Others ascribe it to Machiavelli. It was traditionally the motto of Austria. Under such circumstances its unique pertinence to any historical situation would be difficult to demonstrate, although no doubt its origin lies in some particular event. *No grass grows where the Turk's horse has trod* is cited three times between 1639 and 1732, but, as we might expect, it could not maintain itself long after the Turk ceased to threaten Europe. As a rule, the meaning of an historical allusion cannot long remain generally intelligible. Consequently the life of an historical proverb must be very brief, or the allusion must be rendered so general that it no longer has an identifiable connection with the historical fact. This situation appears in a rhyme about James I of England and Queen Anne:

April 23rd, 1619
Queen Ann departed out this life,
King James the first, his loving wife,
Of whom it hath a proverb been,
A hunting King, a dancing Queen.

a special chapter on French historical proverbs in Leroux de Lincy (*Le Livre des Proverbes Français* [2][Paris, 1859]). Ladendorf (*Historisches Schlagwörterbuch* [Strassburg, 1906]) gives few, if any, proverbs, but confines his collection to words and phrases. Compare also W. L. Hertslet, *Treppenwitz der Weltgeschichte* [8] (Berlin, 1912).

The phrase died when it ceased to have meaning and point. The Swedes still figure in German local tradition and story as ravagers, but have left little trace in German proverbs.

The allusion in *No money, no Swiss* (Kein Geld, kein Schweizer) to the service of Swiss mercenaries in European armies may still be intelligible to the general reader, but it is quite beyond our power to attach it to a particular event. If we do so, there is almost no chance of being right. It is, to be sure, customarily assigned to an event in the siege of Milan in 1521, but it would be difficult to prove tradition to be right or wrong. An explanation of *Those who live in glass houses should not throw stones* can be confidently rejected. It has been referred to the so-called Glass House in St. Martin's Fields where the Duke of Buckingham, a favorite of King James I, resided. The Duke supported attacks against the Scotch followers of the king, and in retaliation a crowd smashed the windows of his house. When he complained to the king, the king replied, "Steenie, Steenie, those who live in glass houses should be carfu' how they fling stones." Clearly we have here an allusion to a proverb which was already in existence and not the origin of a proverb. We must of course distinguish between an historical proverb and a proverb which alludes to a custom or condition which no longer exists. *It's good living under the crozier* (Unter dem Krummstab ist gut wohnen) alludes to the preferred situation enjoyed by serfs of ecclesiastical lords, and not to a particular event.

Possibly the proverb *The lucky man takes home* ('marries') *the bride* (Wer Glück hat, führt die Braut heim) has something to do with events of the year 871; but since the proverb is not reported in contemporary accounts of the abduction which is referred to, and since the connection is first suggested by a chronicler seven centuries later, the explanation is more than doubtful. And the explanation that we have here a reminiscence of the "Brautlauf," a foot-race in which the bride was the stake, is equally dubious, although we know this custom existed at Germanic weddings. The proverb probably means only that luck is often the determining factor in success, and not wealth, rank, or cleverness.

A search for historical proverbs is not profitable. In the several books which have been devoted to the subject, we find much material which does not deserve inclusion. The historical allusion is, as we have seen, often uncertain. The phrase may be a scholar's epigram and lack proverbial currency. Most often, perhaps, such collections have erred in including slogans and catch-words of an age, phrases which never passed as proverbs. Such a phrase as *Rum, Romanism, and Rebellion* may enjoy oral and even traditional currency, but it cannot be termed proverbial in any other senses. Seiler quotes *Möck, Mock und Uhl retteten Rottweil* ('Möck, Mock, and Uhl saved Rottweil') as a Swiss historical proverb, but, lacking all metaphorical values, it cannot be anything but a schoolmaster's epigram which has perhaps won a longer life than usual.

LEGAL PROVERBS [1]

Although the proverbial evidences of legal customs and forms are extremely interesting, and although

1 The collection and study of legal proverbs has dealt chiefly with Germanic sources. Little has been done since the publication of the standard German collection by Graf and Dietherr in 1864 (*Deutsche Rechtssprichwörter*), although much is now to be expected from the excellent introduction of Eberhard, Freiherr von Künssberg, to bibliography and problems ("Rechtsgeschichte und Volkskunde," *Jahrbuch für Historische Volkskunde* I [1925], 69–125). Introductory bibliographical materials will be found in Claudius, Freiherr von Schwerin, *Einführung in das Studium der Germanischen Rechtsgeschichte* (Freiburg i. Br., 1922), p. 47; D. Martin, *Lawyers' Merriments* (Glasgow, 1912), pp. 47–59 (hasty, but informative); and the general bibliographies, e. g. Lundell in H. Paul, *Grundriss der Germanischen Philologie²*, II, i, 1174, for Scandinavia, and, in general, Bonser, *Proverb Literature* (London, 1930), pp. 435–439, Nos. 3798–3838.

Important collections and studies devoted to legal proverbs are chiefly German, e. g. Cohn, *Drei rechtswissenschaftliche Vorträge in Gemeinverständlicher Darstellung, I, Deutsches Recht im Munde des Volkes* (Heidelberg, 1888); Eisenhart, *Grundsätze der Deutschen Rechte in Sprüchwörtern* (Helmstädt, 1759; 2nd ed., Leipzig, 1792; 3rd ed. by C. E. Otto, Leipzig, 1823); Gierke, *Das Humor im Deutschen Recht* (Berlin, 1871); Günther, *Recht und Sprache* (Berlin, 1898) and *Deutsche Rechtsaltertümer in unserer Heutigen Sprache* (Leipzig, 1903); Hillebrand, *Deutsche Rechtssprichwörter* (Zürich, 1858); Koehne, *Gewerberechtliches in Deutschen Rechtssprichwörtern* (Zürich, 1915); Reyscher, "Die Ueberlieferung der Rechte durch Sprichwörter," *Zeitschrift für Deutsches Recht und Rechtswissenschaft*, V (1841), 189–209; Winkler, *Deutsches Recht im Spiegel Deutscher Sprichwörter* (Leipzig, 1927). For other languages and countries see Bouthors, *Les Proverbes, Dictons et Maximes du Droit Rural Traditionnel* (Paris, 1858); Corso, "Kalabresische Rechtssprichwörter," *Zeitschrift für Vergleichende Rechts-*

there already exists a considerable mass of collection, discussion, and interpretation of these evidences, they have rarely been studied effectively. The apt quotation of a proverb will often turn the course of an argument, just as the apt citation of a precedent may win a case at law. In former days the lower courts before which the peasants appeared used proverbs freely. A German legal document of the fourteenth century declares: "Wherever you can attach a proverb, do so, for the peasants like to judge according to proverbs." [1] The act of quotation recognizes the weight of human experience condensed in the proverb. This weight is necessarily greater than that which any individual's utterance can have. Of course the fundamental defect of proverbial wisdom springs from this same universality. Proverbs are bound to

wissenschaft, XXIII (1910), 289–308; "Proverbi Giuridici Italiani," *Archivio per lo Studio delle Tradizioni Popolari*, XXIII (1907), 484 ff., "Proverbi Giuridici Italiani," *Rivista Italiana di Sociologia*, XX (1916), 581–592, and "Usi Giuridici Contradineschi Ricavate da Massime Popolari," *Circolo Giuridici* (Palermo), XXXIX (1908), 35–48; Saverio, "Collana di Proverbi Giuridici ed Economici Pugliesi," *Rivista Italiana di Sociologia*, XXII (1918), 300–322; Solari, "La Vita Economica nei Proverbi Greci," *ibid.*, II (1898), 187–206, 303–320; Corso, "Proverbi Giuridici Abessini," *ibid.*, XXIV (1920), 150–162; van Hall, *Nieuwe Bijdragen voor Regtsgeleerdheid en Wetgiving*, III (1852), 247–314; A. Corvinus, *Jus Canonicum per Aphorismis* (Amsterdam, 1663); Matthaeus, *Paroemiae Belgarum Jurisconsultis Usitatissimae* (Utrecht, 1667); van Hasselt, *Annotationes ad Antonii Matthaei Paroemias* (1780); Ilu'ustrov, *Iuridičeskiya Poslovitsy i Pogovorki Russkago Naroda* (Moscow, 1885); Koskenjaakko, *Sananlaskututkimuksia, I: Laki* (Helsingfors, 1913).

1 Quoted by von Künssberg, *Jahrbuch für historische Volkskunde*, I (1925), 72.

the common level of mankind; above it they cannot rise. Yet they display a sound practical sense which even the law itself has not always been able to put into better words: *Better ten guilty escape than one innocent person suffer*; *The extremity of law is the extremity of wrong* (Summum jus, summa injuria); *Right wrongs no man*; *Two wrongs don't make a right*; *Good laws spring from bad morals* (Leges bonae ex malis moribus procreantur).

In Iceland the law-giver, an official of the All-Thing, recited the code annually at the meeting on Thingvellir. The Frisian codes, the first to be written down in any Germanic language, contain metrical or semi-metrical passages in which the form made the work of memory easier. Yet we must not imagine, as some have done,[1] that such codes were highly poetic rhapsodies, "like the recitation of a heroic lay." On the contrary, they employ the language and manner of business, not poetry. The alliterative formulae had the practical purpose of emphasizing and defining legal ideas. They accomplished this by repeating the word or by using one which was more or less nearly synonymous. The latter procedure, the so-called epic variation, is also characteristic of Germanic alliterative verse. The rhythm of these formulae, a natural speech rhythm, is moreover the same as the rhythm

---

1 R. Koegel, *Geschichte der Deutschen Literatur*, I, 242–259; see further, Siebs, *Zeitschrift für Deutsche Philologie*, XXIX (1897), 405 and "Friesische Literaturgeschichte," in Paul's *Grundriss der Germanischen Philologie*[2], II, i, 527.

of Germanic alliterative verse. But in verse a strict rhythmical regularity and a systematic use of alliteration are required, and, although epic variation is freely employed, the repetition of words is avoided. As we see, alliterative verse and alliterative formulae develop from the same linguistic and rhythmical conditions. The two lines of development are, however, independent, and we must not look upon the formulae as fragments of verse.

Mnemotechnic alliterative formulae [1] which retain the literal words of the law have persisted in common use, and new ones after the same fashion have been invented: *Land und Leute, Haus und Hof, Mann und Maus, hide nor hair, house and home.* We cannot easily distinguish the old from the new in such formulae: *with heart and soul* is Biblical. Not all the old formulae, moreover, are alliterative: *a year and a day* is

---

[1] Typical collections of legal and traditional formulae are Gering (*Zeitschrift für Deutsche Philologie*, XLVIII [1919–20], 304–306 [collected in a review of Feilberg, *Bidrag*]), Willert (*Die Alliterierenden Formeln der Englischen Sprache* [Halle, 1911]), Lean (*Collectanea*, II, 899–940), Heyne (*Formulae Alliterantes ex Antiquis Legibus Frisica Conscriptis Extractae* [Halle, 1884] and "Alliterierende Verse und Reime in den Friesischen Rechtsquellen," *Germania*, IX [1864], 457–499), Koulen (*Der Stabreim im Munde des Volkes zwischen Rhein und Ruhr* [Düren, 1896]), Eiselein (*Die Reimhaften, Anklingenden und Ablautartigen Formeln der Hochdeutschen Sprache* [Leipzig, 1841]), Schulze ("Die sprichwörtlichen Formeln der Deutschen Sprache," *Archiv für das Studium der Neueren Sprachen*, XLVIII [1871], 435–450, XLIX [1872], 139–162, L [1872], 85–122, LI [1873], 195–212, LII [1874], 61–80, 375–392, LIV [1875], 55–74), and Lind ("Rim och verslemningar i de svenska landskapslagarna," *Uppsala Universitets Årsskrift* [1881], No. 3). I have noted only those concerned with Germanic materials. I have not seen Seitz (*Zur Alliteration im Neuenglischen* [Itzehoe, 1883]).

evidently of long standing. Newer formulae are *in any way, shape, or form* (var. *manner*), *to the best of my knowledge and belief.*

Some of these formulae are very interesting. One of the first bits of German lyric verse begins with the formula "Ich bin dein; du bist mein," and, as we might expect, the same words recur constantly in popular love-poetry. But the phrase is more than a mere commonplace: it was part of the wedding ritual. As late as the sixteenth century, Martin Luther knew its use in this connection.

Typical legal proverbs are: *Two words to a bargain*; *Those who will not work shall not eat*; *Root, hog, or die*; *Findings, keepings* (var. *Finders, keepers; losers, weepers*); *Beggars cannot be choosers*; *First come, first served*; *Ein Mann, kein Mann* (i. e. *Testis unus, testis nullus*, 'one witness is no witness.') *My house is my castle* has been declared to be as old as the *Odyssey*, but perhaps not correctly. Curiously enough, parallels do not seem to be very frequent: we may compare the Icelandic *Every man is master at home* (Halr er heima hverr), to which Heusler cites only one parallel, a Gaelic proverb,[1] and the similar and widely known saying *Every cock is proud on his own dunghill*. Sir Edward Coke knew our proverb and puts it: "A man's house is his castle" (Et domus sua est unicuique tutissimum refugium). *Of ill debtours men take oats* means evidently 'Take what you can get in settlement of a bad debt'; oats will do, if wheat is lacking.

---

1 *Zeitschrift des Vereins für Volkskunde*, XXXV (1915), 111, No. 5.

Proverbs which we might scarcely consider as possessing a legal background actually have associations with legal principles. James Howell's important collection of English proverbs (1659) says, for example: "In our Common Law there are some Proverbs that carry a kind of authority with them, as that which began in Henry the Fourth's time, He that bulls the cow must keep the calf." The reference is, of course, to an illegitimate child. In contrary fashion, the legal allusion may be entirely different from what it superficially appears to be: *Necessity knows no law* probably refers, not to necessity in a general sense, but to necessity forced upon one by the need of self-defence. In other words, *Necessity knows no law* means 'in defending one's self all means are legal.' It was in this special legal sense, of course, that the proverb was used by the German chancellor, von Bethmann-Hollweg, in his speech before the Reichstag in defence of the invasion of Belgium.

Certain fields are richly represented in legal proverbs: notably rights in real and personal property, e. g. *Suum cuique*, a venerable saying; the bases on which claims for privileges and consideration may rest; the rules of testimony. Proverbs connected with the handicrafts are relatively abundant, while those associated with mercantile pursuits are less frequent. Legal proverbs dealing with mercantile affairs are ordinarily concerned with the rights of buyer and seller and therefore touch the interests of the common

man closely: *Caveat emptor* ('Let the buyer beware')
— compare the German *Augen auf, Kauf ist Kauf*
('Keep your eyes open; a sale is a sale') — is an ancient warning.[1]

Often the legal principle involved in proverbs is
still valid; e. g. *No receiver, no thief*; *The hailer* ('receiver') *is as bad as the stailer* ('thief'); *Better steal a
horse than stand by and look on* exemplify the legal
principle that aiding and abetting a thief renders
one equally guilty with him. In the oldest form of
The hailer is as bad as the stailer, the assertion is
general and concerns the accessory to any crime.
Later it is restricted, as in the preceding instances, to
thievery or is altered into the assertion, which accords
with mediaeval legal practice, that the accessory after
the fact is more guilty than the criminal. Other legal
proverbs refer to punishments no longer employed,
e. g. *Mitgefangen, mitgehangen* ('Caught with [a crim-
inal], hanged with [a criminal]') or the variant *Mitgegangen, mitgefangen, mitgehangen* ('Those who have
accompanied and have been caught with [thieves] are
hanged with them'). So severe a punishment for
theft (if, as is probable, theft is meant) points to a
considerable age for this proverb, and the same is true
of *As well be hanged for a sheep as a lamb*. The Ger-

1 See the Latin proverbs on business and money collected by Otto,
"Geldverkehr und Besitz im [Lateinischen] Sprichwort," *Archiv für
Lateinische Lexikographie*, VI (1889), 47–58, and p. 15 above. See an
interesting small collection of German proverbs in a merchant's hand-
book: P. J. Marperger, *Nothwendig und Nützliche Fragen über die
Kaufmannschaft* (Leipzig, 1714), pp. 429–446.

mans in Bohemia now say *Mitgehanga, mitgefanga* and explain it as meaning 'He who participates ("mitge-hanga") is called to account with the actual criminal,' but in so doing they have exchanged the meanings of the two words in the proverb. *Service is no heritage* alludes to feudal customs, and has necessarily passed out of use. Similarly *The king can do no wrong* is no longer accepted as true. Some legal proverbs have died even though the idea expressed by them persists: Chaucer said "Promise is dette," which, although now lost, is paralleled by *His word is as good as his bond.*

Many legal proverbs are ultimately Latin in origin: *Ignorance of the law excuses no one*; *Silence gives consent* (Qui tacet, consentire videtur); *Ein Wort, kein Wort* ('One word is naught') or *Ein Mann, kein Mann* (Testis unus, testis nullus).

Those legal proverbs which describe a situation or indicate a course of action which can scarcely ever have been legally justified form an especially interesting group. Such proverbs are *All's fair in love and war*; *A fair exchange is no robbery*; *Einen Kuss in Ehren kann niemand wehren* ('No one can object to an honorable kiss'). Some of these can be explained by reference to the historical background from which the saying sprang or by study of the variants. For example, the obvious literal interpretation of *A fair exchange is no robbery* is of course out of the question legally, until we understand that it refers to an exchange effected by force by a person in flight. In

order to disguise himself a man can exchange clothing
and such a forcible exchange is not reckoned as theft.
Einen Kuss in Ehren kann niemand wehren has been
declared to be a quotation from the German Anacre-
ontic poet, Hölty; but it was in print before he was
born. Our conceptions have changed regarding the
ideas expressed in some proverbs: *Bis an't kni is't fri*
('Up to the knee is permitted') is a Low German
proverb alluding to the degree of liberty permitted.

As in any proverb, the allusion in a legal proverb
may be obscure and call for explanation. Perhaps
Possession is nine points of the law or the older form
Possession is eleven points of the law refers merely to
the ten or dozen conceived of as a unit; in that
case we need not seek to discover what the points
really are.

A very important class of legal proverbs finds comparatively little use today, although it once consti-
tuted a significant part of legal practice. The gist of
the law was condensed into maxims which circulated
in legal groups, were collected in handbooks, and
found a place in pleading and even judicial deci-
sions. In modern times we have something similar in
G. Cohn, *Das Neue Deutsche Bürgerliche Recht in
Sprüchen* (Berlin, 1896–1900), which turns the German
code into brief and easily remembered sentences. For
the most part, popular tradition was unable to take
up and preserve the mediaeval legal maxims because
the precision of their Latin form did not readily per-

mit of translation and because the distinctions involved did not obviously and immediately concern
common folk. Yet we must regard these maxims as
proverbs, although of a very special kind, for they are
anonymous, traditional, and epigrammatic. Every
calling in which the practitioners use freely a body
of relatively esoteric information is likely to possess
such professional maxims. Typical examples of legal
maxims are *Ultra posse nemo obligatur* ('No one is
bound beyond his power') and the variant *Impossibilium nulla obligatio est* ('The impossible is no obligation'), *Socii mei socius meus socius non est* ('The
companion of my companion is not my companion'),
Res judicata pro veritate accipitur ('Things adjudi-
cated are considered true'), *Quod initio vitiosum est
non potest tractu temporis convalescere* ('What is wrong
in its beginnings cannot be remedied by the passage
of time'), *Domus sua cuique est tutissimum refugium*
('A man's house is his safest refuge', *An Englishman's
house is his castle*), *Cessante ratione legis cessat ipsa
lex* ('When the reason for the law no longer exists, the
law ceases to exist'), *Volenti non fit injuria* ('No in-
jury is done to one who is willing'). The examples
cited thus far can be traced back to the great body of
Roman law and its commentators. A few which have
been quoted have established themselves in popular
tradition; others of the same kind are *Ignorance of the
law excuses no one*; *Silence gives consent*. Occasionally
we find maxims which appear to be modifications of

the Roman law or to represent separate English developments: *De minimis non curat lex* ('The law does not concern itself with minor matters'); *Qui facit per alium facit per se* ('He who commits an act by another's agency commits the act himself'); but in such matters we are touching on difficult points in legal history. The origin and use of these maxims is little studied; the best introduction to them, a brief essay by James Williams, concludes in part as follows: "Few students of jurisprudence would be qualified, and probably still fewer would be willing, to devote the time to a careful search among the voluminous and forgotten writings of jurists whose very names are only known to students of the history of the law." [1]

A considerable body of popular law has never crystallized in formulae, and although it is extremely interesting and little known it cannot be examined here. Such legal superstitions, if we may call them so, are: witnesses cannot testify to what is seen through glass (although this belief does not seem to exclude the wearer of spectacles), pregnant women cannot testify, a blow struck against a man wearing glasses is subject to severer punishment than another kind of assault. The collection and study of such notions deserve to be undertaken, but they do not in the main find expres-

---

1 "Latin Maxims in English Law," *The Law Magazine and Law Review*, 4th Ser., XX (1895), 283–295. See a small collection of such maxims in J. Michelet, *Les Origines du Droit* (Paris, 1837), p. lxxiii, note, and L. Volkmar, *Paroemia et Regulae Juris Romanorum, Germanorum, Franco-Gallorum, Britannorum* (Berlin, 1854).

sion in legal proverbs. Possibly we may see allied material in such proverbs as *Don't hit* (var. *kick*) *a man when he is down*; *A taleteller is worse than a thief*; *Among friends all things are common*, which is an idea perhaps to be traced back to the Pythagorean society; *Hands off is fair play*.

"BLASON POPULAIRE" [1]

Men are always ready to mock their neighbors, and from time immemorial witticisms have passed be-

[1] Miscellaneous bibliographical notes will be found in Gaidoz and Sébillot (*Blason Populaire de la France* [Paris, 1884] and the *Catalogus van Folklore*['s Gravenhage, 1919–1922]). The best collections are French. Unfortunately there is no good discussion of the problems in the field of local witticisms; after Schulte ("Spottnamen und -verse auf Ortschaften im nördlichen Oberhessen," *Hessische Blätter für Volkskunde*, IV [1905], 142–167) the best introductions are the prefaces to the collections, notably Dejardin (*Dictionnaire des Spots ou Proverbes Wallons* [Liège, 1863, 2d ed., 1891]). Typical collections are Lean (*Collectanea*, I, 11–343), who gives English and Italian materials; Dejardin, as above; Raadt (*Les Sobriquets des Communes Belges* [Brussels, 1903]); Gittée ("Steden en Dorpen tegen Elkander," *Volkskunde* [Ghent], V [1892], 124–138, 167–179); Barjavel (*Dictons et Sobriquets Patois des Villes . . . du Département de Vaucluse* [Carpentras, 1849]); Canel (*Blason Populaire de la Normandie* [Caen, 1859]); Gaidoz and Sébillot, as above; O. de Watteville (*Etude sur les Devises Personnelles* [Paris, 1888]); A. Ledieu (*Blason Populaire de la Picardie* [Paris, 1905]); Handelmann (*Topographischer Volkshumor* [Kiel, 1886]); Hesekiel (*Land und Stadt im Volksmunde* [Berlin, 1867]); Schlauch (*Sachsen im Sprichwort* [Leipzig, 1905]); Wick (*Geographische Ortsnamen, Beinamen und Sprichwörter* [Leipzig, 1896]); Cornelissen (*Nederlandsche Volkshumor* [Antwerp, n.d.]); Goebel (*De Graecarum Civitatum Proprietatibus Proverbio Notatis* [Breslau, 1915]). Examples of older, related collections are Caviceo (*Urbium Dicta ad Maximilianum Primum Romanorum Regem* [Parma, 1491]) and Ritio (*Le Nomi et Cognomi*, etc. [1585], reprinted in *Due Opuscoli Rarissimi del Secolo XVI* [Scelta di curiosità letterarie, XCII, Bologna, 1865]).

tween man and man, village and village, country and country. A word or a pointed phrase singles out a characteristic trait which seems to be hereditary or at least dominant — the presence or, more frequently, the absence of a quality. Physical peculiarities, the dark hair of southern peoples or the light hair and blue eyes of northern Germany, are rarely commented on. Stupidity, greed, miserliness, and such antisocial qualities are favored subjects. Ordinarily the hearer perceives readily enough the barb in the remark, for the wit is rarely subtle. The attitude is sufficiently illustrated by Nathanael's remark to Philip: "Can there any good thing come out of Nazareth?" (A Nazareth potest aliquid boni esse? *John* i, 46), but we cannot be sure of the proverbial currency of this allusion. Tacitus (*Ann.*, xiv, 7) tells us that the murderous affray in which the inhabitants of Pompeii and Nuceria engaged in the days of Nero took rise in mutual raillery. Although the insults are no longer preserved, we need have little doubt regarding their general nature and intent.

The characterization of races and nations is found both in single descriptive words, *frog-eater*, *squarehead*, *boche*, and in proverbial sayings. With the former we are not particularly concerned, although it is well-nigh certain that curious facts regarding them can be discovered by the careful searcher.[1] Perhaps,

1 See, for example, T. Roth, *Völkernamen in ihrer Entwicklung zu Gattungsnamen*, Friedland i. M., 1909–10; M. Spiegel, *Völkernamen als*

for example, it might be shown that French racial and provincial names are often derived from references to food and eating, while this is less true of other countries. Nor need we linger over the very definite associations which have in many cases attached themselves to certain places. Villages and groups of people have distinguished themselves for their folly, like the three wise men of Gotham. Every country has its Abdera or its Schilda.[1] Bœotia has an immortality of a sort, along with Sybaris and Miletus. The poverty of a village seems to become proverbial more often than its wealth.[2] With such traditional characterizations we might compare the Irishman, Scotchman, or Yankee of stage and story.

The brief characterizations of a neighboring village or people which the French call "blason populaire" and the German "Ortsneckereien," and for which there is no convenient English term, are truly popular. Some are merely traditional insults which have lost all meaning in the course of time. The Greeks and later the Romans said that the Cretans were liars (*Mendax Creta*). The word "Erbfeind," 'hereditary enemy,' which I suppose everyone now thinks alludes to France, once meant the Devil (and is comparable

Epitheta im Gallo-romanischen (extract of a dissertation [Berlin, 1921]); F. Boillot, *Répertoire des Métaphores Français tirés des Noms des Villes et des Pays Étrangers* (Paris, 1929).

1 See a very useful list in Gaidoz-Sébillot, *Blason Populaire*, p. vi, and Schulte's collection for the different provinces of Germany in *Hessische Blätter für Volkskunde*, IV (1905), 146.

2 Schulte, as above, pp. 151–153.

in English to the Arch Enemy) and later the Turk.
The Italians say of the French:

> Tutto fanno, niente sanno,
> Niente sanno, tutto fanno.

> ('They do everything, they know nothing,
> They know nothing, they do everything').

Perhaps most such local nicknames contain a hostile or at least an unfriendly suggestion. There are, however, a few sayings which are simply descriptive; of these the most famous is no doubt *Frisia non cantat* ('Frisia does not sing'). There are, furthermore, some sayings which seem to be the direct opposite in spirit of these local nicknames: one admirable trait is singled out as characteristic. Probably such phrases were invented by the group itself rather than by its neighbors. Typical examples are *Deutsche Treue*; *La belle France*; *Merry England*.

Epigrammatic characterizations of several peoples are frequent enough, particularly in the Romance languages. A typical example is

> Ingles borracho,
>   Frances gabacho,
> Hollandes mantequero,
>   Español gran caballero.

> ('The Englishman a drunkard,
>   The Frenchman a scoundrel,
> The Dutchman a farmer,
>   The Spaniard a gentleman.')

The epigram is interesting for the indication which it gives of the age in which it was invented, an age when Spain was in contact with England, France, and the Netherlands. German examples are rare, but the following characterization of four Hessian villages shows that the form is not entirely unknown:

Niederohme — Dreacksome,
Habach — hatt Kartoffelsaat,
Ermerod — der Bär brummt,
Elperod — die Kaffeestadt.

In explanation we are told that Niederohmen supplied the adjoining territory with flax seed and Habach with seed potatoes; in Ermenrod a peasant once mistook an ass for a bear and called for help, saying, "The bear is growling"; and Elpenrod was the center for coffee and sugar. Such a characterization is not particularly interesting. The examples which are definitely associated with the Romance languages have found a wider dissemination than such local rhymes ever could. The saying *The Jews spend their money at the Feast of the Passover; the Moors, at weddings; and the Christians, in law-suits* is asserted to be originally Spanish, and even more widely known is *The Italian is wise before the deed; the German, in the deed; and the Frenchman, after the deed.* Such a characterization as *England is the paradise of women, hell of horses, and purgatory of servants* is certainly not of English make. The spirit of the Reformation is abundantly apparent in an epigram which is quite probably German in invention: *A Polish bridge, a Bohemian monk, a Swabian nun, an Austrian soldier, Italian reverence, and German fasting are worth a bean* (Pons Polonicus: monachus Boemicus: Suevica monialis: miles Australis: Italorum devotio et Alemannorum ieiunia: fabam valent omnia). It is difficult to know to what extent such epigrams were popular. Many, I suspect, are no more than semi-literary witticisms which enjoyed only a short life.

In longer characterizations, which may now and again be termed proverbial, we recognize many which attempt more or less successfully to name essential or typical merits of various countries. *Italia para nacer, Francia para vivir, España para morir* praises the climate of Italy, the gaiety of France, and the piety of Spain. After the Renaissance, such group characterizations appear to have enjoyed great popularity and to have been translated from one language into another. It is rather doubtful whether many such sayings ever became firmly established among the folk. We know little or nothing about their origin, history, or stylistic peculiarities. A few of these epigrams may well be of local origin, perhaps even without the suggestion of foreign models, e. g. *Cheshire for men, Berkshire for dogs, Bedfordshire for naked flesh, and Lincolnshire for bogs*; and the previously cited German quatrain.

We do not know exactly how these longer epigrams were composed. Apparently certain single characterizations were capable of being transferred from one epigram to another, and perhaps the fashion was transmitted in this way. The power of Venice, for example, appears in more than one connection during the fifteenth and sixteenth centuries. An early mention is in a description of the Italian cities ascribed to Messer Pandolfo Collenuctio, ambassador of Gostanzo Sforza: *Auctoritas pontificis, sapientia regis* (sc. Neapolis), *potentia venetorum, arma mediolanensium, aurum florentinorum* ('The authority of the Pope, the wisdom of the king [of Naples], the power of the Venetians, the arms of the Milanese, the gold of the Florentines'). Such an epigram has a unity arising from the fact that only Italian cities are mentioned. In the next century there is an analogous German saying:

> Nürnberger Witz,
> Strassburger Geschütz,
> Venetier Macht,
> Augsburger Pracht,
> Ulmer Geld,
> Wer dieses hätte, wäre reich in dieser Welt.

('The wit of Nuremberg, the artillery of Strassburg, the power of Venice, the splendor of Augsburg, the money of Ulm: whoever had this would be rich in this world').

The presence in the German epigram of the allusion to Venice suggests very strongly that it was modelled directly or indirectly on the Italian one.[1]

---

1 A long list of feminine charms, ranging in number from seven to thirty, has been handed down by literary tradition rather than by word of

The traditional mockery of certain trades offers many interesting problems, for we do not always clearly understand why some trades should be the object of scorn and suspicion and others go unscathed. Why, for example, should the tailor be a conventional object of ridicule and the cobbler rarely? We also know very little about the variations from country to country; different trades are mocked in different countries, and even when the same trade is being held up to ridicule, different formulae and different associations are employed. The material at our disposal for the study of such problems is comparatively abundant and reliable, but very little has been accomplished as yet.[1] Often a readily intelligible attitude of the peasant is reflected in these sayings. The peasant who deals with the miller doubts the miller's

mouth. Although the occurrences are numerous, their relations have never been studied fully. Since the list is scarcely proverbial, I cannot discuss it here. See Haltaus, *Liederbuch der Clara Hätzlerin* (Bibliothek der Gesamten Deutschen National-Literatur, VIII [Quedlinburg, 1840]), p. lxviii; R. Koehler, *Kleinere Schriften* (ed. J. Bolte), III (Weimar, 1900), 31 ff.; Küffner, *Die Deutschen im Sprichwort*, pp. 200, 253a–c; Wesselski, *Angelo Polizianos Tagebuch* (Jena, 1929), p. 93, No. 195.

1 Albrecht Keller, *Die Handwerker im Volkshumor* (Leipzig, 1912); P. Sébillot, *Légendes et Curiosités des Métiers* (Paris, 1895); H. F. Feilberg, *Bidrag til en Jysk Ordbog* (Copenhagen, 1886–1914); H. Klenz, *Schelten-Wörterbuch* (Strassburg, 1910). L. Ricker (*Zur landschaftlichen Synonymik der Deutschen Handwerkernamen* [Freiburg i. Br., 1917]) gives nicknames for the potter, cooper, and cabinet-maker. In an admirable article, which is soon to appear, Barbara Salditt traces the origin and dissemination of the traditional association of the tailor and the goat; see "Der Schneider und die Geiss im Deutschen Volksmunde bis zum siebzehnten Jahrhundert," *Hessische Blätter für Volkskunde*, XXX (1931).

honesty in taking toll for the grinding of grain: *The miller has a golden thumb*. Similarly the tailor is accused of cutting cloth to his own advantage: *The tailor cuts three sleeves for every woman's gown.*

Equally curious and interesting are those traditional associations which do not spring from the obvious relations of the peasant to the trade, but these associations do not in general take proverbial form. We find cowardice mentioned as a typical trait of the tailor: *It takes nine tailors to make a man*. Other traditional slurs do not appear as proverbs: the association of the tailor and the goat, which is restricted to Germany, has left no record in proverbs. The origin and history of these traditional insults are often interesting problems in the history of culture.

Many traditional sayings show a keen recognition of linguistic resemblances or peculiarities. So far as I have observed, they seem to be more abundant in German than in English. Characteristic similarities between English and the Frisian language spoken on the islands along the coast of the Netherlands, Germany, and Denmark and on the adjoining mainland appear in *Eggs, butter, and cheese are good English and good Freese* and *Gooid brade, botter, and sheese is good Halifax and good Freese.* The rhyme

> Nä, nich und jawol
> is Brôkmer Prôtcoll.
> Nee, neet un jawall
> Seggen de Krummhörners all

indicates certain distinctive peculiarities of the Frisian dialects on the northwest coast of Germany in the vicinity of Emden. The Low German saying *In Friesland one eats Brugge* ('bridges,' 'butter cakes'), *walks on Mühlen* ('mills,' 'slippers'), *and keeps Schaipen* ('sheep,' 'coins worth about ten cents') *in a bag* involves a pun in each of the significant words: the first meaning is Low German and the second Frisian. There is a curious instance in which the explanation does not make the situation clear: we are told that the Swabian proverb *A Swabian has no heart but two Magen* (Ein Schwabe hat kein Herz aber zwei Magen ['stomachs']) rests upon the supposedly Swabian dialectal peculiarity of using *Magen* for *Herz*. Inasmuch as this peculiarity is not registered in the large Swabian dialect dictionary and the same proverb is, furthermore, used of Prussians, the explanation is rather dubious. An English proverb which concerns itself with the peculiarities of local speech is *By Tre, Pol, and Pen, you shall know the Cornish men*, which refers to three words, 'town,' 'head,' and 'top' respectively, frequently found in Cornish place-names and proper names. Those who live in the town of Glarus mock their neighbors with the traditional sentence "Hæidər odər wæidər odər hæidr šu kxæ?" i. e. 'Habt ihr oder wollt ihr oder habt ihr schon gehabt?' [1] This sentence illustrates two striking details in which

---

1 C. Streiff, *Die Laute der Glarner Mundarten* (Beiträge zur Schweizerdeutschen Grammatik, VIII [Frauenfeld, 1915]), p. 36, § 44. So also in Winteler, *Die Kerenzer Mundart* (Leipzig, 1876), p. 192, No. 1.

the neighboring dialects differ from that of Glarus. In Glarus "habt" (hæid) and "wollt" (wænd) cannot possibly rhyme, while in the dialects illustrated by the sentence the rhyme is perfect. The form "kxæ" (gehabt) differs very considerably from that found in Glarus and most Swiss dialects. Obviously we cannot always know when the traditional phrase merely illustrates the linguistic peculiarities of a group and when it serves to mock one's neighbors.

For various regions of Germany we have distinctive traditional sentences of rhymes which indicate characteristic dialectal traits: *Eine jute jebratene Jans ist eine jute Jabe Jottes* exemplifies the spirant [j] for [g] of Berlin speech; *Der Riese Ragi auf dem Rathaus zu Bremen* and *Reiner Roggen, Bremer Brot*, the typical guttural [r] of Bremen; *Es heisst nicht hēst, es hēst heisst*, the pronounciation of [ai] as [ē] in Dresden; and *Anna sass auf einem spitzen Stein*, the Hanoverian [sp] and [st] for [šp] and [št] of standard German. *Heute trägt der Heide Häute über die Heide* plays with Saxon dialectal traits, for "heute," "Heide," and "Häute" are usually pronounced differently. The Norwegian *Boner spiser Böner* ('Peasants eat beans') involves an essential distinction between simple and compound accent. The most famous instance in which a dialectal trait was utilized is recounted as follows: "And the Gileadites took the passages of Jordan before the Ephraimites: and it was so, that when those Ephraimites which were escaped, said,

Let me go over; that the men of Gilead said unto him, Art thou an Ephraimite? If he said, Nay, then said they unto him, Say now 'Shibboleth'; and he said 'Sibboleth': for he could not frame to pronounce it right. Then they took him, and slew him at the passages of the Jordan." (Judges xii, 5–6.) From this incident we have of course the proverbial use of *shibboleth*.

Although we cannot distinguish sharply these various classes of proverbial linguistic observations, there is another group which includes combinations of words difficult to pronounce. Some such combinations contain difficult and characteristic sounds and combinations like the Polish *Chrząszcz brzmi w trzcinie* [xšoⁿšč bžmⁱi f tščⁱinⁱe], i. e. 'Beetle buzzes in reeds,' or the Bohemian *Strč brk skrz krk a krk skrz brk*, i. e. 'Stick a quill through [your] throat and a throat through the quill,' and *Tři a třicet stříbrných křepelek přeskočili tři a třicet stříbrných střech*, i. e. 'Thirty-three silver quails jumped over thirty-three silver roofs.' These sentences illustrate the typical sibilants and the Bohemian syllabic *r*. The English "tongue-twisters," e. g. *Peter Piper picked a peck of pickled peppers*; *She sells sea-shells by the seashore*; *Bill had a billboard and also a board bill, but the board bill bored Bill so that he sold the billboard to pay the board bill*, belong to the more usual type of such phrases. As we see, they do not concern themselves with characteristic and unusual sounds in English speech, for *w*, *th* in "there," and *th* in "thin" are not mentioned. Sentences of this sort are ordinarily composed of sounds which a child finds it difficult to form and not of sounds peculiar to a particular language. In general, linguistic proverbs, shibboleths, and "tongue-twisters" are concerned with consonants rather than vowels, although Finnish, a language in which vowel quantity is all-important, has some sentences involving vowels.

WEATHER PROVERBS [1]

It is of course difficult to separate proverbs about the weather from superstitions and traditions which

1 In addition to the bibliographies in most collections of weather proverbs, e.g. Inwards, *Weather Lore* (London, 1893), there are admirable lists in *Schweizer Volkskunde*, XIV (1924), 16 and Bonser, *Proverb Literature* (London, 1930), pp. 422–429, Nos. 3675–3746. The following collections are important. England and America: Dunwoody, *Weather Proverbs*, Signal Service Notes IX (Washington, 1883); Humphreys, *Weather Proverbs and Parodoxes* (Baltimore, 1923); Inwards, as above; Swainson, *A Handbook of Weather Folk-lore* (London, 1873). France: Corbis, "Recueil des Dictons Populaires sur le Temps," *Bulletin de la Société Belfortaine d'Emulation*, VIII (1886–87), 19–30; XIV (1895), 109–115; F. de Roucy, *Dictons Populaires sur le Temps* (Paris, 1878). Germany: Bahlmann, *Alt-Münsterische Bauern-Reime* (Münster, 1896); Haldy, *Die Deutschen Bauernregeln* (Jena, 1923), a recent popular collection without notes; Müldener, *Das Buch vom Wetter oder das Wetter im Sprichwort* (Bernburg, n. d.); Reinsberg-Düringsfeld, *Das Wetter im Sprichwort* (Leipzig, 1864); Walter, *Wetterssprüche* (Braunschweig, 1920); Wimmert, "Bauern- und Wetterregeln aus dem Rheinlande," *Zeitschrift für Deutsche Mundarten*, 1910, pp. 351–356. The Netherlands: van Hall, *Spreekwoorden en Voorschriften in Spreuken Betreffend Landbouw en Weêrkennis* (Haarlem, 1872); Thijm, *Kalender- en Gezondheidsregels* (Uitgaven der Koninklijke Vlaamsche Akademie, III, 9 [Ghent, 1893]); Beets, "Volkswijsheid over het Weer," *Verslagen en Mededeelingen van het Vlaamsche*

are definite in substance but not in form. The advice
"Don't plant corn until the dogwood is in bloom,"
which is current in eastern Pennsylvania and perhaps
elsewhere, has not received final form as a proverb,
nor has the widespread superstition regarding the
groundhog and his shadow. Many such sayings, furthermore, do not involve a forecast of weather; consequently Frick, who has written extensively on the
style and construction of weather proverbs, excludes
them from consideration. Proverbs which contain no
forecast tell when certain migratory birds arrive or
leave:

> The cuckoo comes in April,
> Sings a song in May;
> Then in June another tune,
> And then she flies away

or

> The first cock of hay
> Frights the cuckoo away;

Akademie, XXI (1908), 553–592 (an essay which is little more than a paraphrase of Yermoloff). Portugal: Thomaz Pires, *Calendario Rural* (Elvas, 1898). Russia: Yermoloff, *Die Landwirtschaftliche Volksweisheit in Sprichwörtern, Redensarten und Wetterregeln*, I (Leipzig, 1905). Spain: Rodríguez Marín, *Cien Refranes Andaluces de Meteorología, Cronología, Agricultura y Economía Rural* [2] (Seville, 1894) and *Los Refranes del Almanaque* (Seville, 1896). Sweden: Hildebrandsson, "Samling af Be-märkelsedagar, Tecken, Märken, Ordspråk och Skrock Rörande Väder-leken," *Antikvarisk Tidskrift för Sverige*, VII, pt. 2 (1883), 1–106. Switzerland: Seelig, *Die Jahreszeiten im Spiegel Schweizerischer Volks-sprüche* (Zürich, 1925). Most studies of weather proverbs deal with their meteorological aspects. The most significant studies are by Frick ("Le Peuple et la Prévision du Temps," *Schweizerisches Archiv für Volkskunde*, XXVI [1926], 1–21, 89–100, 171–188, 254–279); Hellmann, "Uber den Ursprung der Volkstümlichen Wetterregeln (Bauernre-geln)," *Sitzungsberichte der Preussischen Akademie, Physikalisch-Mathematische Klasse* (1923), 148–170; and Yermoloff, as above.

what weather characterizes certain months (*March comes in like a lion and goes out like a lamb*);[1] when crops should be planted; how the days grow longer or shorter; or what hygienic precautions are necessary at certain seasons:

> When the wind is in the east,
> It is good for neither man nor beast.

All these sayings and the weather proverbs which involve a forecast differ in a significant matter from ordinary proverbs: they contain no metaphorical shift of meaning. A weather proverb of whatever kind means what it says and no more. Of course there are proverbs taken from weather conditions which employ a metaphor, e. g. *Every cloud has a silver lining*; *The darkest hour is just before dawn*; *It never rains but it pours*, but these cannot properly pass as weather proverbs.

Many traditional forecasts of weather conditions can be called truly proverbial: *April showers bring May flowers*; *Rain before seven stops before eleven*;

> Mackerel sky, mackerel sky,
> Never long wet, never long dry.

1 The longer form of this proverb,

> March hack ham ('black ram')
> Comes in like a lion,
> Goes out like a lamb,

is clearly derived from verses in a calendar. The obscure reference to Aries, the ram, in the zodiac has been lost in later forms. Today, the proverb is perhaps more often regarded as a prophecy: "*If* March comes in like a lion, it goes out like a lamb."

> As the days begin to lengthen,
> The cold begins to strengthen.

It is interesting to note that the old rhyme

> Evening red and morning gray
> Will speed a traveler on his way;
> But evening gray and morning red
> Will pour down rain upon his head

appears, perhaps for the first time, in the New Testament: "When it is evening, ye say, It will be fair weather: for the sky is red. And in the morning, It will be foul weather today: for the sky is red and lowring" (*Matt.* xvi, 2–3). Occasionally a proverb bears within itself an indication of the circumstances under which it arose:

> A rainbow at night
> Is the sailor's (*var.* fisher's, shepherd's) delight;
> A rainbow in the morning
> Is the sailor's (*var.* fisher's, shepherd's) warning.

On the whole, weather proverbs which clearly belong to the sea and sailors are surprisingly few; perhaps the manner in which our collections of proverbs have been made has hindered their discovery and preservation. The few classical Greek instances of weather proverbs are, as Hellmann [1] points out, typically concerned with the winds and the sea and in this way reflect the sea-faring life of their inventors.

1 Hellmann, *Sitzungsberichte der Preussischen Akademie, Physikalisch-Mathematische Klasse*, 1923, p. 159.

Most weather proverbs refer to certain signs which are believed to forecast the weather. They mark the beginning of spring by the appearance of migratory birds or the growth of characteristic plants. Others give directions about the planting of crops or foretell the weather of certain later weeks or months from the weather on certain days. If they are taken in a sufficiently general sense, some truth may ordinarily be found in them — but then the observation is so readily apparent or conveys so little of a definite sort that it has small value in the meteorologist's eyes. Even the weather proverbs themselves suggest that the speaker did not take his own words too seriously:

> Wenn der Hahn kräht auf dem Mist,
> Wird's anders oder es bleibt wie's ist.

> ('When the cock crows on the dunghill,
> The weather will change or it will stay as it is'.)

The doubt here expressed is no new trait in weather proverbs: in a manuscript of the fourteenth or fifteenth century in the Brunswick city library we read

> Si pluit in festo processi martiniani
> Quadriginta dies continuare solet
> Hoc intelige sic si non pluit hic pluit illic.

('If it rains during the feast of the procession of St. Martinianus, it usually continues for forty days. Understand it thus: if it does not rain here, it rains there'.)[1]

All signs fail in dry weather expresses a similar idea of the value of popular weather forecasts.

1 Hellmann, as above, p. 152. I have expanded abbreviations.

We distinguish proverbs which deal solely with crops, storms, and fair weather at sea, and forecasts of the weather from natural signs, from proverbs in which the days of the calendar play a part. Hellmann, who writes learnedly on the origin of weather proverbs, believes that proverbs of the more general sort in which the calendar is not mentioned are perhaps ultimately classical in their beginnings, although he is able to cite only one Latin instance, a parallel to *April showers bring May flowers*, and a few Greek instances of a very special kind concerned with the winds and the sea. In the *Saturnalia* (v, 20, 18) Macrobius preserves for us this Latin example, "an old rustic saw" (rusticum vetus canticum): "Hiberno pulvere verno luto grandia farra, Camille, metes" ('With winter dust and spring mud you will reap, Camillus, big harvests'), which we may compare to the English *A bushel* (var. *peck*) *of March dust is worth a king's ransom*. A characteristic trait which appears in this and many other weather proverbs is the description of the weather in terms of its effects: "winter dust" instead of "drought." Perhaps we may conclude with Hellmann that Macrobius' saying belongs to dry central Italy rather than to lower Italy or Sicily, where a more definite rainy season prevails.

Proverbs in which reference is made to the calendar — and ordinarily to specific days — must have originated at a time when knowledge of the calendar was common property. They cannot be extremely old, for the general use of any form of calendar indicating the separate days dates only from the late Middle Ages. The peasant still thinks in terms of Lammastide and St. Martin's Day rather than those of our calendar. In such proverbs a remarkable agreement over a wide area can often be observed, and not infrequently we can see that the proverb has been carried to a region where it is quite out of place. An adaptation to different climates appears in the English *March grass never did good* and the Norwegian *April's growth is rarely good* (Aprils grode er sjelden til gode).[1]

The inapplicability of weather proverbs in regions to which they have been carried by cultural currents appears in meteorological matters. Hellmann, for example, believes that *A green Christmas, a white Easter*, which is widely known in all the Western European languages, must have arisen in a region where snow ordinarily lies on the ground at Christmas. It cannot be native to regions where the ground is bare at Christmas, since snow at Easter is unusual in most parts of Europe. Probably this argument is correct. Nevertheless, it is hard to understand why the proverb is so widely disseminated in the Romance languages, spoken in countries where the meteorological conditions are even more unfavorable than in Germany. It may be that the proverb was invented in a region where snow is usual at Christmas; and its

1 Kock and Petersen, *Ostnordiska och Latinska Medeltidsordspråk* (Copenhagen, 1889–94), II, 88.

persistence may be ascribed to contrast, both in form and substance: undue warm weather will be balanced by cold.

In weather proverbs which mention a particular day in the calendar, a conflict between the facts and the day named may make it possible to assign an approximate age to the tradition. For example, English, French, and German proverbs connect St. Barnabas' Day (June 11) with the summer solstice, e. g. *Barnaby bright,the longest day and the shortest night.* Clearly this refers to dates in "old style" and enables us to fix the origin of the proverb in the fifteenth century, when the calendar was about ten days behind the true time. In the same way *Lucy Light, the shortest day and the longest night,* which is a companion in form to the proverb just quoted, and the German saying *St. Lucy's* (December 13) *makes the days stop getting shorter* (Sankt Luzen macht den Tag stutzen) refer to the winter solstice and must have originated about A.D. 1350, when the Julian calendar was eight days behind. Before the calendar was changed on the continent, i. e. before 1581, St. Lucy's Day had come to be celebrated on what is now December 23. Flemish tradition remedies the matter by substituting St. Thomas' Day (December 21) for St. Lucy's: *On St. Thomas' the days lengthen* (Op St. Thomas lengen de dagen). A widely known version of the Lucy proverb expresses the thought in novel fashion, and seems to have provided a model for other proverbs based on days later in the winter:

On the festival of St. Lucy
The day grows by the leap of a flea.

('A la feste de Sainte Luce
Le jour croist du saut d'une puce'.)

The "leap of a flea" refers to the lengthening shadow on the sun dial. At a later season (New Year's) the measure is a cock's stride,[1] and when the proverb ceased to be understood, it became *On Epiphany the days lengthen by a cock's crow* (Op Driekoningendag sijn de dagen een hanengekraai gelongen).

As a matter of fact, one argument advanced against the introduction in 1581–82 of the Gregorian calendar was that the weather proverbs based on saints' days would no longer guide the husbandman. One of our important early sources of calendar proverbs, *New Lösstag. Nvtzliche bedencken vnd vnterscheidung der pöflischen alten Lösstag, die feldregel vnd Bawrenpractic angehend* (Rorschach am Bodensee, 1590), is designed by its author to meet this very difficulty. The author, Johann Rasch, kept some proverbs as they stood; others he altered by the addition of the necessary ten days. With a truly scientific spirit he printed both the new and the old proverbs to show what he had done.

In the proverbial weather forecast we discern four essential elements which are associated in pairs: the sign with its time of appearance, the weather with its

1 See further examples in Beirens, "De folklore van het weer," *Nederlandsch Tijdschrift voor Volkskunde*, XXIX (1924), 35–36.

time of appearance.[1] No importance attaches to the
order in which these pairs are coupled: we may have
Rain before seven stops before eleven, in which the
sign and its time of appearance come first, or *April
showers bring May flowers,* in which they follow. Of
course one or the other indication of time may be
implied rather than expressed, as in:

> Mackerel sky, mackerel sky,
> Never long wet, never long dry.

Only a few proverbs fix the time of the sign as New
Year's Day. Obviously they can have been invented
only after January 1 had become the first day of the
year. Charlemagne, it will be remembered, had
moved the beginning of the year to March 1; the
Church dated the year from Easter. From the thirteenth century on, there were sporadic efforts to bring
the beginning of the year back to January 1, but the
movement was not generally successful until after the
Reformation, indeed not until the end of the sixteenth
century. Clearly the age of this small group of proverbs cannot be much greater than 350 years.

The forces which are operative in the creation of
weather proverbs are not altogether clear. Some seem
to reflect a principle of equalizing extremes of temperature: a warm summer balances a cold winter or
a green Christmas a white Easter. Although some
meteorologists claim quite positive periodicities, such

[1] Frick, "Le Peuple et la Prévision du Temps," *Schweizerisches Archiv
für Volkskunde,* XXVI (1926), 1 ff.

a principle seems to have little or no authority: over a long term of years the variations in temperature and rainfall are equalized, but the balance is not always restored within the space of twelve months. Etymological puns have a share in the invention of weather proverbs: the Russians say that flax should be sowed on St. Helena's Day (August 18). The maxim is obviously suggested by the similarity of Helena and "l'en" ('flax'). The association of St. Lucy and the winter solstice may possibly have some connection with the well-established association of Lucy and "lux" ('light'). In general, the love of rhyming does not appear to have created many weather proverbs, which, however, are like all other proverbs in the facility with which they use or imitate already existing proverbial types. A very curious adaptation of a saying which has originally no connection at all with the weather is seen in *Heute rot, morgen tot* ('Red today, dead to-morrow'), or *Morgen rot, abend tot* ('Red in the morning, dead at evening'), which in oral tradition signifies that a red morning is followed by a windless evening. This is a strange misapplication of a saying which ordinarily refers to the fate of soldiers.

Frick believes that traces of magic can be discerned in the oldest strata of weather proverbs, but as mankind has become more skeptical of magical powers the popularity of weather proverbs has declined. So far as we can see, few proverbs of the sort have been invented in the last three centuries. Perhaps one group, which can be termed local meteorological proverbs, deserves exemption: proverbs which refer to local signs may have developed more recently and often have a foundation in fact. A famous example of this sort is the passage at the beginning of *Wilhelm Tell* where the fisher, the hunter, and the shepherd are discussing the weather:

> Der graue Talvogt kommt, dumpf brüllt der Firn,
> Der Mythenstein zieht seine Haube an,
> Und kalt bläst es her aus dem Wetterloch;
> Der Sturm, ich mein', wird da sein, eh' wir's denken.

> ('The grizzly monarch of the vale is near,
> There's a deep muttering in the angry sky,
> Old Mytenstein puts on his cloudy cap,
> And icy blasts from the storm-cavern howl!
> Quicker than thought, the tempest will be here'.)
>   ll. 38–41.[1]

English proverbs of the same sort exist, but of course enjoy only a very restricted circulation:

> When Billing Hill puts on its cap,
> Calverley Mill will get a slap;
> As long as Helsby (Hill) wears a hood,
> The weather's never very good.

The examination of Scotch weather proverbs of this sort shows that there is a considerable measure of truth and sound meteorology in them.[2]

1 The translation, published at Providence in 1838, is anonymous.
2 Dunwoody (*Weather Proverbs* [Signal Service Notes IX, Washington, 1883], pp. 9 ff.) reprints an article on this subject by Abercrombie and Marriott from the *Quarterly Journal of the Meteorological Society*.

Among others, the following examples are cited. Clouds gathering on the tops of hills, although the weather is otherwise clear, are a sign of rain:

> When Bredon Hill puts on his hat,
> Ye man of the vale, beware of that;
> When Cheviot ye see put on his cap,
> Of rain ye'll have a wee bit drap.

Windy cirrus clouds follow after a storm and betoken wind rather than rain:

> Mackerel sky and mare's tails
> Make lofty ships to carry low sails.

Under certain special circumstances an unusually clear atmosphere indicates rain: *The further the sight, the nearer the rain.* All these, we are assured, rest upon meteorological facts.

MEDICAL PROVERBS [1]

Another type of proverbial wisdom deals with health and its maintenance. Like weather proverbs,

---

[1] Such proverbs are not very abundant and have not been rendered easily available for study. See bibliographies in Bonser, *Proverb Literature* (London, 1930), pp. 432–433, Nos. 3778–3786, and pp. 439–442, Nos. 3839–3865a. The English proverbs are collected in a special section in Bohn, *A Hand-book of Proverbs*, London, 1855 (almost this entire section is taken from Ray's collection of 1670). Further materials are brought together in Benham, *Book of Quotations, Proverbs and Household Words* (London, 1924), s. v. Health, and Lean, *Collectanea*, I, 478–509. Proverbs of various origins are translated into English in W. K. Kelly, *Proverbs of All Nations* (1859), pp. 203–207; Christy, *Proverbs, Maxims, and Phrases of All Ages* (1890), I, 489–492. There are special books devoted to these proverbs, as follows. Catalan: Miró y Borrás, *Aforística Médica Popular Catalana* (Manresa, 1900).

such maxims are not always easily distinguished from traditions and superstitions. Medical proverbs have in general aroused little interest, although everyone knows a rhyme like

> After dinner rest a while,
> After supper walk a mile.

This rhyme, which we can fairly call a proverb, traces its origin from a rule of the medical school of Salerno, the *Regimen Sanitatis Salernitanum*: Post coenam stabis vel passus mille meabis ('After dinner rest or walk a mile'), and has still older antecedents in the writings of Plutarch. We do not know the extent to which proverbial rules of health derive from this Latin handbook of medical lore. Inasmuch as it reached more than 150 editions and was widely translated, we might expect its influence to be consider-

Flemish: Thijm, *Kalender- en Gezondheidsregels* (Uitgaven der Koninklijke Vlaamsche Akademie, III, 9 [Ghent, 1893]). French: Couché, *Essai sur quelques Expressions Proverbiales et Sentences Populaires Relatives à la Médicine* (Paris, 1808). German: Bremser, *Medizinische Parömien* (Wien, 1806); Bücking, *Versuch einer Medicinischen und Physikalischen Erklärung Deutscher Sprichwörter und Sprichwörtlichen Redensarten* (Stendal, 1797); Ofellus, *Philosophie des Magens in Sprüchen aus Alter und Neuer Zeit* (Leipzig, 1886); Sepp, *Wichtige Gesundheitsregeln* (Augsburg, 1893). Italian: Bernoni, *L'Igiene della Tavola dalla Bocca del Popolo* (Venezia, 1872). Spanish: Monlau, *Elementos de Higiene Privada* (Madrid, 1870); Sorapan de Rieros, *Medicina Española Contenida en Proverbios Vulgares de Nuestra Lengua* (Granada, 1615–16). Curiously enough, several dissertations on medical proverbs were submitted to the University of Altdorf for the degree of Doctor of Medicine. I have noted nine in the first quarter of the eighteenth century; see Bonser, as above, Nos. 3844, 3847, 3848, 3853, 3854, 3858, 3861, 3862, 3865.

able. I have noted only a few survivals in oral tradition: *Plenus venter non studet libenter* ('A full stomach does not work willingly'), which we may compare with *Inanis venter non audit verba libenter* ('An empty stomach does not willingly listen'); *Contra vim mortis non est medicamen in hortis* (*Gegen den Tod ist kein Kraut gewachsen*, 'For death there is no medicine'). Clearly the *Regimen* is borrower in the case of *A tree is known by its fruit*, as in

> Fructibus ipsa suis, quae sit, dignoscitur arbor,
> Saepe solet similis filius esse patri.

Although this is not a health proverb, it may serve as an illustration of the other materials on which the *Regimen* draws.

A few health proverbs are international in their currency, but their number is apparently small. It is perhaps chance that I have noticed more examples of

> Milk before wine,
> I wish't were mine;
> Milk taken after
> Is poison's daughter

than of any other internationally known health proverb; the Germans say

> Wein auf Bier, das rat ich dir;
> Bier auf Wein, lass das sein;

the French,

> Lait sur vin est venin,
> Vin sur lait est souhait;

and the Spanish, *Dexo la lache al vino: bien seas venido, amigo* ('Milk says to Wine, "Welcome, friend"').

What truth inheres in health proverbs remains to be discovered; no one, so far as I am aware, has looked into the matter. They have received thus far step-motherly treatment at the hands of those interested in proverbs, and the few books on health proverbs which are named in the bibliographies are rarely significant contributions to the subject, unless the titles and other indications wholly belie the contents. At present we cannot make any generalizations regarding the history, form, typical characteristics, or subject-matter of these admonitions.

Health proverbs give the most varied kinds of advice. Some deal with sleep: *Six hours sleep for a man, seven for a woman, and eight for a fool; Early to bed and early to rise/Makes a man healthy, wealthy, and wise,* which is at least as old as 1554: *Sanat, sanctificat et ditat surgere mane; An hour's sleep before midnight is worth two after.* A greater number, I suppose, deal with food and eating: *You must eat a peck of dirt before you die; An apple a day keeps the doctor away; Un œuf n'est rien, deux font grand bien, trois est assez, quatre est trop, cinq donnent la mort* ('One egg is nothing, two are very good, three are enough, four are too much, five will kill');[1] *Chair fait chair et poisson, poison* ('Meat makes flesh and fish, poison').[2] The play on

1 Le Roux de Lincy, II, 191; Polites, Παροιμίαι (Athens, 1899–1902), III, 202.
2 Le Roux de Lincy, II, 205; Polites, II, 601–602.

the words "poisson" and "poison," which occurs again in *Poisson sans boisson est poison* ('Fish without drink is poison'), mark the forms as French. The proverb just quoted we find again in the English *Fish should swim thrice*, i. e. in water, sauce, and wine, and the belief involved is old: Petronius tells us in his famous description of a Roman banquet that "Fish should swim" (Pisces natare oportet).

So far as I can see, the more recently introduced articles of food do not give rise to proverbs: potatoes and coffee seem not to be mentioned. Tobacco has little or no place in proverbs. Butter, bread, meat, and cheese, on the other hand, appear frequently. *Bread and cheese* is traditionally a meal in English, and the French say *Fromage et pain est médecine au sain* ('Bread and cheese is medicine for the well'), and

> Pain et beurre et bon fromage
> contre la mort et le vray targe
>
> ('Bread and butter and good cheese
> are a true buckler against death'),

which is evidently closely related to the English *Bread and cheese be two targets against death*. So essential, indeed, is cheese that the French can say

> C'il qui mange du fromage,
> S'il ne le fait, il enrage
>
> ('He who does not eat cheese, will go mad'.)[1]

[1] Le Roux de Lincy, II, 198.

Vegetables are rarely mentioned, although the French say

> Qui vin ne boit après salade
> est en danger d'être malade

> ('He who does not drink wine after
> his salad is in danger of falling sick')[1]

and the Scotch, *Good kail is half the meal.*
  Some health proverbs give only general advice:

> Disne honnestement et soupe sobrement,
> Dors en hault et vivras longuement

> ('Dine rightly and sup moderately,
> Sleep upstairs and you will live long').[2]

I cannot say how well established is the superstition that sleeping upstairs is healthful. Familiar general advice in England is *An ague in the spring is physic for a king*; *Laugh and grow fat.* Occasionally we have an observation regarding the climate: *A green winter* (var. *Christmas*) *makes a fat churchyard*, which is evidently the model for *A hot May makes a fat churchyard.* Rare is such an observation as *Never rub your eye but with your elbow*, and prognostications are not usual:

> Quickly too'd ('toothed') and quickly go,
> Quickly will thy mother have moe.

1 Le Roux de Lincy, II, 216. Cf. Otto, *Archiv für Lateinische Lexico-graphie*, IV (1887), 351.
2 Le Roux de Lincy, II, 195; Wander, *Deutsches Sprichwörter-Lexikon*, V, col. 1545.

Some health proverbs are utterly obscure: *Parsley fried will bring a man to his saddle, and a woman to her grave*, which is evidently concerned with some superstition and may involve the aphrodisiac qualities of parsley. Only a very few proverbs concern themselves with the health of animals:

> Uphill spare me,
> Downhill forbear (*var.* ware) me,
> Plain way (*var.* level ground) spare me not,
> Nor let me drink when I am hot.

In general, proverbs concerned with physical peculiarities are rare.[1] Even those traditional sayings which describe or mock one's neighbors give little room to remarks on physical traits. It is worthy of note that proverbs mentioning physical traits are found most frequently among the Romance peoples. Recognition of such traits appears to be characteristic of a comparatively high culture which distinguishes individual details in the surrounding world; the savage and the peasant show little interest in physiognomic observations. Some traditional sentences

1 Hentig, "Physiognomik im Sprichwort," *Archiv für Kriminologie*, LXXX (1927), 136–144; Sartori, "Körperliche Merkmale im Westfälischen Volksmunde," *Volk und Rasse*, II (1927), 28–34; Bahlmann, "Der Menschliche Körper und seine Funktionen im Westfälischen Glauben, Brauch und Sprichwort," *Zeitschrift des Vereins für Rheinische und Westfälische Volkskunde*, XXIII (1926), 2–19, XXIV (1927), 46–52; Gittée, "De Volkshumor tegenover Lichamelijke Gebreken," *Volkskunde* (Ghent), VI (1893), 1–9; Otto, "Der menschliche Körper und seine Teile im [Lateinischen] Sprichwort," *Archiv für Lateinische Lexikographie*, VI (1889), 309–34c; O. Scarlattini, *L'huomo e sue parte figurato e simbolico*, Augustae Vindelicorum, 1695.

relate physical attributes to psychical traits: *Curled heads are hasty*;

> Lange Nase, spitzes Kinn;
> Da sitzt der Teufel leibhaft drin
>
> ('Long nose, pointed chin;
> The Devil himself sits within');
>
> Cheshire born and Cheshire bred,
> Strong i' th' arm and weak i' th' head.

It might be possible to discover the extent to which sayings concerned with a relationship between physical and mental traits draw on the stock of physiological information associated with the Renaissance belief in "humours." The distrust and even fear of red hair is ancient and universal: *Rotbart nie gut ward* ('A red-beard was never good'), but the association with treason very probably involves an allusion to the traditional color of Judas's hair.[1] Apparently the proverbial warnings against red hair concern only a man. An analogous tradition, also of international currency, is *Crazy people don't turn gray, but asses are born gray* (De gekken grijsen niet, maar de ezels worden grijs geboren).[2] The lack of a beard or its scanty growth marks a man, particularly in southern lands, as suspicious. Certain physical traits are proverbially indices of other physical qualities, e. g. *Vir pilosus aut fortis aut luxuriosus* ('A hairy man, either

---

1 P. F. Baum, "Judas' Red Hair," *Journal of English and Germanic Philology*, XXI (1922), 520–529.
2 Hentig, *Archiv für Kriminologie*, LXXX (1927), 138.

strong or lustful'), and the traditional comparisons based on the length of nose or size of mouth. Typical illustrations of these proverbs, illustrations which are perhaps less offensive than most examples, have been collected to prove that the description of Juan Ruiz in an old Spanish poem contains more traditional elements and fewer bits of actual descriptive detail than we might at first believe.[1]

CONVENTIONAL PHRASES

Phrases and sentences customarily used in a single special situation form a special class of proverbs.[2] Although a metaphor is often present, its purpose is to describe the situation, not to convey an ethical or moral lesson. The Romans said *An ass from Aesop's pit* (Asinus de Aesopi puteo) of an unwelcome, noisy person. The allusion is entirely obscure. When the Scotch say *Either the tod* (fox) *or the bracken-bush* to silly people who speak vaguely and uncertainly, they are contracting an older proverb: *It is a blind goose that knoweth not a fox from a fern-bush.* The German sentence *An angel flew through the room* (Ein Engel

---

1 E. K. Kane, "The Personal Appearance of Juan Ruiz," *Modern Language Notes*, XLV (1930), 103–109.
2 I have noted special collections of conventional phrases only in Scandinavian languages; see, e. g., E. T. Kristensen, *Danske Ordsprog* (Copenhagen, 1890), pp. 532–555; anon., "Ordlekar från Åkers och Österrekarne Härader," *Bidrag til Södermanlands Äldre Kulturhistoria*, I, pt. 1 (1884), 94–99, II, pt. 6 (1886), 86–92; Nordlander, "Svenska Barnvisor ock Barnrim," *Nyare Bidrag till Kännedom om de Svenska Landsmålen*, V, pt. 5 (1886), pp. 254–280.

flog durchs Zimmer) is widely used of the sudden silence which falls on a social group, but its origin is not clear. Another equally obscure phrase with the same meaning is *Ein Leutnant bezahlt seine Schulden* ('A lieutenant pays his debts'), which has not yet found universal acceptance. In the same situation the Dutch say "The pastor is going by" (De domine gaat voorbi) and Americans say "Quaker meeting" or "It's twenty minutes past." *Let her go, Gallagher* is, I believe, unexplained.

Many fixed, conventional phrases exist in English: *I have other fish to fry,* i. e. 'I cannot undertake a proposed task'; *His eyes are bigger than his stomach,* i. e. 'he cannot eat all he asked for'; *Boys will be boys,* i. e. 'a boyish prank is a minor fault and one to be overlooked'; *You're the doctor,* i. e. 'you, the more competent person, and not I, should make the decision'; *Sent a boy to mill,* said when a low card, which the player thought high enough to win the trick, is exceeded by the opponent; *Heads I win, tails you lose,* said of an undertaking in which only one participant profits; *It's six of one and half a dozen of the other* or *It's as broad as it's long,* said when there is no reason for preferring either of two alternatives; *What's yours is mine and what's mine is my own,* said of a selfish child; *Fingers were made before forks*; *Take while the taking is good,* said to a person who hesitates to accept something when it is offered; *Put that in your pipe and smoke it,* said as impudent repartee; *That's no skin off my elbow*, i. e. *My withers are unwrung*, 'the event or remark does not injure or refer to me'; *Keep that under your hat*; *Do as I say and not as I do*, which has parallels in Livy and the New Testament. *Tell it to the marines!* which may be compared to the Horatian *Credat Judaeus Apella* ('Let the Jew Apella believe it,' *Sat.* 1, 5, 100), a "learned" proverb, was parodied for a season as "Tell it to the Danes," when F. A. Cook's story of the discovery of the North Pole was accepted by the Danish Academy.

Generally speaking, such fixed phrases as we are now considering rarely deal with superstitions. The ordinary English form of refusal to give the name of one's informant is *A little bird told me*, while on the continent it is *My little finger* (var. *thumb*) *told me* (*Mein kleiner Finger* [var. *Daumen*] *hat es mir gesagt*). The third witch in *Macbeth* alludes to the superstition underlying the continental phrase, but her remark is hardly proverbial in form:

> By the pricking of my thumbs,
> Something wicked this way comes.
> Act iv, sc. 1.

Ask me no questions and I'll tell you no lies is a brutally frank formula with the same general meaning. Old and widespread is the phrase *A hair of the dog that bit you* for a drink of liquor taken on the morning after a night of dissipation. It displays curious and typical variations: Ben Jonson says in *Bartholomew Fair* "pluck a hair of the same wolf" and Hermann Kurz, a German poet of the nineteenth century, alludes to the hair of a cat in a similar connection. These variations illustrate once more the substitution of analogous and contrary details in oral tradition. In both these examples of superstitions in fixed phrases we have very ancient and widely known tradition.

Evasive descriptions of childbirth have in some cases become standing formulae.[1] The stork is proverbial in English, and the German phrase is even more specific: *The stork has bitten mother's leg* (Der Storch hat der Mutter ins Bein gebissen). A wholly satisfactory explanation is not forthcoming. Obviously the phrase cannot have been invented in England, where storks are rarely, if ever, seen. There may be some primitive symbolism in the mention of the stork. Another form, which is characteristically English, but has not spread to America, assigns the origin of children to the parsley bed; it is equally inexplicable. A more careful examination of the superstitions and medical lore associated with parsley would probably throw light on the matter. An analogous German tradition names the cabbage bed, and is very likely connected more or less directly with the English phrase.

1 See the collectanea entitled "Woher kommen die Kinder," *Am Urquell*, IV (1893), 224 ff.; V (1894), 80 f., 162, 254, 255, 287; VI (1895), 41, 125, 159, 218 f.; H. F. Feilberg, *Bidrag til en Ordbog over Jyske Almuesmål, s. v.* Barn (see also Tillæg); Boekenoogen, "Waar de Kinderen vandaar Komen," *Volkskunde* (Ghent), XXII (1911), 18–24, 143–151, 193–198, XXIII (1912), 29–37.

PROVERBIAL PROPHECIES

A few proverbs forecast the future in politics or war. Perhaps the most famous example is *Austria erit ultima in orbe* ('Austria shall be the last thing in the world') or, arranged in the order of the vowels, *Austria erit in orbe ultima.* English proverbs are particularly concerned with military affairs: *He that England will win must with Scotland* (var. *Ireland*) *begin*; *The vale of Holmsdale was never won and never shall*;

> When the black fleet of Norway is come and gone,
> England, build houses of lime and stone,
> For afterwards you shall have none;

> When hemp is spun,
> England is done.

> Nene and Welland
> Shall drown all Holland.

Spenser knew the last of these prophecies. Such sayings are probably fragments of mediaeval or later prophecies; we might understand them better if the whole were before us. Some chance has dictated the preservation of these prophecies. A still more curious prophecy was current in Germany before the recent war and during its early years:

> 1911 ein Flutjahr,
> 1912 ein Blutjahr.

When the Balkan War scare of 1912 passed over, the rhyme could of course no longer serve as a prophecy and it was revised to read:

> 1911 ein Flutjahr,
> 1912 ein gut Jahr,
> 1913 ein Blutjahr.

And still further additions and alterations were needed in the further course of events. So far as we may see in proverbs a summing up of a prevailing popular mood, this proverb illustrates the fatalistic attitude which preceded the war of 1914.

III

THE STYLE OF PROVERBS

ALTHOUGH rigidity of form constitutes an essential characteristic of proverbs, scholarly efforts to describe and study it have been unavailing and profitless. Metrical studies have been uniformly tedious and uninspired. The examination of other important stylistic factors has not yielded important results. We may consider the proverbial vocabulary: a few words are interesting as relics of former days, and a few others as nonce-formations. In the main, however, proverbs are rarely distinguished by peculiarities in diction. They must necessarily restrict their choice of words to the simplest and most obvious materials. Except for Heusler's remarks concerning the stylistic differences between the Viking proverb and the humbler vulgar proverb and the previous mention of *Faint heart ne'er won fair lady* as an instance of stylistic contrast, the question of proverbial style as a reflection of the speaker's social background has been neglected. Still other matters call for our attention. Although the rhetorical details in proverbs have been often discussed, the subject is not exhausted. The figures of speech, notably contrast and metaphor, and the kinds of sentences used in proverbs are especially interesting bits of rhetoric. Certain proverbial types which are important for their origin, history, or peculiarities may be distinguished on stylistic grounds. And finally, I shall discuss the subject of proverbs in their literary relations, a subject which extends beyond the merely stylistic in its importance.

Metrical studies of proverbs have rarely escaped the temptation to employ the elaborate classical system of metrics, and have consequently failed to discover the essential traits.[1] The chances of winning significant results in this field are good, if hairsplitting classical metrical formulae are avoided. As we might expect, proverbs conform to the general rhythm of the language in which they have been taken down. So far as we can determine and describe the prevailing rhythm of a language we have a standard with which we can compare each individual proverb. It might be possible, in the case of a proverb borrowed from another language, to trace a gradual adaptation to a new rhythm of speech. Conceivably we might find in similar fashion a development in the passage from the mediaeval to the modern vernacular proverb, a development which avoided certain metrical types and preferred others. The importance of such conclusions for the history of metrics and poetics — if they can be established — is obvious. Of course we must deal

[1] See Seiler, *Deutsche Sprichwörterkunde* (Munich, 1922), pp. 194 ff.

with deep currents in linguistic and stylistic habits, and the investigation must be conducted in such a way as to emphasize broad tendencies.

The metrical device of alliteration is an untrustworthy mark of age in a proverb. Alliteration is a familiar characteristic of early Germanic verse, and for a long time scholars regarded alliterative formulae as ancient.[1] A long list of such formulae will be found in the early pages of Grimm's *Deutsche Rechtsaltertümer*. We are no longer tempted to regard an alliterative formula or proverb as necessarily reaching back to that early period in Germanic literary history when alliterative verse prevailed. Some alliterative phrases are old, while others have arisen in much more recent times from the love of a jingle. There is no easy way to distinguish between old and new alliterative expressions; we are forced to rely largely on the historical evidence. Alliteration is not sufficient to prove the antiquity of a proverb: *Many men, many minds* is a classical and not an early Germanic proverb. An investigation of the facts concerning alliteration in proverbs would begin by discussing what signs prove a phrase to be old. With stylistic, chronological, linguistic, and other tests at our disposal, we might learn that there are two groups of alliterative proverbs, one old and one new, with different characteristics. In such an investigation one must bear constantly in mind that apt alliteration's artful aid marks

1 See pp. 89 ff.

both simple speech, as we see in children's rhymes, and highly elaborated diction.

The typical form of the mediaeval Latin proverb is the leonine hexameter: *Arbor per primum quaevis non corruit ictum* ('A tree does not fall at the first stroke'); *Parvus pendetur fur, magnus abire videtur* ('The little thief is hanged, the big one is seen to go off'). These examples, which have been chosen merely because we have already referred to them above, illustrate a conspicuous fault of such proverbs. In order to fill the hexameter, the versifier adds u eless words: "quaevis, videtur." Even clumsier expansion is seen in *Ius est implere promissa decentia vere* ('Promise is debt') or *Auri natura non sunt splendentia plurq* ('All is not gold that glitters'), and occasionally a whole clause is needed to fill the line: *Sunt pueri pueri, vivunt pueriliter illi* ('Boys will be boys'); *Luscus praefertur caeco, sic undique fertur* ('Better the eye to be sore than all blind'); *Res miranda nova, picae fur abstulit ova* ('An egg is stolen even from a witch'); *Quod male lucratur, male perditur et nihilatur* ('Ill gotten, ill spent'). Even when the composer had a brief and effective model in classical Latin before him, he did not hesitate: *Quot homines, tot sententiae* ('Many men, many minds') yields *Quolibet in capite viget ingenium speciale*. Although a stylistic examination of proverbs in leonine hexameters leads into arid and untrodden fields, it is worth undertaking. No one has sought to learn what standards existed, whether proverbs were actually composed in this form in addition to being translated from the vernacular, or what local stylistic variations and habits or developments in the form can be found. It has been pointed out, for example, that leonine hexameters with feminine rhymes are probably later in origin than those with masculine rhymes.[1] Altogether useless are the emendations which Suringar [2] and Seiler [3] make to correct the versification of these mediaeval Latin proverbs. The versifiers gave little thought to such matters: some wrote carefully and others not.

The linguistic peculiarities of proverbs have never received thorough examination.[4] As we have seen, old or dialectal words are kept. New words which go beyond the ordinary bounds of word-formation are occasionally found. *He is one of the McTak's, not one of the McGie's* rests on the pun involved in "McGie" and the family name McGee. The compound McTak is unusual, indeed unnatural, for the component Mc- is never used with a verb. German seems to make new compounds more freely than English, and the results in proverbs are more interesting. *Ein Kaufmann ist kein Schenkmann* illustrates the readiness with which "Mann" is used as second member in

---

1 See Kock and Petersen, *Ostnordiska och Latinska Medeltidsordspråk* (Copenhagen, 1889–94), II, 65.
2 *Over de "Proverbia Communia"* (Leiden, 1863).
3 *Deutsche Sprichwörterkunde, passim.*
4 See Seiler, as above, p. 179. Tetzner (*Die Wortbildung im Deutschen Sprichwort*, Gelsenkirchen, 1908) includes many plays on words which can scarcely have been proverbial.

compounds; normally "Mann" is compounded with another noun, e. g. "Amtmann," "Fuhrmann," but in this case the speaker has regarded "Kauf-" as derived from the verb "kaufen" and not from the noun "Kauf," and has formed an analogous, but new and unusual, compound "Schenkmann" from the verb "schenken." The punning proverb *Vorrat ist besser als Nachrat* is comparable to the English *Hindsight is better than foresight*. In both instances the noun which served as a basis, i. e. "Vorrat," 'foresight,' has yielded a new compound with a first member of opposite meaning. "After wit" in *After wit is dear bought* is a nonce-form of similar origin; it is of course a compound word and should be so printed, although the collections print it otherwise. New words are made in ways which are no longer used: *Many a mickle makes a muckle* contains the word "muckle" formed by vowel gradation from "mickle" in the same way that "sing" and "sung" are related. New formations are especially frequent in coining whimsical place-names for proverbial use. With one place-name as a model a second one is invented for the sake of contrast: *Er stammt nicht aus Schenkendorf, sondern aus Greifswald* ('He does not come from Giversville but from Graspers' Grove'). So, too, the historical proverb *Nimmweg, Reissweg und Unrecht* ('Take away, snatch away, and injustice') twists the names Nimwegen (the final *n* is silent), Ryswick, and Utrecht to describe the treaties of 1678, 1697, and

1713. Such nonce-proverbs are widely used in Germany, but are not so familiar elsewhere. The English proverbs *He is none of the Hastings*, i. e. 'he is slow,' and *He was born at Little Wittham* illustrate a similar punning use of a proper name, but contain no new formations. With them we may compare the German "Drückeberger" ('one who avoids an issue or responsibility') and "Schlauberger" ('a person who is adroit in attaining his ends'); "Schlaumeier," which has the same meaning as "Schlauberger," is a different kind of formation, since it does not suggest a place-name.

The figures in proverbs have not been studied profitably. An application of the classical rhetorical rules and subdivisions will hardly bring to light anything of interest or importance.[1] Seiler tries another tack. He distinguishes three classes of metaphors in proverbs: (1) proverbs in which the idea preceded the image, e. g. *Those who will live in glass houses should not throw stones*; (2) those in which the image preceded the idea, e. g. *New brooms sweep clean*; (3) those in which the image and the idea are conceived simultaneously, e. g. *Still waters run deep*. The first group is recognizable, he asserts, by its employment of an impossible image: glass houses do not exist. A collection and a close study of proverbs in which an impossible situation is described would certainly be fruitful.

---

[1] See the literature, which is rather discouraging in its achievements, in Seiler, *Deutsche Sprichwörterkunde*, pp. 153 ff.

Seiler is perhaps inclined to go a little too far in regarding a situation as impossible: *Too many cooks
spoil the broth* can hardly be considered as depicting
an impossible situation. The distinction between the
second and third groups is, as Seiler acknowledges,
entirely metaphysical and is therefore better discarded. Proverbs develop from the generalization of a
simple scene, and it is useless to discuss whether the
perception of the scene and its application are simul-
taneous or separated in time.

Simple metaphors which verge on personification
are of course common to proverbs in all lands: ab-
stractions are assigned the powers of human beings,
e. g. *Truth will out*; *Lies have short legs*; *Walls have ears*
(compare *Campus habet oculos, silva aures*); *Hunger
breaks stone walls*; *Misery loves company*; *Hunger is
the best cook*. A freer use of personification and in
a form which is more dramatically effective marks
German proverbs, e. g. *Trauwohl reitet das Pferd weg*
('Easymark rides off with the plug,' i. e. 'the trusting
man is cheated'); *Herr Pfennig geht voran* ('Mr.
Penny heads the procession'); *Borghard ist Lehnhards Knecht* ('Mr. Borrow is the servant of Mr.
Lend'), which involves a pun on the family names
"Borghard" and "Lehnhard." The type is infrequent in English, e. g. *Brag is a good dog, but Holdfast
a better*. Apparently the popularity of such proverbs
in which a whole scene is dramatized without naming
an abstraction — although the abstraction is the

subject of the proverb — has declined in modern use. The proverbs in which it appears in most characteristic form are not frequently used; no new proverbs, so far as I can see, are being made on the same model. As is evident, the history of this stylistic device is unknown. In fact, we know very little about the development and spread of any particular stylistic peculiarities in proverbs.

A rhetorical trait which is found in the simplest proverbs, even in those simple aphorisms which do not rise to the dignity of a metaphor, is parallelism of structure with its almost inevitable accompaniment, contrast. Parallelism and contrast are found in words, structure, and thought. Simple proverbial forms like *Many men, many minds*; *Like master, like man*; *The more he has, the more he wants*; *Nothing venture, nothing win*; *Testis unus, testis nullus* are dominated by parallelism. The repetition of the same word in two phrases heightens the effect of the contrasting second members. Many proverbs employ contrast alone by separating contrasting words with a colorless predicate: *Hindsight is better than foresight*; *The longest way round is the shortest way home*. A more complicated use of these devices is seen in *Young saint, old devil*; *Man proposes, God disposes*; *The nearer the church, the farther from God*; *Spare the rod and spoil the child*; *Where ignorance is bliss, 'tis folly to be wise*. Here we have parallelism of structure used to emphasize the contrast in words. *Where ignorance is bliss, 'tis folly to be wise* illustrates a chiastic use of contrast with parallelism of structure.

The stylistic peculiarities of very brief proverbs offer problems which have not yet been seriously attacked. Archbishop Trench conjectures [1] that those sayings which lack a verb are characteristic of classical tradition: Χρήματ' ἀνήρ ('Money [makes] the man');[2] *Sus Minervam* ('The sow [teaches] Minerva,' i. e. 'the fool claims the ability to teach the learned'); *Fures clamorem* ('Thieves [fear] uproar'). He is of course well aware of *Forewarned, forearmed*, which is *Praemonitus, praemunitus*, and he praises the terseness of *Voll, toll* ('A drunken man is a mad man'). It is by no means certain that we may venture to assign proverbs of this form to any one source. No doubt they originated in different ways: *Sus Minervam* may very well be the residuum of a lost fable, and Χρήματ' ἀνήρ represents an old aphoristic sentence type which we cannot use now. Heusler[3] observes that the disinclination to use this old aphoristic form like the German *Viel Feind, viel Ehr* ('Many enemies, much honor') or the English *Young saint, old devil* makes itself felt in the early Middle Ages in Icelandic literature. The form has not been able to maintain itself with any notable success. Yet there are proverbs

1 *On the Lessons in Proverbs*, p. 17.
2 Attributed to Alcæus. Cf. Erasmus, *Chiliades*, ed. 1598, p. 563; Burckhardt, *Arabic Proverbs* (London, 1830), p. 198, No. 680.
3 *Altgermanische Dichtung* (Handbuch der Literaturwissenschaft), p. 68, § 61.

made on this model which, I conjecture, are not very ancient, e. g. *Good hand, good hire,* a phrase which is used of a farm laborer employed only at rush seasons. The proverbs which contain no verb but are held together by correlatives, e. g. *The more, the merrier; The fewer, the better fare,* may be mentioned. The brevity of Russian proverbs, on which Altenkirch [1] comments, is of a different sort, and illustrates what can be accomplished in compression by a language which has no article, which dispenses with the verb "to be" in the present tense, and which employs a very condensed participial idiom.

The rhetorical device of connecting two abstract ideas in terms of a family relationship appears to spring originally from Greek personifications of abstract qualities. Directly or indirectly, the many classical Latin examples seem to imitate Greek constructions. Homer (*Iliad*, xvi, 231) calls sleep the brother of death, and Virgil (*Aen.*, vi, 278) repeats the thought. Apuleius wrote "Poverty . . . is the discoverer of all the arts" (Paupertas . . . omnium artium repertrix, *De Magia* [*Apologia*], 18), a phrase which may have been only an epigram to its author but one which has given rise to the most familiar of all proverbs made on this model: *Necessity is the mother of invention.* From the very beginning this rhetorical device keeps a level a few degrees above the unmistakable popular proverb so that we are

1 *Archiv für Slavische Philologie,* XXX (1909), 19.

always a little conscious of art in its use. The Terentian "Subservience begets friends, truth hatred" (Obsequium amicos, veritas odium parit) was often quoted, if it was not actually proverbial, and its similarity to *Familiarity breeds contempt* is obvious. The two sayings are combined, of course in their Latin forms, by Pope Innocent III; and not content with that, Angelo Poliziano reports a still longer version which springs from the same root: "Veritas odium, prosperitas superbiam, securitas periculum, familiaritas contemptum, id est, parit" ('Truth breeds hate, prosperity pride, safety danger, familiarity contempt'). The notion that fame brings envy in its train finds expression in "Invidia gloriae comes [est]," and Seneca and St. Jerome said "Vicina sunt vitia virtutibus" ('Vices are neighbors of virtues'), which is of similar form. Quintillian has "Avarice is the mother of cruelty" (Crudelitatis mater avaritia est). The variety and freedom with which the formula is used in these early instances are worthy of note, and seem to indicate that it was by no means a rigid rhetorical convention.

In later periods, particularly after the Renaissance, the number of examples of the form increases greatly in the handbooks of apothegms and sententious remarks, but the formula, which rarely occurs in proverbs collected in oral tradition, has little elasticity and is, with one or two exceptions, an outworn framework with no popular associations. The Rule of St.

Benedict has *Discretio mater virtutis* ('Discretion is the mother of virtue'), which is evidently the model for the popular Italian proverb *Discretion is the mother of asses* (La discrezione è la madre degli asini).[1] Heinrich Bebel, a German humanist and the first man to record (although in Latin) German proverbs, has *Veritas temporis filia* ('Truth is the daughter of time'), and Angelo Poliziano, an Italian humanist of the preceding generation, *La notte è madre de pensieri* ('Night is the mother of thoughts'), a thought which is more simply expressed as *In nocte consilium*. Notwithstanding the evidence of the Italian parody of the Rule of St. Benedict, almost all proverbs on this model have an artificial, bookish sound, and rarely occur in collections derived from oral sources. The legal proverb *Actio est filia obligationis* ('The act is the daughter of the obligation') seems a learned maxim rather than a traditional proverb. I give by way of conclusion some phrases which are cited with more or less plausibility as traditional proverbs: *Pity is akin to love*; *Ingratitude is the daughter of pride*; *Diligence is the mother of good luck*; *Idleness is hunger's mother and theft's brother* (Ledigheid is hongers moeder en van dieverij een broeder), which seems to belong to a widely distributed group represented by the English and French proverb *Idleness is the mother of all the vices* (L'ennui est mère de toutes les vices); *Experience is the mother of wisdom*; *Ignorance is the mother of devotion* (var.

1 Wesselski, *Poliziano*, p. 244, No. 398.

impudence); *Sorrow is laughter's daughter*; *Disuse is sister to abuse.* I have made no effort to collect examples outside of English and the classical languages, although the type is a familiar one in all the languages of western Europe, e. g. *Distrust is the mother of safety* (La défiance est mère de sureté),[1] the Low German *Luck is luck's mother* (Glück is glückes moder),[2] or the whimsical *Vorsicht ist die Mutter der Porzellankiste* ('Caution is the mother of the porcelain chest'). The actual contribution made by the formula to the traditional proverbial stock is slight: *Necessity is the mother of invention*, which is actually one of the earliest recorded instances of the type, stands almost alone except for *The thought is father to the deed.*

Another proverbial type is distinguished by the use of correlatives, e. g. *Ubi timor, ibi pudor* ('Where there is fear, there is modesty') — which is first reported in Greek; *Ubi amici, esse ibidem opes* ('Where friends are, there also is wealth'). Although the examples in the Greek and Latin classics are not numerous, they seem to have provided the models for a rather abundant development in the Middle Ages, a

---

1 Quitard, *Dictionnaire des Proverbes* (Paris, 1842), p. 290.
2 See the many German examples collected in Seiler, *Deutsche Sprichwörterkunde*, p. 155. See also the Dutch *God wolts is alder bede moeder* ('"Would to God" is the mother of all prayers,' *Proverbia communia*, No. 354) and *Voorzigtigheid is de moeder der wijsheid* ('Caution is the mother of wisdom'). The first of these is the only example in the 803 proverbs in the late fifteenth-century *Proverbia communia*. Perhaps the form had not yet established itself.

development which, to be sure, accorded with the native genius of Latin and Greek. Characteristic mediaeval examples of the type are: *Ubi crux, ibi lux* ('Where the Cross is, there is light'); *Ubi mala fortuna, ibi mala fides* ('Where there is bad luck, there is bad faith'); and the expanded form: *Ubi timor, ibi pudor; ubi pudor, ibi honor* ('Where there is fear, there is modesty; where there is modesty, there is honor'). We may perhaps see the difference between this type and the modern traditional proverb in the contrast between *Ubi bona custodia, ibi bona pax* ('Where there is good guarding, there peace is kept') and *Good fences make good neighbors*. Modern representatives of the type are not very frequent, but we may note such familiar proverbs as *Where there's a will, there's a way*; *Where there's smoke, there's fire*. The relative popularity of the type appears from the list in Bohn's *Handbook of [English] Proverbs*, where the proverbs are arranged alphabetically according to the first words: those beginning with "where" are not especially abundant.

Other correlatives are used somewhat less often. We have classical models in *Qualis dominus, talis et servus* ('Like master, like man') from Petronius, which is the model for *Qualis hera, tales pedissaeque* ('Like mistress, like maid'), and the Plautine *Quot homines, tot sententiae* ('As many men, so many opinions'), and furthermore in *Qualis grex, talis rex* ('Like company, like king') and *Qualis homo, talis sermo* ('Like man, like speech'). A humanistic imitation is *Quot regiones, tot mores* ('As many regions, so many customs'). The modern languages have few correlatives or, at least, few correlatives which translate neatly and effectively the Latin formulae. Even when it was possible to translate *ubi . . ., ibi . . .* satisfactorily, modern tradition has generally failed to take advantage of the opportunity. For *quot . . ., tot . . .* there is no translation which rings true in popular speech; and consequently *Quot homines, tot sententiae* becomes *Many men, many minds.* The effect of the correlatives is produced by parallelism. It might perhaps be maintained that correlatives live on in such proverbs as *The nearer the church, the farther from God;* but the parallel structure and the contrast of "nearer" and "farther" rather than the correlatives "the . . ., the . . ." hold the proverb together.

Forms which are characteristic of Germanic proverbs have not as yet been generally recognized. An old type began with the words "One must" (or "ought") and was perhaps a general Germanic type.[1] In fact, we can see in Icelandic a still older formula which had no subject: *At kveldi skal dag leyfa* ('At evening one should praise the day,' *Hávamál*, 81, 1). When, however, the use of "skal" without a subject became less natural and idiomatic, the indefinite pronoun was used as subject. In the Germanic languages

---

[1] Taylor, "The proverbial formula *Man soll . . .*," *Zeitschrift für Volkskunde*, XL (1930), 152–156.

in which the indefinite pronoun is little used in popular speech, as in English, the formula necessarily fell into disuse. The formula "mon sceal" is frequent in Old English didactic verse, and the freedom of its use suggests its proverbial popularity then. The disappearance of the formula is almost complete in Middle English. The Middle English *Proverbs of Hendyng* have *Under boske shal men weder abide*, and those who used it may have understood "men" as plural. In the German Middle Ages the formula seems not to have enjoyed particular favor, although instances are not entirely wanting: the proverb *Turn your coat according to the wind* finds formulation in the later Middle Ages as *Man sol den mantel keren nach der wind wehet*. Modern German still uses sayings of this type, e. g. *Man soll den Tag nicht vor dem Abend loben*. Since the formula so readily lends itself to various uses, it is often difficult to know whether we are dealing with a sententious remark, a maxim, or a proverb.

Along with the disappearance of proverbial types, we must also reckon with the possibility of the creation of new patterns. It will require some study to prove that a new pattern has been created, and no one has yet made such an attempt. It is entirely conceivable, for example, that the declarative sentence beginning with "You" is a new pattern, e. g. *You can't spoil a rotten egg*; *You can never tell till you've tried*; *You can lead a horse to water but you can't make him drink*. I am inclined to believe that early examples of this pattern are not frequent and that the form now enjoys a greater popularity and wider use than ever before. Obviously the formula with "You" replaces older impersonal forms like *There's small choice in rotten apples*; *It's ill halting before a cripple*; *One may live and learn.*

Details of style often give a hint regarding the age or the history of a proverb, but our methods of study and the criteria on which we can rely are as yet little developed. Rhyme, alliteration, idiom, or peculiar verbal tricks of style often mark a version in one language as the source of a version in another. Of these indications, rhyme and alliteration are less reliable than idiom.

Ordinarily the rhymed proverb is the source of the unrhymed proverb: *Mieux vaut en paix un œuf, qu'en guerre un bœuf* yields *Besser ein Ei im Frieden als ein Ochs im Kriege* ('An egg in peace is better than an ox in wartime'); and *Les morts ont toujours tort* gives *Die Toten haben immer Unrecht* ('The dead are always wrong'). The rule is not without exceptions: *Morgenstunde hat Gold im Munde* is not the original form because it is rhymed or because it alliterates. *Necessity knows no law* and *Not kennt kein Gebot* are both translations of *Necessitas dat legem. A friend in need is a friend indeed* illustrates how a proverb is padded to obtain a rhyme. The employment of useless words for metrical purposes is especially frequent in mediaeval Latin proverbs in leonine hexameters. Appropriately enough, one collection, which belongs to the end of the eleventh or the beginning of the twelfth century, entitles itself: *Proverbia Rusticorum Mirabiliter Versificata*, although the humor which we see in the name was entirely unconscious.

The effort to produce a rhyming formula, as, for example, in the transformation of *Fortis ut mors dilectio* ('Love [is] as strong as death') into *Amour et mort, rien n'est plus fort*, is often very successful. Abraham à Sancta Clara, court preacher in Vienna in the last quarter of the seventeenth century, displayed a great fondness for rhyming epigrams and proverbs. He was, it will be remembered, the model for Schiller's Capuchin in *Wallensteins Lager*. Abraham's native liking for rhymes and puns makes it hard to know whether his sayings are actually proverbial: "Ehestand, Wehestand" ('The state of marriage [is] a state of misery') is no doubt his own invention. In the case of "Man thut halt die grossen Dieb perdoniren, und die kleinen stranguliren" ('The big thieves are pardoned and the little ones strangled'), which is his version of *Die kleinen Diebe hängt man und die grossen lässt man laufen* ('The little thieves are hanged and the big ones are allowed to run away'), we cannot readily discover how wide an acceptance the rhymed form enjoyed. Whatever the status of this illustration may really be, oral tradition is very likely to make such changes in order to find a rhyme. *Homo proponit, Deus disponit* ('Man proposes, God disposes') yields a rhyming proverb readily enough in English and the Romance languages; the Germans say *Der Mensch denkt und Gott lenkt*; the Dutch, *De mensch wikt, maar God beschikt*; and the Swedish *Menniskan spår och Gud rår*. Clearly the Latin rhyme was a model in the invention of these proverbs. *Sauf oder lauf* ('Drink or run') is evidently translated from the Ciceronian "Aut bibat aut abeat," and it in turn is ῍Η πῖθι ἤ ἄπιθι.

A play on words or an allusion often identifies the age or home of a proverb. Clearly *While there's life, there's hope* comes from the Latin *Dum spiro, spero* ('While I breathe, I hope'), although the force of the English proverb is somewhat different from that of the Latin. *Forewarned, forearmed* is the Latin *Praemonitus, praemunitus*. *Amore, more, ore, re firmantur amicitiae* ('Friendships are strengthened by love, manners, the mouth, and deed'), which is perhaps an ingenious rhetorical invention rather than a proverb, can only be Latin, and the use of rhyme shows, furthermore, that it is a mediaeval construction. The allusion to gender in *Le parole son femine, e fatti son maschi* ('Words are feminine; deeds are masculine') [1] has a point in Italian which it would not have in German or English. In *Acht is meer dan duizend* ('Eight [also: 'care, watchfulness'] is more than a dozen') [2] the pun is possible only in Dutch or German

1 Wesselski, *Poliziano*, p. 214.
2 Stoett, *Nederlandsche Spreekwoorden* (Zutphen, 1923–25), No. 45.

and identifies the home of the proverb. There is no mistaking the source of the Swedish *Föra swin til Rhin, det blijr antå swin* ('Lead a pig to the Rhine; it remains a pig'),[1] in which the need of a rhyme preserves the proper name. Such allusions to places or persons often give us invaluable hints: *Die Zeit ist vorbei, da Bertha spann* ('The time is past, when Bertha span') must be a translation of *Ce n'est plus le temps que Berthe filoit*. An unusual, obsolete, or foreign idiom is ordinarily an insuperable handicap to a proverb and causes its early disappearance. There are nevertheless instances in which the idiom tells the origin of a proverb. The Bohemian *Když ovce pošly, i kozy ke cti přišli* ('Where sheep are lacking, the goats are honored')[2] preserves, we are told, a German idiom in the second clause. The Middle High German *Zwêne sint eines her* ('Two are an army for one,' i.e. 'two can overpower one') soon became unintelligible in German and the proverb disappeared from use. It has been conjectured that *her* 'army' was construed as *Herr* 'master' and that the phrase *Herr werden eines Dinges*, 'to become master of a thing,' arose from the proverb. Although the principle involved in this explanation is correct, the absence of a direct connection between the two phrases and the readiness with which the second could have developed independently (as in English) make the explanation improbable.

1 Krohn, *Die Folkloristische Arbeitsmethode* (Oslo, 1926), p. 139.
2 Altenkirch, *Archiv für Slavische Philologie*, XXX (1909), 13, 321–322.

Proverbs are of course distinguished by individual stylistic traits. It is perhaps more difficult for us to discern the characteristic traits in proverbs which are familiar to us. Foreign and unusual forms are easily recognized. Two such forms will be described as illustrations of the possible variations in proverbial style. One of these forms, the dialogue proverb, is Levantine in its distribution and has found only chance acceptance in Western Europe. The other form, a special type of epigrammatic proverb, enjoyed a remarkable popularity in Europe after the Renaissance, but it is no longer in particular favor.

Dialogue Proverbs

A very curious proverbial form which is utterly strange to us is that of a brief dialogue. A typical instance, which has been taken down in Greek, Ruthenian, and Russian, is *How sweet the milk is! — Where did you see it? — My uncle saw another man drinking it on the other side of the river.* Even more widely distributed is the dialogue: *I have caught a bear. — Bring it here. — It won't come. — Then come yourself. — It won't let me go.* The Poles have altered the proverb by substituting a Tartar for the bear. A similar form is the Arabic *They said to the camel-bird (the ostrich), "Carry." It answered, "I cannot, for I am a bird." They said, "Fly." It answered, "I cannot, for I am a camel."* Others are *They brought the wolf to school and read " A, B, C" to him; but he said,*

"*Lamb, she-goat, kid*"; and *They said to the lazy man, "Today is a holiday." Then he answered, "Tomorrow and the day after, too."* The European equivalent is *Lazy people always have holidays* (Ignavis semper feriae). The fact that family quarrels are often marked by bitterness is thus expressed: *Who knocked out your eye? — My brother. — That's why the blow went so deep.* The saying *The Lord helps those who help themselves* is *St. John, help me! — Put out your hand yourself.* This unfamiliar form can be converted into the ordinary European type. The French *The ass invited to a wedding ought to bring wood or water* (Asne convié à nopces eau ou boys y doibt aporter) [1] probably retains a trace of the original Arabic narrative form: *They asked the ass, "Whither?" He answered, "To fetch wood or water."*

In these proverbs we may perhaps see the differences between the European and the Greek proverb which Krumbacher and Hesseling have pointed out.[2] These differences lie in the form rather than in the content. In Western Europe popular wisdom sums up the situation in a general, didactic observation, while the Eastern proverb often shows a liking for a more concrete form. On the one hand we have a

1 Le Roux de Lincy, I, 139.
2 Krumbacher, "Mittelgriechische Sprichwörter," *Sitzungsberichte der Münchner Akademie, Phil.-Hist. Klasse,* 1893, II, No. 1; Hesseling, "Grieksche en Nederlandsche Spreekwoorden," *De Gids,* LXVI, pt. 4 (1902), 89–108 (reprinted in *Uit Byzantium en Hellas* [1911], pp. 169–195).

maxim and on the other an anecdote. The international proverb *Don't look a gift horse in the mouth* will serve as an illustration. The modern Greek version, which may stand for the Levantine forms generally, is *A man gave another an ass and he looked at its teeth* (Κάποιου χάριζαν γομάρι καὶ τὸ τήραε 's τὰ δόντια).[1] As Krumbacher, who cites the Greek proverb, points out, this difference enables us to distinguish the Western and Eastern forms of the proverb in Greece and thus to recognize the infiltration of Western tradition. In German the proverb *Out of the rain into the drip* (Aus dem Regen in die Traufe) expresses much the same idea as our *Out of the frying pan into the fire*; the Arabs put it in narrative form: *He fled the rain and went to sit under the drip of the gutter.* Cervantes uses a familiar proverb in this narrative form: *Said the pot to the kettle, "Get away, blackface"* (Digo la sarten á la caldera, quitate alla ojnegra, *Don Quijote*, ii, ch. lxvii). To this the Arabic parallel is *The kettle reproached the kitchen spoon. "Thou blackee,"* he said, *"thou idle babbler,"* and Abraham à Sancta Clara knew a similar version. And we may also compare the little known English proverb: *The raven said to the rook, "Stand away, black coat."*

The difference is striking, but it is by no means so generally true as these illustrations might lead us to think; the great majority of Greek and Arabic

1 Krumbacher, *Sitzungsberichte der Münchner Akademie, Phil.-Hist. Klasse*, 1893, II, 23.

proverbs resemble in form those current in Europe.[1] Hesseling is inclined to believe that the proverbs in the form of a dramatic dialogue are especially characteristic of Greek tradition; but it is rather a Levantine peculiarity of unknown origin. A more exhaustive description of such proverbs might throw light on questions of origin and style.

EPIGRAMMATIC PROVERBS

The structure of proverbs is simple or complex. The great majority of proverbs make only a single assertion, although this assertion may be made regarding a combination of things and may not apply to them separately, e. g. *To promise and give nothing is comfort for a fool.* Such proverbs with compound subjects are not particularly frequent in English and German.[2] A more interesting class is that in which the same quality is assigned to two disparate objects, e. g. *A groaning horse and a groaning wife never fail their master; Children and fools speak the truth; Time and tide wait for no man.* The whimsical union of objects which have no relation at first sight imprints the proverb more deeply on our minds. Some prov-

---

1 Hesseling errs, I believe, in comparing such proverbs as "*Everything in measure,*" *said the tailor, and beat his wife with the yardstick* ("Alles met mate," zei de kleermaker, en hij sloeg zijn vrouw met de el); see *De Gids*, LXVI, pt. 4 (1902), 94. Such proverbs will be discussed later as Wellerisms. I do not see the resemblance to the Eastern form. He explains the Eastern proverbs as condensed narratives, but the process is more or less doubtful since the narratives are not cited.

2 See Seiler, *Deutsche Sprichwörterkunde*, p. 222.

erbs of this sort have no doubt originated from natural causes. Others, which approach more nearly the epigram, are recognizably foreign in origin and have never become truly popular, e. g. *England is the paradise of women, hell of horses, and purgatory of servants*. It is probably safe to say that when the proverb begins with an indication of the number of members involved, as in *Three things drive a man out of the house: smoke, rain, and a scolding wife*, it is foreign in origin or made on a foreign model; this special form I shall discuss at length. Although sporadic examples are found in the Middle Ages, epigrammatic characterizations seem to have become the fashion after the Renaissance and seem to have spread from Italy. A careful examination of the history of this fashion would be interesting and profitable.

Seiler was the first to recognize as a special group those epigrammatic proverbs which are composed of several members with specific indication of their number.[1] An old and famous example of the type is *Three things drive a man out of his house: smoke, rain, and a scolding wife*. Seiler makes it clear that the type began as an imitation of the Biblical "There be three things" (Tria sunt . . ., *Prov.* xxx, 15, 18, 21, 29; *Ecclus*. xxv, 9). Although the first indications of the form are found in the Middle Ages, its greatest popularity came in the sixteenth century. At that time proverbs which we know to have existed earlier in

1 *Deutsche Sprichwörterkunde*, pp. 222 ff.

other shapes were recast in this mould. In general, the form remained an artificial one which could not establish itself firmly in oral tradition. Two instances from oral tradition are: *There be three things that never comes to no good: Christmas pigs, Michaelmas fowls, and parsons' daughters* and *Three things are thrown away in a bowling green, namely, time, money, and oaths*, which Sir Walter Scott mentions in *The Fortunes of Nigel*, ch. xii.

A later development, which was also suggested directly by the Biblical model, is the mention of a fourth member, e. g.

> A smoke, a storme, and a contentious wife,
> Thre ils are found, that tire a husband's life:
> To which a fourth is by the proverb sed,
> When children cry for hunger, wanting bread.

Although the model lay ready to hand in "There be three things which are too wonderful for me, yea, four which I know not" (Tria sunt difficilia mihi et quattuor penitus ignoro, *Prov.* xxx, 18), it was not widely used. So far as my observation goes, this expanded form seems to have been employed almost exclusively in Germany and the adjoining Germanic countries. The English example which I have quoted seems to go back to a German source. In the *Figure of Foure* (1636, reprinted in 1654), Nicolas Breton gives many instances of the expanded form, but it is not easy to guess how firmly it had established itself in oral tradition. Much the same may be said of the earlier, anonymous *Les quatre choses*, which may have been printed at Lyons about 1490, and of Orazio Riminaldo's little-known *Libro di quatro cose* of uncertain date.[1]

As I have said, the form is semi-literary and the proverbs cited from the sixteenth century hardly have the ring of oral tradition, e. g. *Three things are unsatiable, priests, monckes, and the sea* (A.D. 1560); *Three thinges a man lendeth rife, His horse, his fighting sword, his wife* (A.D. 1577). The German examples run into the hundreds,[2] but sound quite as artificial as the English. In the heyday of its popularity Ulrich von Hutten wrote a bitter satire on Papal Rome entitled *Trias Romana* (1520) which betokens the currency of the form. Another scrap of evidence which shows how the form struggled to establish itself is seen in the conversion of a fable into a proverb of this type: *In their behavior three things are more steadfast than others: suspicion, the wind, and loyalty; the first never leaves a place it has entered; the second never enters when it cannot see a way of escape; the third never returns to a place it has left* (Tre cose inanimate sono più ferme che l'altre nel loro uso: il sospetto, il vento e la lealtà; il primo mai non entra in luogo, donde poi si parta, l'altro mai non entra, d'onde non vegga l'uscita, l'altra, d'onde un tratto si parte, mai non vi ritorna).[3]

---

1 See Bonser, *Proverb Literature* (London, 1930), p. 131, No. 1093, and p. 273, No. 2237.
2 See Wander, *Deutsches Sprichwörter-lexikon, s. v.* Drei.
3 Wesselski, *Poliziano*, p. 232, No. 403.

It does not seem to be possible to trace this saying beyond a fable of Petrarch's in which fire, wind, water, and suspicion travel together and on taking leave of one another give signs by which they may be recognized.

Probably the most popular of all proverbs in this form is *Three things drive a man out of his house: smoke, rain, and a scolding wife.* A brief review of its history will be illuminating. The germ from which it sprang is the Biblical "A continual dropping in a very rainy day and a contentious woman are alike" (Tecta perstillantia in die frigoris et litigiosa mulier comparantur, *Prov.* xxvii, 15), which Pope Innocent III remoulded into "Tria sunt quae non sinunt hominem in domo permanere: fumus, stillicidium et mala uxor." No doubt he recalled an allegorical interpretation by Petrus Cantor. The actual words of Solomon could not establish themselves in tradition, while Pope Innocent's version was taken up by the *Facetus*, a handbook of admonitions regarding manners and morals, the *Dialogue of Solomon and Marcolf*, a rude satirical dispute between a wise man and a fool, and the Goliardic *De conjuge non ducenda*. Although these works belong to the lower levels of literature, they were very widely disseminated in the Middle Ages. Chaucer took our proverb into the *Tale of Melibeus* from the moralizing of Albertanus of Brescia. So general an acceptance of the proverb and so wide a publication ensured its general adoption: we find it expanded into more than a thousand lines of mediaeval Latin verse, we find it in a Welsh wedding ceremony, in a shrove-tide play of Hans Sachs, and in a diatribe against immorality and corruption based on the legendary life of Judas (Abraham à Sancta Clara, *Judas der Ertz-Schelm* [1686]), and finally, much altered, in Shakespere's *1 Henry IV*. It also appears that the development of the formula *There are three evil things, . . . and the fourth is . . .*, which we have already quoted, comes very late in the history of the proverb. Even this proverb, which had an unusually wide distribution early in the Middle Ages, does not seem to have left much mark on oral tradition; other proverbs which were less fortunate are preserved for us only by the collections of the seventeenth and eighteenth centuries.

NATIONAL AND RACIAL TRAITS

Many have sought to identify national or local traits in proverbs and to use them in describing and defining national or racial temperament. Perhaps no side of proverbial study has been prosecuted so long and so vigorously, but the results are insignificant.[1]

[1] See such essays as Kradolfer, "Das Italienische Sprichwort und seine Beziehungen zum Deutschen," *Zeitschrift für Völkerpsychologie*, IX (1877), 185–271; Berneker, "Das Russische Volk in seinen Sprichwörtern," *Zeitschrift des Vereins für Volkskunde*, XIV (1904), 75–87, 179–191; N. Gerbel, "Nationale Sprüchwörter der Franzosen," *Das Ausland*, XLIII (1870), 93–95; XLIV (1871), 226–229; V. Granlund, "Svenska Folket i sina Ordspråk," *Svenska Fornminnesföreningens Tidskrift*, I (1871), 27–45.

All the endeavors are fruitless and unavailing. Before they are likely to attain useful results we must have exhaustive studies of the history and distribution of individual proverbs. A few proverbs can be recognized as regional, e. g. *Day follows even on the winter night* (Dag följer även på vinternatten); *A life without love, a year without summer* (Ett liv utan kärlek, ett år utan sommar); *The sun shines even into a little room* (Solen skiner också på liten stuga); *Midsummer night is not long, but it sets many cradles rocking* (Midsommarnatten är icke lång, men den sätter många vaggor i gång) [1] are from the far North. Archbishop Trench says that *Make hay while the sun shines* is truly English. After all, the gain from collecting such proverbs, when they can be recognized, is likely to be slight. We must not put much reliance in such assertions as that *Love me little, love me long* is a Southern and not a Scandinavian proverb. We can put no reliance in them when they are not based on detailed investigations of history and dissemination. *The Devil is not as black as he is painted*, when it is found in Swedish, does not prove that the trait of justice, even to the most undeserving, is typically Swedish.

Essays on the national traits exhibited in proverbs give abundant evidence that their authors found examples to support preconceived notions. Few of these essays determine their objectives and the means to

[1] Ström, *Svenskarna i sina Ordspråk* (Stockholm, 1926), pp. 307, 38, 62, 34.

attain them. It would seem obvious that the deductions which can be made from proverbs with international distribution are different from the deductions which can be made from a proverb restricted to a single country or province. Ordinarily these essays do not set out to discover new facts. Perhaps the observation that ancient Greek proverbs contain many allusions to mythology is significant: the contrast with the sobriety and practical sense of Roman proverbs seems to give it force and meaning.[1] The Castilian *pundonor* is surely to be found in Spanish proverbs by one who looks for it. The employment of proverbs to determine characteristic or essential racial traits is neither the easiest nor the most reliable means of defining qualities so difficult to appraise. If proverbs are to be used, it is very likely that the estimates recorded in the traditional comment of neighboring peoples would throw light in dark corners.

Long ago Francis Bacon said, "The genius, wit, and spirit of a nation are discovered in its proverbs," and many have repeated it after him. But proverbs which are international in their currency can scarcely reveal and illuminate national traits unless we argue that the acceptance of a bit of international property constitutes in itself a defining of national characteristics. We should know, moreover, that we are dealing with an international proverb before we use it as evi-

---

1 Otto "Die Götter und Halbgötter im [Lateinischen] Sprichwort," *Archiv für Lateinische Lexikographie*, III (1886), 207–229, 384–387.

dence. We must also reckon with a large stock of proverbs resting on fundamental human traits which transcend the national. It might seem that Erasmus was asserting the contrary when he compared proverbs to wines which cannot be transported out of the land in which they have grown. It is apparent, however, that we cannot make much use of the fact that proverbs possess peculiarities which bind them to the soil until we know what those peculiarities are. The first step is obviously a minute examination of each individual proverb or formula. With a large number of special studies in hand, we may hope to draw some general conclusions of value, and we may ultimately be able to define a specifically German and a specifically French group of proverbs; but even when we have done so, it may turn out that the two groups do not show striking or significant psychological and stylistic differences. If the aim of our studies is to discover such differences, the game is scarcely worth the candle.

Perhaps we may see exemplified in proverbs a difference between the spirit of one epoch and that of another, but again we are likely to find the results for which we are looking rather than results based on objective facts. On the whole, the differences in proverbs of various ages seem somewhat easier to discover than do the differences in proverbs of different countries. Certainly the collection of the materials and the presuppositions are less difficult and complicated. Yet it is interesting to observe that there have been few attempts to find strata of different ages in the proverbs of any country. In contrast to the more recent Germanic proverbs, Heusler [1] characterizes the Old Germanic proverb as calm, confident, manly, and distrustful. Fate dominates its ethical ideas. The rare flashes of humor are not kindly. Modern sayings, he believes, turn on simple, everyday events and show a hesitant, renunciatory mood mingled with kindliness and whimsicality. It would be interesting to notice whether contradictory proverbs belong to different cultural epochs or whether, as has been suggested, they only mark out the middle way. The difference between the older and newer strata of Germanic proverbs has been brought about, Heusler believes, by the passing of the viking spirit and by the handing on to the common man of the fashion of proverb-making. It exemplifies what happens when a literary fashion or artistic device passes from higher to lower levels of society.

ETHICAL TRAITS

The most striking trait in the ethics of proverbs is the adherence to the middle way, and indeed their reason for existence lies in that fact. Proverbs will not champion martyrdom or villainy, although *I'll try anything once* and *You never miss a slice from a cut loaf* have no doubt brought much misery in their train.

1 *Altgermanische Dichtung* (Handbuch der Literaturwissenschaft), p. 68.

Just as reflective men see life in the light of eternal truths and formulate them in apothegms and aphorisms, so the folk seeks and finds support in the common humanity of proverbial philosophy. It is perhaps a poor sort of consolation to say *It will be all the same in a hundred years*; *Misfortunes never come singly*; *It will all come out in the wash*; *Be good and you'll be happy*, or, with whimsical irony, *The worst is yet to come* and *You can't keep a good man down*, but life has little more encouragement for the ordinary man and the thought has served the needs of simple folk. Of course the middle way is marked on both sides by contradictions. A sound skepticism pervades proverbial wisdom and ventures to show itself in assertions which no member of the folk would dare utter as his own. Formal doctrine receives short shrift, but God is treated with respect. Empty show is condemned, even though proverbs recognize that it often wins success. A more detailed illustration of such contradictions is unnecessary, and the labor of assembling them may satisfy antiquarian curiosity, but it is not likely to yield useful results.

Obscene Proverbs

Sayings offensive to good manners are comparatively rare, although we must recognize that taste alters with the passage of time. Many proverbs which seem inelegant today once offended no one. Ray puts the situation briefly in the preface to the second edition of *A Collection of English Proverbs* (1678): "But though I do condemn the mention of anything obscene, yet I cannot think all use of slovenly and dirty words to be such a violation of modesty, as to exact the discarding all Proverbs of which they are ingredients. The useful notions which many ill-worded Proverbs do import, may, I think, compensate for their homely terms; though I could wish the contrivers of them had put their sense into more decent and cleanly language." Alterations in taste in language are difficult to discover; and it is even more difficult to know how significant they are as indications of tendencies in manners. So far as inferences regarding the course of manners are permissible, offensive words tend to disappear from proverbs. The vulgar metaphor does not long maintain itself. Of course, the folk does not display a fastidious taste in choosing materials and metaphors, but there are, I believe, signs that a purificatory process goes on in tradition. Apparently the contraction *Peor es mene- allo* ('It is worse to stir it') is created to avoid a vulgar word and *One ill weed marreth a whole pot of pottage* has variants of a more offensive form. *The pot calls the kettle black* and the proverbial phrase *To sit* (var. *fall*) *between two stools* exist in older and well-established versions, which may even be original; they were evidently an offense to good taste.

We really know very little about outspokenly obscene and erotic proverbs. The collections which exist seem to be more concerned with preserving offensive materials than with selecting traditional proverbs. It is hard to estimate the number, distribution, and importance of such proverbs. Two kinds are to be distinguished: superstitions which have in some way acquired a fixed form and proverbs which make some ethical or moral observation regarding appetites or passions, e. g. *P. erectus non habet conscientiam* or a variant form made on the model of *Necessity knows no law*. Obscene proverbial superstitions, which have already been discussed under the head of health proverbs, deal chiefly with comparisons of the proportions of different parts of the body. As in all traditional material, we must expect to find a good deal about simple functions in proverbs. Of course proverbs dealing with these matters are likely to escape print, but that is no argument for their non-existence.[1] Although we cannot examine the subject further here, the old saw *Naturalia non sunt turpia* ('What is natural is not vile') finds appropriate application.

PROVERBS AND LITERATURE

In works of literature the use of proverbs varies in manner and degree from age to age. At all times proverbs have meant more to the folk than to the learned. Erasmus speaks as a scholar and conscious

[1] The collections printed in *Kryptadia* and *Anthropophyteia* offer little enough of value; I have not troubled to run down the *Bibliotheca Scatologica* cited in the Bernstein catalogue, No. 294. See Kainis, *Die Derbheiten im Reden des Volkes* (Leipzig, n.d.).

literary artist when he calls proverbs "condimenta" which must be used intelligently when one writes or speaks. Proverbs are used freely in writings which make an appeal to the folk and in those in which the folk is characterized; in those classes of literature which are far removed from the folk, proverbs rarely occur. We see these distinctions already in classical writers: Aristophanes, Theophrastus, Lucian, and Plautus use proverbs easily and naturally. Writings which make a conspicuous effort at literary style generally avoid them except as details characterizing the folk. Our Saviour quotes proverbs readily, and the Church Fathers use them in writings with a popular appeal. Throughout the Middle Ages proverbs were frequently used in literature, and individual preferences manifested themselves then as now. The German court epic, which is a relatively artificial and cultured product, shows a disinclination for them; writings nearer to the folk use them freely. Yet we must not carry these distinctions too far: Chaucer's *Troilus*, a very sophisticated, anti-popular poem, bristles with proverbs. Didactic writers naturally show a great liking for proverbs. A satirical tone and an appeal to fundamental emotions encourage the use of proverbs. A proverb is often a ready-made epigram, sums up the situation effectively, drives home the point, and appeals to the reader's or hearer's sense of humor. Consequently proverbs are much used in ages of controversy and satirical criticism: the German and Latin literature of the Reformation abound in them.

In later literary history we do not see any significant variations in these fundamental ways of using proverbs. Calderon, on the one hand, eschews them and Lope de Vega, on the other, quotes them freely. This variation reflects the essential difference of the two dramatists. Cervantes characterizes Sancho Panza by the ease with which proverbs drop from his lips, and similarly Shakespere puts the proverb in the mouth of the folk. It becomes a mannerism in the figure of Nicholas Proverbs in Henry Porter's *Two Angry Women of Abingdon*. These differences persist: Dickens uses proverbs more easily and naturally than Thackeray.

We can observe different attitudes toward proverbs in different ages. Before the *Collectanea Adagiorum* (1500) of Erasmus the attitude was primarily one of didacticism. In the beginning and among savage peoples proverbs often have religious associations, and later they find a place in the schoolroom. Then Erasmus aroused an interest in the proverb for its own sake, and for the next two centuries proverbs were translated from one language into another, huge collections were assembled, and dissertations of all kinds were written about them. During the eighteenth century a reaction set in: the rationalistic temper found little to admire in proverbs. Finally, a new interest sprang up in the nineteenth century along with nationalistic or racial strivings and the awakening interest in the folk and its ways of self-expression.

We must also mention those literary works in which the interest in proverbs is of primary, not subsidiary, importance. In early times proverbs were collected for their didactic value, as rules and guides for life. Such collections in the Old Testament, Old English, and Icelandic pass as literary monuments and not as mere assemblings of proverbial material. So similar are the proverbs and the incidental editorial comment that we cannot always separate them. The Middle Ages used proverbs in instruction in foreign languages and rhetoric, and although Humanism and the Renaissance cast aside the collections on which such exercises were based, the method still persists. Textbooks in foreign languages often include proverbs, and the German school-boy still writes themes based on proverbs. After mentioning some efforts to invent proverbs we shall return to certain closely allied literary forms.

A curious accompaniment of long familiarity with proverbs often appears in the belief that new proverbs can be invented. Intimate acquaintance with the manner of proverbs awakens confidence in the ability to create others. In almost every case the results have given the lie to the belief. James Howell, who in 1659 published the first very large English collection, ventured to compose "Divers centuries of new sayings, which may serve for proverbs to posterity." Not one of them has, I dare say, found a place in oral or even learned tradition. It would perhaps be difficult to say just why the vital spark is lacking, but its absence is beyond question. Benjamin Franklin may have hit the popular vein more successfully with the aphorisms in *Poor Richard's Almanac* (1732–1758), but even of these only a few have survived in oral tradition, e. g. *A penny saved is a penny earned*; and this proverb, which was already known in the sixteenth century, owes its form and not its thought to him. Perhaps we can credit Franklin with the invention of *Three removes are worse than a fire*. We must remember that Franklin drew freely on Ray's collection (1670) and such others as were available to him. At the beginning of his literary career K. F. W. Wander, the compiler of a huge lexicon of German proverbs, issued several volumes of original proverbs which died still-born: *Scheidemünze, ein Taschenbuch für Jedermann, Oder: 5000 Neue Deutsche Sprichwörter* (1831), and a second volume of the same work, which appeared in 1835 along with *Nüsse für Kinder aufs Ganze Jahr Oder Turnübungen für Verstand, Scharfsinn und Witz, in einer Sammlung Neuer Sprichwörter*. As a matter of fact, Wander's inventing of proverbs has cast some suspicion on his lexicon, for he does not always give sources for his quotations. Many proverbs which are not supported by quotations seem to be his translations from other languages; perhaps he thought that tradition would make them its own. Alexander F. Chamberlain, long the editor of the *Journal of American Folk-lore*, collected and invented maxims suggested by modern life and science in the hope that one or another might become proverbial; but his efforts are not notably successful.[1] The "literary" proverb, if one can speak of such a thing, is a dreary chapter in both literary and proverbial history.

On a somewhat higher artistic plane we find collections of aphorisms and emblems. Although these do not pass themselves off as actual proverbs, they employ more or less closely the form and subject-matter of proverbs. The rise of emblem-books and their age of popularity agree with the rise and popularity of proverb collections. After the Renaissance, collections of engravings with accompanying inscriptions in prose or verse became very popular. In many instances one finds it hard to say whether the engraving illustrates the inscription or the inscription explains the engraving. The model for later collections was Andrea Alciati's *Emblemata* (first complete ed. 1551). Emblem-books were especially favored by the Dutch; some of the greatest Dutch poets of the seventeenth century composed them. Proverbs were used to some extent in emblem-books, and the subject-matter and the aphoristic view of the world have much in common with the temper of proverbs. Compositions in the

1 "Proverbs in the Making: Some Scientific Commonplaces," *Journal of American Folk-lore*, XVII (1904), 161–170, 268–278.

proverbial vein are not infrequent. Goethe set his aphorisms apart in his works under the caption "Sprichwörtliches"; presumably he regarded them as efforts in the proverbial manner. The same may be said of Edward Fitzgerald's *Polonius*. More ambitious endeavors in the same direction are Martin Tupper's *Proverbial Philosophy*, a book which summed up the sententious observations and notions of the middle of the last century, or the writings of such men as J. F. Castelli and J. N. Vogl of Vienna in the first half of the century. Such compositions are unendurably dull today.

It is not surprising that the most interesting and important literary monument associated with proverbs should bear the name of Solomon. The Old Testament collects his wise sayings, many of which have found new currency in the oral tradition of Western Europe. Legend associates with Solomon stories of a combat of wits in which his opponent was the Queen of Sheba, Hiram of Tyre, or another less familiar figure. Although the early development of this legend is extremely obscure, we find it widely known in the Middle Ages. From almost the beginning of its history the legend is separated into two branches, one predominantly narrative and the other predominantly proverbial in subject and treatment. With the narrative branch we need not concern ourselves further, although its complicated and extensive history needs elucidation. In the proverbial branch we see a

definite trend from the serious to the comic and obscene. The Old English *Salomon and Saturnus* is a
sober disputation on religious matters. In the course
of time, Solomon's opponent becomes his foil and is
degraded to a jester who stops at nothing. In the mediaeval dialogue of Solomon and Marcolf the shrewd,
witty, and vulgar fool caps each wise saying of Solomon's with an obscene proverb or parody. Almost
every country in Europe possessed translations of
this dialogue. Special developments in French are
dialogues which have become almost entirely obscene. Although the full history of this transformation of the Biblical Solomon and the legends about
him can never be written, the main outlines of the
deterioration are clear.[1]

We have already noticed the tendency of proverbs
to form models for the invention of parallel proverbs.
In some instances these parallel proverbs exist in con-
junction with the original proverb. Thus the saying
Praise the fair day at even probably began as a simple
assertion, but it is often found in compound form:
*Schöne Tage soll man abends loben, schöne Frauen mor-
gens* ('One should praise beautiful days in the evening, beautiful women in the morning'); *Sed vero laus*

[1] See J. M. Kemble, *The Dialogue of Salomon and Saturnus* (Ælfric
Society, London, 1848); F. Vogt, *Salman und Morolf* (Halle, 1880);
A. Ritter von Vincenti, *Die Altenglischen Dialoge von Salomon und
Saturn* (*Münchener Beiträge*, XXXI), 1904; W. Benary, *Salomon et
Marcolfus* (Sammlung Mittellateinischer Texte, VIII [Heidelberg,
1914]).

in fine canitur, et vespere laudatur dies ('But, truly, praise should be sung at the end, and the day should be praised in the evening'); *Vespere laudatur lux, hospes mane probatur* ('The light should be praised in the evening; the host is tested on the morrow'). In fact, the oldest instance of the proverb in a Germanic language occurs in a series:

> At kveldi skal dag leyfa, kono, er brend er,
> mæki, er reyndr er, mey, er gefin er,
> ís, er yfir kømr, ol, er drukkit er.

> ('Praise the day at even, a wife when dead,
> a weapon when tried, a maid when married,
> ice when 'tis crossed, and ale when 'tis drunk.')
>
> *Hávamál*, 81.

This listing resembles a curious literary form, the Priamel, which enjoyed remarkable literary vogue in Germany during the fifteenth century and a little later. The exact nature of this literary form is difficult to define: it consisted in an accumulation of assertions, usually unrelated in appearance, which are often united at the end by a single remark binding them together in an epigram.[1] Since the form is so indeterminate, scholars have sought and found its origins in many other ages and countries. Indeed the similarity of the Old Norse verses which have just been quoted to some Finnish verses on the one hand and to some Sanskrit epigrams on the other have led

---

1 See Euling, "Priamel," *Reallexikon der Deutschen Literaturgeschichte*, II (1926–28), 723–725.

Comparetti and others to declare that these are relics of an ancient verse-form.[1] The Finnish verses are

> Praise your new horse in the morning,
> Your wife in the second year,
> Only in the third year your brother-in-law,
> And yourself never in your life,

and the Sanskrit epigram is "Praise food when it is digested; the wife, when her youth is past; the hero, when he has returned from battle; the grain, when it is harvested." Whether we can safely make such an excursion as this into literary prehistory must remain more than doubtful.

In essence the Priamel is an epigrammatic improvisation which uses proverbs in part. If we conceive the form so simply, — and it is difficult to make a better working definition, — it has existed from time immemorial and is closely allied to all early aphoristic writing. Even in the fifteenth century, when the Priamel flourished in the hands of Hans Rosenplüt, a Meistersinger of Nuremberg, it failed to establish itself as a distinct and permanent literary form. Apparently it stood so close to improvisation that it was unable to separate itself. In this way the literary form which most nearly expressed the genius of the proverb failed to come to full realization.

An interesting use of proverbs appears in *La*

---

1 R. M. Meyer, *Die Altgermanische Poesie* (Berlin, 1889), p. 434 (quoting H. Paul, *Kanteletar*, p. 143); Heusler, *Zeitschrift des Vereins für Volkskunde*, XXVI (1916), 43.

Comédie des Proverbes, which is ordinarily ascribed to Adrien de Montluc, Comte de Cramail. It is variously dated between 1609 and 1632. In the simplest and most conventional sort of plot, the author inserts all the proverbs at his command. With surprising wit and ingenuity he fits the proverbs to the situation. The comedy was translated as the Zugabe to the second volume of G. P. Harsdörffer's *Frauenzimmergesprächspiele* (2d ed., 1644). It seems to follow the traditions of French and Italian farce, closer to the former in style, to the latter in characters and plot. Why the author hit upon the trick of using proverbs so freely remains uncertain. Even earlier than Montluc's comedy is the anonymous dialogue, *Les Menus Propos*, of the end of the fifteenth century.[1] Cervantes wrote a similar composition, *El Entremés de Refranes*. There is enough plain speech to give the thread of the story, but proverbs are quoted wherever possible. According to Tuinman,[2] the Dutch dramatist Paffenrode (1618–1673) wrote a dialogue in proverbs, but I have not found it in his *Gedigten* (Amsterdam, 1711). A prose example of the same sort, Francisco de Quevedo Villegas's *Cuento de Cuentos*, tells of a family quarrel involving an unruly daughter and her lover. A somewhat similar device is seen in the figure of Nicholas Proverbs in Henry Porter's *Two Angry Women of Abingdon* (1598). From painting I

1 See Bonser, *Proverb Literature* (London, 1930), p. 127, Nos. 1059, 1060.
2 *De Oorsprong en Uitlegging van Dagelyks Gebruikte Nederduitsche Spreekwoorden*, Eerste Voorrede, p. [vii].

might call to mind the parallel in Pieter Breughel's marvelously ingenious and dramatic assembling of more than a hundred proverbs on a single canvas.[1] Small collections of proverbs, farragoes without a thread of dramatic or narrative interest to hold them together, are often used to gain more or less successfully a particular effect. To this end François Villon wrote a "Ballade en Proverbes," [2] John Heywood composed *A Dialogue Conteyning the Number of the Effectuall Prouerbes in the English Tonge, Compact in a Matter Concernynge two Maner of Mariages* (1562), Jean Antoine de Baïf wrote four books of sestets (*Les Mimes, Enseignements et Proverbes* [1581]), Rabelais (*Pantagruel*, V, ch. xxii) described the "Proverb Island," [3] the sixteenth-century *Faustbuch* devoted a chapter to proverbs,[4] and Carl Sandburg heaps them up in "Good Morning, America."

Another dramatic use of proverbs is found in the *proverbes dramatiques*, so widely known in the latter half of the eighteenth century. In these plays, which are something after the manner of a charade, the audience is led by degrees to guess the proverb on

---

1 See W Fraenger, *Der Bauern-Bruegel und das deutsche Sprichwort* (Erlenbach-Zürich, n.d. [1923]). G. P. C. van Breugel, *Gedenkschrift wegens een Schilderij van Spreekwoorden* (Haarlem, 1876), seems to have been overlooked by later writers.

2 Conveniently reprinted in Duplessis, *Bibliographie Parémiologique* (Paris, 1847), p. 125.

3 See Fraenger, as above, pp. 11 ff.

4 See Fränkel and Bauer, "Entlehnungen in ältesten Faustbuch. 1. Das Sprichwörterkapitel," *Vierteljahrschrift für Litteraturgeschichte*, IV, (1891), 361–381.

which the play depends for its point and purpose. Ordinarily the invention of this sort of play is credited to Carmontelle (1717–1806), but Leroux de Lincy (I, p. lxxx) asserts that its beginnings reach back into the seventeenth century, when Mme. de Maintenon wrote no less than thirty-nine such plays. There seems to be more or less question about the plays of Mme. de Maintenon, and certainly the first author who made a name in the genre was Carmontelle. Similar plays began to be written in the latter part of the eighteenth century; and in the nineteenth, Théodore le Clercq, Alfred de Musset, and Octave Feuillet continued the tradition. The German imitations, e. g. M. G. Saphir, *Narreteisprichwörter*, which I have been unable to see; C. J. Pulvermacher, *Taschenbuch Dramatischer Sprichwörter* (Berlin, 1835); C. E. von Benzel-Sternau, *Das Hoftheater von Barataria* (Leipzig, 1828); Luise Hölder, *Dramatische Sprichwörter zur Schauspielmassigen Darstellung* (Munich, 1838), never attained an equal level of literary importance. After all, we are very ill informed regarding the history and nature of this minor literary genre.[1]

1 See R. Werner, *Zur Geschichte der "Proverbes Dramatiques"* (Berlin, 1887), and Deiardin, *Dictionnaire des Spots ou Proverbs Wallons* (Liege, 1863), p. 37. I have not seen P. R. Faiex, *La Chasse aux Proverbes* (n. p., n. d.), which is cited in the Bernstein catalogue, No. 1073.

IV

PROVERBIAL PHRASES, WELLERISMS, AND PROVERBIAL COMPARISONS

Proverbial Phrases [1]

THE proverbial phrase exhibits the characteristic rigidity of the proverb in all particulars except grammatical form. A proverb does not vary in any regard, while a proverbial phrase shifts according to time and person. *He pulls the chestnuts out of the fire* may vary according to tense and subject. In general, the problems which arise in connection with the proverbial phrase are the same as for the proverb. Interest turns chiefly on the history and dissemination of individual phrases and on their origin and meaning. It is

---

1 Although many collections make no sharp distinction between proverbs and proverbial phrases, the latter are generally more difficult to collect. The best annotated collections are Dutch, and are valuable for any European language because of the international distribution of the more important and interesting proverbial phrases. Significant collections of proverbial phrases are Hyamson, *A Dictionary of English Phrases* (London, 1922); de Cock, *Spreekwoorden en Zegswijzen, Afkomstig van Oude Gebruiken* (Ghent, 1905, 1908), *Spreekwoorden en Zegswijzen over de Vrouwen, de Liefde en het Huwelijk* (Ghent, 1911), and *Spreekwoorden en Zegswijzen op Volksgeloof Berustend* (Ghent, 1919); Stoett, *Nederlandsche Spreekwoorden, Spreekwijzen, Uitdrukkingen en Gezegden* (Zutphen, 1923–25); Borchardt-Wustmann, *Die Sprichwörtlichen Redensarten im Deutschen Volksmund nach Sinn and Ursprung Erläutert* (Leipzig, 6th ed., 1925); Richter, *Deutsche Redensarten* (Leipzig, 4th ed., 1921); Schrader, *Der Bilderschmuck der Deutschen*

ordinarily more difficult to trace the history of a proverbial phrase than of a proverb, since the sources are
very hard to assemble. Older collections of proverbs
only occasionally include proverbial phrases; dictionaries mention them infrequently and carelessly;
and even modern collections of proverbs often show
equally little interest in them.

Many proverbial phrases can boast of a very long
and respectable history. Some which have a surprisingly modern and popular ring are first mentioned in
the Latin and Greek classics: *to open his eyes* [to a
situation]; *to be as hungry as a bear*; *to touch a sore
spot*; *to have eyes in the back of his head*; *to be full of
vinegar*, i. e. 'to be high-spirited.' Aristophanes used
the phrase *to quarrel over the ass's shadow* (*Wasps*,
l. 191), and it is still current in Italy.[1] Biblical sources
gave their share: *to be a thorn in the flesh* (Lanceae in
lateribus, *Num.* xxx, 55); *to build on sand* (Similis erit
viro stulto, qui aedificavit domum suam super are-

Sprache (Weimar, 6th ed., 1901); Otto, *Die Sprichwörter und Sprichwörtlichen Redensarten der Römer* (Leipzig, 1890); Caballero, *Diccionario de Modismos* (*Frases y Metáforas*) (Madrid, 1905). Wander
(*Deutsches Sprichwörter-Lexikon*) gives many German proverbial
phrases and distinguishes them with a star. A great deal of information
about the proverbial phrases is available in *Notes and Queries* (London),
but the lack of a cumulative index makes reference difficult. Comprehensive studies, e. g. L. P. Smith, *Words and Idioms: Studies in the
English Language* (Boston, 1925), and W. Gottschalk, *Die Sprichwörtlichen Redensarten der französischen Sprache* (Heidelberg, 1930), are
rare.

1 Seiler, *Die Entwicklung der Deutschen Kultur im Spiegel des Deutschen Lehnworts*, V [Halle, 1921], *Das Deutsche Lehnsprichwort*, Pt. I,
p. 125.

nam, *Matt.* vii, 26); *to wash one's hands of a thing* (Lavi inter innocentes manus meas, *Ps.* lxxii, 13); *to heap coals of fire on his head* (Carbones ignis congeres super caput eius, *Rom.* xii, 20). Especially interesting are the fortunes of *to cast pearls before swine* (Neque mittatis margaritas vestras ante porcos, *Matt.* vii, 6), which is the source of the Dutch *to scatter roses before swine* (Roozen strooien voor de varkens). Very probably we have a confusion of Latin "margarita," 'pearl' and French "marguérite," 'daisy, flower.' St. Jerome appears to be responsible for *to make a virtue of necessity*. Seneca knew the saying *to sit between two stools*. Allusions to Aesopic fables are frequent: *to burst with envy*; *to blow hot and cold*; *to get the lion's share*; and to other classical stories, e. g. *to hang by a thread*. Although the English phrase *to cut the Gordian knot* has lost the original idiom, which is preserved in the German *den gordischen Knoten lösen* ('to loosen or untie the Gordian knot'), it gives us a better and clearer picture.

Many proverbial phrases are international in their currency, and for this reason the excellent Dutch and German treatises on proverbial phrases are often very useful in studying English or American turns of speech. Typical international proverbial phrases are: *to get out of bed with the wrong foot first*; *to break the ice*, i. e. 'to overcome a social stiffness'; *to jump from the frying pan into the fire*; *to hear the grass grow*; *to put* (var. *set, harness*) *the cart before the horse*. It is inter-

esting to note the variations in *to buy a pig in a poke*.
The earliest forms, which were already current in the
Middle Ages, speak merely of "buying in a sack,"
i. e. 'buying sight unseen,' as in

> Swer inme sack koufet,
> und sich mit tòren roufet,
> und borget ungewisser diet,
> der singet dicke klageliet.

> ('Whoever buys in a sack,
> and quarrels with fools,
> and lends to unreliable people,
> often sings a song of sorrow.')
>
> Freidank, lxxxv, 5.

Luther still uses the mediaeval form. The cat, which
is of course a dishonest substitute for the hare, early
enters the phrase.[1] The pig, which is evidently a
sucking pig, appears in both English and German
forms from the seventeenth century on and is apparently the latest development.

The internationally used phrase *to sell the skin before you have caught the bear* goes back to a fable introduced into the Aesopic collections by Laurentius
Abstemius in 1495. Although several have seen in
this phrase the origin of the term "bear" for one who
sells shares of stock he does not possess, the explanation is scarcely to be accepted. A satisfactory explanation would account for "bull" at the same time.

Especial interest attaches to the origin and cultural

---

[1] Compare "Bien lor savoit chat en sac vendre" (*Joufrois*, l. 1674).

background of proverbial phrases. Many phrases, to be sure, offer nothing of interest, and once they are pointed out as proverbial, can be passed over without more ado, e. g. *to wind him around your finger, to pour out one's heart, to blow one's own horn, to be tarred with the same stick, to build castles in Spain,* which is first found in mediaeval French, *to be caught red-handed, to set the North River* (var.: *Thames*) *on fire.* Some phrases are amusing for their whimsicality: *to know which side his bread is buttered on*; *to look as if butter would not melt in his mouth*; *to feel like a fish out of water*; *to make two bites of a cherry* (said of a fastidious person). These, like proverbs and proverbial phrases generally, involve a simple metaphor which gives a scene a general instead of a specific application.

A classification of the fields of human activity from which tradition draws proverbial phrases is illuminating, although it is difficult in the absence of a good English collection. What can be said here is only by way of suggestion and owes much to the remarks of L. P. Smith.[1] Mediaeval punishments evidently imprinted themselves on popular fancy: *to curse with bell, book, and candle*; *to put him on the rack*; *to run the gauntlet*; *to put the screws on.* From the procedure of canonization we have *to be the Devil's advocate* and *to be on the side of the angels.* The phrase *to fly false*

---

1 *Words and Idioms: Studies in the English Language* (Boston, 1925), ch. v.

colors suggests a piratical trick or a warlike stratagem, and the origin of *to walk the plank* is obvious. Many proverbial phrases are taken from card-playing: *to have an ace up his sleeve*; *to lay all the cards on the table*; *to stack the cards*; *to hold all the cards*; *to pass the buck* (the "buck" is any object used to designate the dealer, and as the deal passes from one player to another, the buck is passed); *to euchre*; *to stake everything on the turn of a card*; *to call his bluff*; *to trump his ace*. Others refer to gambling of different kinds and particularly to horse-racing: *to have little (nothing, everything) at stake*; *to be out of the running*; *to bet on the wrong horse*; *to be left at the post*; *to hold the whip-hand*; *to play with loaded dice*; *to stake everything on one throw*; *to bank on*; *to draw the short straw*. Many are derived from sports: *to be at fault* and *to be in at the death* (fox hunting); *to bark up the wrong tree* ('coon hunting); *to hold* (var. *run*) *with the hare and run* (var. *hunt*) *with the hounds*; *to draw a red herring across the trail*; *to beat about the bush*; *to fall into a trap*; *to have shot one's bolt*; *to have him in the nine hole* (billiards); *to have two strikes on him*; *to be caught with his foot off first base*. From boxing and wrestling we have *to be down but not out*; *to take the count*; *to give him a body blow*; *to hit below the belt*; *to have him on the hip*; *to throw up the sponge*. Cock fighting yields *to live like a fighting cock*; *to stand steel*; *to show the white feather*; and perhaps even *to turn tail*.

Proverbial phrases from seafaring life seem to be

more frequent proportionally than proverbs from the same source. Typical examples are: *to be in the same boat with, to steer clear of a thing, to put in an oar, to sail close to the wind, to pour oil on troubled waters,* and perhaps *to carry it through to the bitter end.* Many others owe their origin to military life: *to pass muster, to fall into line, to steal a march on a person, to stand one's ground, to bear the brunt of the attack.* Country life contributes a large share: *to kick over the traces, to put one's shoulder to the wheel, to feel his oats, to take the bull by the horns, to put a spoke in his wheel, to tar with the same brush, to go the whole hog, to feather one's nest, to clip his wings, to crow over, to pull in his horns,* i. e. 'to be less arrogant,' *to take to a thing like a duck to water, to lie fallow, to break fresh ground.* Others are taken from the household: *to lay on the shelf, to go like clockwork, to put the lid on, to stew in one's own juice, to have a finger in the pie, to be on pins and needles, to look for a needle in a haystack, to be at loose ends, to pin him down.* The phrase *to rule the roost* is really "to rule the roast." The trades and modern mechanical devices yield an abundance: *to put through the mill, to go at it hammer and tongs, to work like a nailer, to throw on the scrapheap, to have an axe to grind, to hit the nail on the head, to have a screw loose, to blow off steam, to keep his nose to the grindstone.* Cf. *a live wire; to step on it; a high flier,* etc. Characteristic idioms from the arts are: *to put the finishing touches to a thing, to change one's tune, to buy for a song, to act a part, to be in the limelight, to give the show away.* Mercantile proverbial phrases are more frequent than mercantile proverbs, e. g. *to strike a balance, to get more than one bargained for, to make the best of a bad bargain, to make capital of, to turn the scales, to talk shop, to call to account, to take into account, to pay him back in his own coin, to ring true, to give it the acid test* (the pawnbroker tests gold with acid). The number derived from schools and books is comparatively small: *to give chapter and verse, to turn over a new leaf, to take a leaf out of his book, to gloss over, to read a lecture to, to read between the lines, to put a period to.* Even the American Indians have given us *to smoke the pipe of peace, to bury the hatchet, to go on the warpath.*

Many such phrases are extremely obscure in their origins and offer unsolved problems. Of course the meaning and history of a phrase can only be determined on the basis of a careful and relatively large collection of instances. A thorough familiarity with the age of a saying, its degree of popularity, and the circles in which it is known are of invaluable assistance in discovering its meaning. Unfortunately the dictionaries and collections of proverbs at our disposal often fail or mislead us in just these respects. Proverbial phrases are very often passed over with slight attention by lexicographers.

It is instructive to examine briefly a number of proverbial phrases for which we have no adequate explanation. The Elizabethan *to lead apes in hell* was synonymous with being an old maid, and, although it was once a commonplace, we no longer understand the allusion. The German synonyms *Giritzenmoos* and *Flederwische feilhalten* ('to offer dustbrushes for sale') are equally obscure. Other imperfectly understood English proverbial phrases are: *to be at sixes and sevens, to leave one in the lurch, to be in a brown study, to be up to snuff*, i. e. 'to be clever,' *to cast sheep's eyes on, to make no bones about a thing*, i. e. 'to treat it without formality,' *to have a rod in pickle, to fight like Kilkenny cats*, which may involve an old story with parallels in Icelandic saga, *to kick the bucket* and *to go West*, i. e. 'to die,' *to give him the sack* (in England: *bag*), i. e. 'to discharge from employment,' *to be duck soup for him*, which resembles its German equivalent *Das ist ihm ein gefundenes Fressen* in form and substance, *to be an Indian giver*, i. e. 'to demand the return of a gift,' *to paint the town red*, which, although not recorded before 1877, may have some connection with the ancient use of red as a festival color, *to take French leave* (the French idiom is *Filer à l'anglaise*). *To read him the Riot Act* refers to the actual reading aloud which precedes the dispersing of a mob in England.[1] The phrase *to call a spade a spade* may allude to a spayed dog, and possibly we can find support for this explanation in the synonymous Italian *to call a cat a cat* (chiamar gatta gatta). On the other hand, the

---

1 See Act for Preventing Tumults and Riotous Assemblies, 1714. 1 George I, St. 2, ch. 5, §2, par. 2 (13 Statutes at Large, p. 143).

German *to show him what a rake is* (einem zeigen was eine Harke ist) suggests that "spade" means a garden implement. Chaucer has several obscure phrases for which no one has found an explanation: *Farwel feldefare, to pipe in an ivy leafe, hazlewodss shaken.*

Often the explanations given for proverbial phrases are scarcely convincing or involve matters which after all we do not understand much better than the phrase itself. There may be an allusion to a forgotten game in *to hold a candle to,* i. e. 'to be compared with.' In the case of *to get a thing by hook or by crook* it is not quite clear what significance attaches to the fact that the earliest instances have ecclesiastical associations. Certainly that fact has been neglected by those who find in it an allusion to a manorial privilege granted certain dependants of using a hook to cut the green wood and a crook to break off the dry. Perhaps *to be driven* (var. *beaten*) *from pillar to post* refers to the treatment of Christ before the Crucifixion. The scene was presumably a familiar one from the representations of Biblical dramas. But an allusion from the end of the sixteenth century does not accord well with this explanation: "tossed from post to pillar like an espial or runagate" suggests rather an origin in a punishment like running the gauntlet. Much greater probability attaches to the explanation of *to make ducks and drakes of his money,* which finds in it an allusion to the term "ducks and drakes" for the circles made by a stone skimming across the water. Perhaps to mind your P's and Q's refers to the innkeeper's account of P[ints] and Q[uarts], although some have maintained that it is an idiom of the dancing school where attention was constantly being called to "pieds" and "queues." An explanation which is more probable than either of these finds the origin in the difficulty which the typesetter has in keeping P's and Q's from getting mixed. Obviously more knowledge of the circumstances under which a proverbial phrase is used (particularly in its early occurrences) helps greatly to make such matters clear. As it now is, in many instances *yo' pays yo' money and yo' takes yo' choice.*

Many unexplained phrases are internationally known and offer especially attractive opportunities for investigation. With the light thrown on the phrase from different angles it ought to be possible to discover its meaning easily. Yet the many long discussions of the phrase *to wear horns*, i. e. 'to be a cuckold,' have not made its origin clear; probably the trick of grafting spurs on a capon will explain it. One of the most interesting of such phrases is *wissen wo Barthel den Most holt* ('to be very sly and clever'; 'to know ways and means to attain one's end,' often with sexual implications; lit. 'to know where Barthel gets new wine'), for which several explanations have been offered. It may involve an allusion to St. Bartholomew's Day (August 24), which marks the beginning of autumn (although new wine is not made at that time), or to the marriage at Cana in Galilee which, according to tradition (but not *John* ii), was held in the house of Bartholomew. Probably the most generally accepted explanation bases itself on thieves' jargon and interprets "Barthel" as 'jimmy' (a thief's tool) and "Most" as 'money'; hence the phrase may have originally meant 'to know where one can get money by housebreaking.' If this explanation is correct, then the Dutch variant *weten wel waer Abraham de mostaerd haelt* ('to know well where Abraham gets mustard') is merely a corruption in popular speech. *To put a spoke in his wheel* is said to be a mistranslation of the Dutch *Er is eene spaak in het wiel gestoken.* The phrase *leben wie der liebe Gott in Frankreich* ('to live like the blessed Lord in France'), which is current both in Germany and in the Netherlands, has found no convincing explanation. Since it is at least as old as 1771, it cannot refer to the leisure given to God by the atheists of the French Revolution.

Ordinarily the distribution of phrases which are difficult to explain does not extend beyond the boundaries of a single language. In addition to the English examples of obscure phrases, I cite a few from the German: *einen Metzergang machen,* i. e. 'to make a journey in vain'; *im Schwabenalter stehen,* i. e. 'to be forty years old'; *auf keinen grünen Zweig kommen,* i. e. 'not to prosper.' From the fifteenth century on, and apparently more frequently in southern than in northern Germany, one summoned vexatious opponents to the valley of Josaphat (*ins Tal Josaphat laden*), but an explanation of the phrase is not forthcoming beyond the fact that the Last Judgment is meant. We may compare the English exclamation *Go to Jericho!* The phrase *von Pontius zu Pilatus schicken* evidently alludes to the treatment of Christ before the Crucifixion, but the exact way in which the phrase arose is not understood. Perhaps it alludes to scenes in the mediaeval Passion Play in which Christ goes from Herod to Pontius Pilate and from Pontius Pilate to Herod. The proverbial phrase *flöten gehen*, i. e. '[he can] whistle for it,' has been the occasion for much fruitless discussion.

Of course great interest attaches to proverbial phrases which concern themselves with the life of former days. Examples have already been given incidentally, but additional illustration is not out of place here. Perhaps *to take the cake* (or *That takes the cake*), a phrase which Aristophanes uses more than once, alludes to a cake as a prize for the man who stayed awake until sunrise in a drinking bout; we of today are more likely to find in it an echo of the custom of the "cake-walk." An older phrase of the same meaning is *to bear the bell*. The phrase *to throw dust in his eyes*, which is first found in classical writers, refers to a trick of gladiators. When Chaucer's Wife of Bath says "As by the whelp chasted is the leoun" and Iago, "Even so as one would beat his defenseless dog to affright an imperious lion," they use a Latin proverbial phrase based on the animal tamer's way of taming a lion by example. The English idiom *to curry favor* refers to a famous horse, Fauvel, in a forgotten French romance. *To pay on the nail* is an old French legal phrase. German humanists who read Tacitus' description of heathen German life with keen interest are supposed to have invented *auf der Bärenhaut liegen*, i. e. 'to be idle.' *Den armen Judas singen*, i. e. 'to sing the air of "Poor Judas,"' and then 'to suffer great humiliation,' was an idiom current in the sixteenth century and used, appropriately enough, of Faust just before his death. The queer German phrase *einen Korb bekommen*, i. e. 'to get a basket, to be refused in marriage, to fail in an examination,' is now explained as an allusion to a mediaeval story of Virgil. He was left suspended in a basket by a lady to whom he was paying court. Other idioms meaning 'to refuse in marriage' are *to give him the mitten*, the Spanish *dar una calabaza*, i. e. 'to give him a calabash.' More or less obvious paraphrases like *to give him his walking papers* or *ticket* (compare the Dutch *iemand zijn pasport geven*) and the French *faire promener* are less interesting.

In proverbial phrases perhaps even more frequently than in proverbs we have allusions to traditional superstitions and the beliefs of former ages: *to be born under a lucky star* refers to astrological notions; *to be in the seventh heaven* involves the old cosmology; and *to shed crocodile tears* is explained by the old belief that crocodiles enticed unwary men into their power by imitating a weeping child. The proverbial phrase *Some one is walking over my grave*, which involves a widely known superstition, is used on feeling a sudden shiver. *Mit einem Helm geboren sein* ('to be born with a caul') alludes to the belief that such children are unusually lucky; we have an analogous phrase in English: *to be born with a silver spoon in his mouth*. A legal allusion persists in *to come under the hammer*, which refers to the auctioneer's hammer.

The explanation of historical allusions in proverbial phrases often leaves much room for doubt, although it seems likely that historical details are better preserved in phrases than in proverbs. Perhaps the German *to burn his ships behind him* (Seine Schiffe hinter sich brennen) refers to Cortez in Mexico in 1519, but the existence of parallel incidents extending so far back as 310 B.C. makes the identification uncertain in the extreme. The English *to burn his bridges behind him* also stands in some unexplained relation to the German idiom. The appropriation of the lands of St. Peter at Westminster to pay for the repair of St. Paul's in the reign of Edward VI can hardly account for the phrase *to rob Peter to pay Paul*. In French and German, the allusion would be unintelligible, and furthermore the early variant form, French and English, *to rob St. Peter to clothe St. Paul*, must be considered in any explanation of origins.

As is already abundantly apparent, proverbial

phrases come into being in the same ways as proverbs. A phrase with limited application acquires by metaphorical use a meaning in new fields: *to kill two birds with one stone* acquires in addition to its literal meaning the connotation of accomplishing two ends with the same instrument. Most proverbial phrases have arisen in this way. Proverbial phrases are also derived from narratives, e. g. *to bell the cat,* i. e. 'to undertake a dangerous task.' Often these narratives have a long and checkered history. In Arabic the story behind the phrases *to pull the chestnuts out of the fire* and *to be a cat's paw* has a crab instead of chestnuts, and this form found its way into Italian in the *Fables of Bidpai* (the *Pañcatantra*). Other variants in Italian and in Dutch read "snake" instead of "crab" or "chestnuts." The substitution of the cat seems to have occurred in France. Perhaps, as has been conjectured, "cat" is a misunderstanding of the Latin *catellus* 'whelp,' for a dog is found in several texts.

Although probably less frequent, the changes which occur in proverbial phrases during their life in oral tradition are of the same general character as the changes in proverbs. Ordinarily proverbial phrases do not accumulate expansions by parallelism and contrast with the same readiness as do proverbs, but such an extension as *to have a crow to pluck with you and a poke to put the feathers in* is analogous to the whimsical enlargement of proverbs. Of course substitutions of similar and contrasting objects after the manner of associative thought take place readily.

Analogous to proverbs which are used only in certain definite connections are proverbial phrases with a single connotation. An important class of such phrases is found in paraphrases for drunkenness, e. g. *to be jingled, soused, half seas over, all teed up, lit, pickled, pie-eyed, crocked, corned* (referring to corn whiskey), *three sheets in the wind, over the bay, to pass out.*[1] It is possibly true that synonyms for drunkenness are more abundant in German than in English or French, but the fact, if it is one, is an uncertain basis for conclusions regarding the temperance of a people.

WELLERISMS [2]

A very curious proverbial type has, so far as I am aware, no English name, although it is well repre-

[1] Proverbial phrases signifying "drunken" have been collected in several places: Bohn, *A Hand-book of Proverbs*, 1855, p. 63; Prenner, *American Speech*, IV (1929), 102–103; H. Schudt, "Er ist betrunken," *Hessische Blätter für Volkskunde*, XXVII (1928), 76–89; Friedli, *Bärndütsch*, V (1922), 455–494; Unfeld, *Zeitschrift für Deutsche Mundarten*, VII (1906), 177–182; K. Rother, *Die Schlesischen Sprichwörter und Redensarten* (Breslau, 1928), pp. 103–108; H. Schrader, *Das Trinken in mehr als 500 Gleichnissen und Redensarten* (Berlin, 1896); Woeste, "Niederdeutsche Ausdrücke für 'trunken sein,'" *Die Deutschen Mundarten*, V (1858), 67–74; Harrebomée, *Bacchus in Spreekwoordentaal* (Gorinchem, 1874); J. Cornelissen, "De dronkenschap in de volkstaal," *Ons Volksleven*, IX (1897), 48–49.

[2] Collections devoted solely to Wellerisms are not numerous and are limited to German and Swedish: Hoefer, *Wie das Volk Spricht: 524 Sprichwörtliche Redensarten* (Stuttgart, 1855; the recent undated eighth edition contains more than 2, 100 Wellerisms); G. H[olmström],

sented in English and American oral tradition.[1] Yet curiously enough when Moritz Haupt, professor of classical languages and literatures at Berlin, lectured on a line in Theocritus in which one of these proverbs occurs, he said "A certain Samuel Weller of Dickens uses many English [proverbs of this sort]" (Anglicis plurimis utitur vel unus ille Dickensii Samuel Wellerus).[2] With such authority to support us we may call these proverbs Wellerisms. To be sure, the observation that they are characteristic of Sam Weller is by

Sa Han och Sa Hon (Stockholm, 1876, 2nd ed., 1880, 3rd ed., 1890); Schultz, *Sex Hundra Ordstäv* (Stockholm, ca. 1860); Woeste, *Die Deutschen Mundarten*, III (1856), 253–264, V (1858), 57–66; H. Herzog, *Beispielssprichwörter*(Aarau, 1882). Collections of ordinary proverbs often give Wellerisms a place apart, e. g. Norway: R. T. Christiansen, *Gamle Visdomsord* (Oslo, 1928), pp. 83–87; Denmark: E. T. Kristensen, *Danske Ordsprog* (Copenhagen, 1890), pp. 633–650; England: Lean, *Collectanea*, II, 741–752. Particular interest attaches to collections from certain regions in Germany where Wellerisms are less frequent than in northern Germany; see, e. g. Berthold, *Hessische Blätter für Volkskunde*, XXIII (1924), 113–115; A. Becker, *Pfälzer Volkskunde* (Bonn, 1925), p. 169.

Studies devoted to Wellerisms are, as follows. General: Seiler, *Lehnsprichwort*, VIII, 1ff.; Classical: M. Haupt, *Opuscula* (Leipzig, 1876), II, 395–406; Low German and Danish: P. Bartels, as cited by Seiler, *Zeitschrift für Deutsche Philologie*, XLVIII (1920), 87, n. 1; Swedish: Cederschiöld, *Om Ordstäv och Andra Ämnen* (Lund, 1923), pp. 5–33; Kalén, "Några Utbyggda Ordstäv från Halland," *Folkminnen och Folktankar*, XII, part 2 (1925), 27–38. Hoefer's introductory essay to *Wie das Volk Spricht* is not in the first, anonymous edition (*pace* Seiler) and is alluded to as an omission from the eighth edition; the long introduction by Max Bruns in the recent undated edition under the title *Der Volksmund* is not particularly helpful.

1 German has also struggled with the problem of naming this type of proverb and has called it variously "Beispielssprichwort," "apologisches Sprichwort," and "Sagwort."

2 *Opuscula* (Leipzig, 1876), II, 405.

no means original with Haupt. The examples in the
Pickwick Papers had already been brought together
in 1867, and presumably the proverbs collected under
the title "Samwelleriana" in a Dutch periodical, *Het
Leeskabinet*, of 1863, belong to the same class.[1] But
long before Dickens the existence of the type in England is attested by a story about Queen Elizabeth and
the first collection of English proverbs. Tradition re-
lates that John Heywood presented his collection to
her. She asked whether every English proverb was
included and he assured her that he knew of no omission. She in turn offered to wager that she could
name a proverb he had overlooked. The proverb
which she had in mind, namely, *Bate me an ace, quoth
Bolton,* was actually missing. Heywood might have
defended himself by saying that it belonged to a very
special class of proverbs which he would have found
it difficult or even impossible to use in his verses,
although he does find room for "*Backare,*" *quoth
Mortimer to his sow.* Essential characteristics are
the phrase "quoth Bolton" and the humorous turn,
which in this particular instance escapes us. The
meaning and connotation of Queen Elizabeth's proverb are now entirely lost, notwithstanding its frequent occurrence in writings of that age. Heywood's
Wellerism is, moreover, not the earliest example in

1 Maass, "39 Odd Similes aus dem Pickwick Papers von Charles
Dickens," *Archiv für das Studium der Neueren Sprachen,* XLI (1867),
207–215; Harrebomée, *Spreekwoordenboek der Nederlandsche Taal*
(Utrecht, 1858–70), III, cccxv.

English. Nearly two centuries before, Chaucer wrote in *Troilus and Criseyde*:

> Lat this proverbe a lore unto you be:
> "To late y-war!" quod Beaute, whan it paste.
>
> ii, 397–398.

In the *Canterbury Tales* he uses "'Soth play, quad play,' as the Flemyng saith."

Wellerisms are far older than these English quotations, for examples from Latin and Greek literature can be pointed out. Indeed Seiler even goes so far as to maintain that the modern traditional forms have descended to us from classical antiquity. Latin and Greek examples are not very numerous, but their resemblance to the type is unmistakable. A few illustrations are "*All the women we need are inside,*" *said the bridegroom and closed the door on the bride* (Theocritus, xv, 77); "*The water will tell you,*" *said the guide when the travelers asked him how deep the river was* (Plato, *Theaet.*, 200 E); "*Farewell, dear light,*" *said the lustful old woman as she undressed and put out the light* (Zenobius, vi, 42);[1] "*That is too much business,*" *said the broker; he had seen six policemen* (Laberius, frag. 63, in Aulus Gellius, xvi, 7, 12). Perhaps Livy

---

1 The point of the witticism lies in the fact that she used the conventional dying words of a tragic figure. We may compare the conventional farewell in ballads of executions, e. g.

> Got gesegne dich, Sunn! Got gesegne dich, Mon!
> Got gesegne dich, schönes Lieb, wa ich dich hon!
> Ich muss mich von dir scheiden.

See O. Böckel, *Handbuch des Deutschen Volkslieds* (1908), p. 132.

(xxiii, 47) alludes to a proverb of this sort in his account of the meeting of Taurea and Claudius: 'when Taurea finds that Claudius takes him at his word, he pretends that his proposal to fight on the road was merely a joke, saying, "By your leave, I will not throw my horse into a ditch" (Minime, sis, inquit, cantherinum in fossam).' These words, Livy tells us, became a proverb. Less than a score of classical examples are known. It is not clear whether classical rhetoricians recognized the form. Possibly Quintilian was referring to it when he said: "παροιμίας that sort which is briefer like a fable and is understood allegorically: '*It is not our burden,*' *said the ox,* [*looking*] *at the saddle*" (παροιμίας genus illud, quod est velut fabella brevior et per allegoriam accipitur: "non nostrum," inquit, "onus," bos clitellas, v, 11, 21). The use of a Greek term suggests that the concept was not familiar to him and possessed no Latin name.

The historical significance of these classical Wellerisms, and indeed the whole history of the form, is obscure. Seiler asserts categorically that the form is classical in origin, notwithstanding its apparently native vigor and originality in Germany and the adjoining Germanic countries. Cogent proof of classical descent is not forthcoming, unless it lie in the almost complete neglect of the form in the Middle Ages and its reappearance in the sixteenth century. The four oldest mediaeval examples, which are found in the monastic *Fecunda Ratis* of Egbert of Liège, show some affinity to classical story. But direct descent from the few classical Wellerisms cannot be made out. Between this time — the end of the eleventh century — and the rise of German Humanism in the sixteenth century instances are extremely rare. Seiler notes two, which are distinctly mediaeval and monastic rather than popular, and I may add "*Something is better than nothing," said the wolf when he swallowed the louse* ("Plus valet il quam nil," pulicem gluciens lupus inquit) and others.[1] Perhaps this historical evidence supports Seiler's conjecture.

Yet we need not see a relation of cause and effect in the appearance of Wellerisms after the rise of Humanism in Germany. Here the *argumentum ex silentio* can, however, have little value. For at least two reasons Wellerisms found no place in the earliest German collections; in the first place, these collections are by south German authors who had little opportunity to know Wellerisms; and in the second

---

1 Examples of mediaeval Latin Wellerisms are much more frequent than Seiler's discussion would imply. The following instances have come to my attention: Müllenhoff and Scherer, *Denkmäler*², I, 45, No. 84 (In discendo lupus nimis affirmans ait "agnus '); 48, No. 161 ("Phi," sonuit fuscum ridens ardaria furnum); J. Werner, *Lateinische Sprichwörter und Sinnsprüche des Mittelalters* (Heidelberg, 1912), p. 9, No. C 42 (Clamat ocellus: "amat!" "dolet hic" manus anxia clamat); p. 25, No. D 189; p. 57, No. N 154; p. 96, No. S 211; J. Klapper, *Die Sprichwörter der Freidankpredigten* (Wort und Brauch, XVI), 1927, Nos. 61, 87, 151, 174, 329. The Wellerism which Goethe uses, "*Es ist schlecht Wasser*," sagte der Reiher und konnte nicht schwimmen ("'Bad water,' said the heron and couldn't swim'), was known in the Middle Ages; see Seiler, *Zeitschrift für den deutschen Unterricht*, XXXIII (1919), 383–386; Müllenhoff and Scherer, *Denkmäler*², I, 59, No. 13 and the note, II, 138.

place, the aims of these collections conflicted with the characteristic temper and tone of Wellerisms. The peculiar qualities which characterize the form, its often obscene humor and its lack of a moral or didactic turn, render it unsuitable for school use. Consequently there was no place for it in the early collections with primarily pedagogical or didactic aims. According to Seiler,[1] Luther believed the Devil was hostile to proverbs and seduced people by turning them into an evil form, the Wellerism. It is clear from Luther's marginal notes to his collection of proverbs that he regarded Wellerisms as malicious perversions, but there is no convincing evidence that Luther regarded Wellerisms as the work of the Devil.

The obvious conflict with morality causes the exclusion of Wellerisms from most later German collections of the sixteenth and seventeenth centuries. Their relative abundance in Neander's compilation of 1590 leads Seiler to believe that many Wellerisms were invented in the sixteenth century; but this is the *argumentum ex silentio*. Unfortunately the hundred instances from sixteenth-century literature which J. Franck said he could readily quote are lost along with the 250,000 sheets of collectanea.[2] Macaronic Weller-

1 *Lehnsprichwort*, VIII, 13.
2 See F. Latendorf, *L. v. Passavant gegen Agricola's Sprichwörter* (Berlin, 1873), p. 28. The collectanea of Franck were, from all reports, the most extensive ever made, but all trace of them has been lost; see Seiler, *Deutsche Sprichwörterkunde*, p. 147. Latendorf (*Michel Neanders Deutsche Sprichwörter* [Schwerin, 1864]) gives some fifty Wellerisms from the sixteenth century.

isms like "*Barbati praecedant*," *sagte Magister Fuchs,
stiess einen Bock die Treppe hinunter* ('"Let gray-
beards go first," said Master Fox [and] pushed a goat
down the steps'); "*Virtus in medio*," *sagte der Teufel,
sass zwischen zwei alten Huren* ('"Virtue in the middle," said the Devil [and] sat between two old har-
lots'), which Seiler quotes from Neander, are cited to
show the humanistic associations of the form. But
these macaronic witticisms seem to be clever inventions rather than the germ from which the type developed. We can certainly conclude that humanists were
well disposed toward the Wellerism, but the evidence
does not permit us to declare that they were responsible for it. Inasmuch as Neander came from Silesia, a
region in which the folk still show a marked predilec-
tion for Wellerisms, it is difficult to know whether his
evident liking for the form is better explained by his
humanistic training or by his native bent. The latter
seems much more probable.

In sum, the history of the Wellerism as a type is
obscure and difficult to trace. We have thus far been
concerned only with classical, mediaeval, and German
instances. Examples from other countries and ages
are little known and studied. Before going farther, it
will be wise to examine the distribution of the type.

The distribution of Wellerisms is very curious. We
have more information about the state of affairs in
Germany than elsewhere. A liking for Wellerisms dis-

tinguishes northern Germany as far south as Hesse. Hoefer's *Wie das Volk spricht*, which is the most important collection, contains nearly 2,100 numbers, and of these more than half are Low German. The Wellerism is popular along the Rhine and in the later-colonized areas in the East, notably Silesia. As we have seen, this fact may explain Neander's liking for the form; he was born at Sorau, in Lusatia. Sebastian Frank's large collection and the others of the sixteenth century with which Seiler makes comparisons are without exception middle and south German. The first north German collections are didactic and have no room for Wellerisms. The exact southern boundary is not known, nor is it possible of determination like the boundary of a linguistic detail. Instances are known from Hesse, Baden, and even from Bavaria and Switzerland. Certainly the manner in which they are mentioned implies that the form is rare in those regions. A careful study of local proverb collections might give us more information, although the frequency with which Wellerisms are excluded must be reckoned with. A close examination of the forms reported from southern Germany might be instructive: we might find them awkward and unskilfully made. A study of the variants of some widely known Wellerisms might reveal the ways in which they spread.

In northern Germany and Scandinavia the Wellerism is very popular. We know very little about its

currency in other regions. The few mediaeval instances owe their dissemination to Latin and have for
the most part become extinct. The toad and harrow
supply the materials for perhaps the only mediaeval
Latin Wellerism which still has any importance in
tradition. In English it circulates as "*Many masters,*"
*quoth the toad to the harrow when every tine turned her
over.* This saying goes back as far as the eleventh-
century *Fecunda Ratis*. The long history of "Nos
poma natamus," which is perhaps known to English
readers in the mistranslation "*We apples are swimming,*" *said the horse-chestnut and swam down the
stream with the apples* or in the utterly unintelligible
"*How we apples swim,*" is international and begins in
the sixteenth century. Martin Luther did not disdain
to use it against an opponent; and before him it finds
an appropriate place in the satiric handbooks of in-
verted etiquette: Dedekind's *Grobianus* (1549) and
the translation by Kaspar Scheit (1551).

Generally speaking, parallels to Wellerisms from
several countries are much rarer than parallels to ordinary proverbs. There are, to be sure, Swedish and
Dutch variants and even a Frisian one of 1691 for the
English "*Many a thing is made for a penny,*" *as the
old wife said when she saw the black man.* Ordinarily
we can speak of the international dissemination of
Wellerisms only with reservations and with reference
to particular sayings.

English Wellerisms are collected by Lean.[1] John Galsworthy uses one in the *Forsyte Saga*, III, i, ch. xii: "'Fini,' as the French girl said when she jumped on her bed after saying her prayers," and Thomas Hardy has others in his Wessex novels. In addition to those cited already, we may mention *"Nay, stay," quoth Stringer, when his neck was in the halter*; *"Ahem!" as Dick Smith said, when he swallowed the dishcloth*; *"I'll tent* (probe?) *thee," quoth Wood*; *"If I can't rule my daughter, I'll rule my good"*; *"Go away here, go away there," quoth Madge Whitworth, when she rode the mare in the tedder*; *"I'll make one," quoth Kirkham, when he danced in his clogs*. In the *Shortest Way with the Dissenters* Defoe used one which has a long history: *"Pray, good folk, let us not step on each other," said the cock* [*to the horse*]. Although examples in modern British and American oral tradition have not been recorded in any abundance, the type is not entirely unknown, e. g. *"Everyone to his taste," said the farmer and kissed the cow*; *"Neat but not gaudy," said the monkey* (var. *Devil*) *when he painted his tail blue*; *"All's well that ends well," said the peacock when he looked at his tail*.

So far as I can learn, French Wellerisms have never been collected. Probably the rarity of the form in French accounts for this lack of interest. In a notice

1 *Collectanea*, II, 741–752. See others in Apperson, *English Proverbs and Proverbial Phrases: A Historical Dictionary* (London, 1929), under "I"; Bohn, *Handbook*, pp. 42, 51, 53, 56, 61, 62, 169, 171, 176, 177, 210, 225, 334.

of one of Seiler's books on proverbs, Arnold van Gennep declares that proverbs of this sort are found in French tradition, but he cites only one example: *"Oh! Oh!" said the Portuguese* ("Oh! Oh!" dit le portugais). Perhaps Rabelais was using a Wellerism when he wrote *"Appetite comes from eating," said Angest on Mans, "and thirst from drinking"* ("L'appetit vient en mangeant," dit Angest on Mans, "et la soif en buvant," *Gargantua*, I, ch. v). In Balzac's *Les Paysans* we find the following example: *"You mustn't spit on the harvest," as Papa Noah said* ("Faut pas cracher zur la vendange!" a dit le papa Noé, ch. iv). Since we have a collection of Spanish proverbial and traditional phrases containing proper names (L. Montoto y Rautenstrauch, *Personajes, personas y personillas que corren por las tierras de ambas Castillas* [Seville, 1911–13]) in which Wellerisms should be recorded if they exist, we may conclude that they are practically unknown. Italian examples are difficult to find, e. g. *"Saran quest' anno di molte pere," diceva l'orso, perchè n'harebbe volute* ("'There will be many pears this year," said the bear because that was his wish'); *"Adagio," disse il Fibbia* ("'Slow," said Fibbia'). A few others, which do not seem to be very characteristic examples, have been mentioned in the remarks on the connections of fables and proverbs.

Scandinavian tradition revels in the Wellerism. Many of the important collections of Danish, Icelandic, Norwegian, and Swedish proverbs devote a special section to it. The early vernacular examples are interesting and historically important, e. g. *"Such things often happen at sea," said the seal, [when] it was shot in the eye* (Opt verðr slíkt á sæ, kvað selr, var skotinn í auga), which occurs in the *Fornmannasögur* of the late twelfth century.[1] At the end of the twelfth century King Magnus Barfot sent one of his followers to southern Bohuslän to induce the people to submit peacefully to his authority. After listening to the emissary's speech to the assembly, someone in the audience answered, *"The snow will come soon, lads," said the Finns [and] had skis for sale* ("Snart kommer snön, svenner," sa finnarna, hade skidor till salu). And on the same occasion another man said, *"No roller is needed," said the raven [and] pulled a mussel-shell on the ice* ("Behövs ingen rulle," sa räven, drog musselskalet på isen). An allusion to a house raising or some similar custom in which neighbors join to help one another is found in a Wellerism in a fifteenth century Swedish collection: *"The assistance would be good, if they only didn't eat so much," said the old woman* (Hjälpen vore nog god, ginge bara inte maten åt," sa käringen).[2]

It has not been noticed that the Celts employ the Wellerism with evident ease and freedom, as the fol-

1 Finnur Jónsson ("Oldislandske Ordsprog og Talemåder," *Arkiv för Nordisk Filologi*, XXX [1914], 71, No. 44; 105, No. 228) gives two later Icelandic examples.
2 The language is slightly modernized.

lowing Gaelic examples show: *"If this be human, it's light,"* as the waterhorse said; *"I'm not a soldier and don't wish to be,"* as the fox said to the wolf; *"Mair haste, the less speed,"* quo' the wee tailor to the lang thread; *"Blow for blow,"* as Conan said to the Devil. A few Lettish examples are quoted by Gustav Meyer in commenting on the preference which Greek proverbs show for the narrative form, e. g. *"Now we have rowed well,"* said the flea, when the fisher drew the boat on land.[1] To this we have an English parallel in *"What a dust I have raised,"* quoth the fly upon the coach, which Bacon (Essay 54) credits to Æsop: "It was prettily derided by Æsope; *The Fly sate upon the Axle-tree of the Chariot wheele, and said, What a dust as I raise?"* [2]

The Wellerism describes a scene with such vividness that it is clearly brought home to us, although we may not be able to catch the full implications, as in the Elizabethan *"Backare,"* quoth Mortimer to his sow. Its relation to historical fact is often close. Cederschiöld is able to trace a number of Swedish instances back to their origins: *"Inte ett dugg,"* sa Settervall refers, for example, to an incident in the Swedish financial crisis of 1857. Settervall examined

---

1 "Zu den Mittelgriechischen Sprichwörtern," *Byzantinische Zeitschrift,* III (1894), 400. Meyer, who is following Crusius ("Märchenreminis-zenzen im Antiken Sprichwort," *Verhandlungen der 40. Versammlung Deutscher Philologen zu Görlitz* [1889], p. 40), seems to confuse the Greek narrative proverb with the Wellerism; see also p. 159 above.

2 The reference to Æsop is found in Romulus, ii, 17 (ed. Oesterley, p. 60).

the accounts in the presence of his partner, Dugge. Dugge asked anxiously, "Can you find anything left?" "Not a drop" (Inte ett dugg), said Settervall. In *Hemsöborna*, a novel of peasant life on the small islands along the Swedish coast, Strindberg gives a graphic description of the origin of a Wellerism: neither of the farm-hands, Carlsson and Rundqvist, liked to work, but in order to gain favor they did many small tasks about the house. Finally Carlsson seemed to have won the day by painting the fireplace white. Not to be outdone, the duller Rundqvist painted an outhouse a brilliant red. The household saw the humorous side of it all and someone coined the phrase: "One should begin at the right end," said Rundqvist, and painted the outhouse first ("Man ska börja i rätta ändan," sa Rundqvist, strök avträdet först, *Hemsöborna*, ch. iii). We need not try to show that this is actually a traditional Wellerism. It suffices that the manner of invention suggests the ways in whichth e traditional forms arise. A Dutch Welerlism, "*Give me time*," *said Koekkbakker* ("Geeft tijd," zei Koekkbakker), which is more than two centuries old, can also be traced to a definite incident in business. When his creditors suspected his honesty, Koekbakker, a resident of Middelburg (a town near the mouth of the Schelde), reassured them by saying, "Give me time," and fled with all his money the next night. We need not fear greatly to trust the story or one of the stories told to explain "*The case is altered*," *quoth Plowden.* I tell the shorter one: Edmund Plowden, an eminent barrister in Queen Elizabeth's time, answered a neighbor that there was very good remedy in law for hogs that trespassed. But when the neighbor went on to say that the hogs were Plowden's own, "Nay, then, neighbor," quoth Plowden, "the case is altered." Probably we cannot verify the truth of this narrative, but we need not hesitate to believe that the saying sprang from this incident or a similar one. *"Bate me an ace," quoth Bolton* becomes more intelligible when we know that a John Bolton was "one of Henry VIII's diverting rascals."

Kalén declares that he has been able to trace practically every Wellerism in oral tradition in the Swedish province of Halland back to a definite personal allusion when the Wellerism gives a clue in a proper name. Notwithstanding this close relation to historical events, it does not appear that many Wellerisms have arisen as condensations of fables and apologues. *"I punish my wife with good words," said the peasant and threw the Bible at her head* (German and Danish) is probably a reminiscence of an old story which has attained international currency as a Wellerism. The same is true of *"That's strong tobacco," said the Devil, when the hunter shot off his rifle in the Devil's mouth.* Seiler is inclined to regard the narrative element as often being present, but it is very slight in some of his examples. Tuinman, a very sensible Dutch commentator on proverbs in the first quarter of the eighteenth century, regarded Weller-isms as closely related to Æsopic fables.[1] Such explanations apply to a very small number of Weller-isms. An interesting illustration is "*It's a day too late,*" *said the widow, when a servant-man proposed to her at the funeral dinner; she had engaged herself to the man who had made the coffin* ("De' er ein Dag for-seint," sa Enkjan, daa Drengen friade till henne i Gravölet — ho hadde lovat han, som gjorde Likki-stan). This is an allusion to the world-old story of the Ephesian widow which has been told from China to Iceland.[2]

Probably the life of the ordinary Wellerism is very short. An incident gives rise to a witty remark which perpetuates itself for a space of time, but when the circumstances have been forgotten or the names and persons of those concerned have ceased to be suggestive, the saying passes out of existence. Only a few Wellerisms enjoy a wide currency, and these are often based on some internationally intelligible allusion or a witticism so obvious that it needs no commentary. The great majority of Wellerisms probably never gain currency beyond very narrow confines.

We may examine the Wellerism as regards subject

1 See Seiler, *Sprichwörterkunde*, p. 27; *Lehnsprichwort*, VIII, 3–4; Tuin-man, *De Oorsprong en Uitlegging van Dagelyks Gebruikte Nederduitsche Spreekwoorden*, I, 176. An illustration of Seiler's method will be found in *Zeitschrift für Deutsche Philologie*, XLVIII (1919–20), 87, No. 1.
2 For references to this story see Killis Campbell, *The Seven Sages of Rome* (Boston, 1907), pp. ci–cviii; Chauvin, *Bibliographie des Ouvrages Arabes* (Liège), VIII (1904), 210; IX (1905), 92.

and form. Essential to it is the incongruity of combining a sober assertion with an utterly inappropriate scene. This incongruity often leads to obscenity and sardonic humor. Typical examples of humor are *"These are fine cuffs,"* said the thief of his handcuffs ("De va fina manchetter," sa tjuven om handklovarna); *"This week is beginning splendidly,"* said one *who was to be hanged on Monday* ("Den här veckan börjar trevligt," sa han, som skulle hängas på måndagen). Seiler's detailed analysis of the kinds of incongruities employed in Wellerisms does not, it seems to me, reveal significant facts, and it does not encourage one to pursue the subject further.[1]

The freedom and scant respect which Wellerisms display toward women, particularly old women, show that the form is a masculine invention in which women have had little share. Such sayings as *"Give her her will or she will burst,"* quoth the good man, when his *wife was dinging him* are characteristic. Perhaps this attitude toward women reflects the temper of an earlier age. We see something of the same sort in the treatment of the priest: *"Virtue in the middle,"* said *the Devil and seated himself between two priests;* "Bad *company,"* said the thief, *as he went to the gallows between the hangman and the monk* (Dutch). Such attitudes may merely represent the manners and thoughts of the peasant of any age. In the last two

1 Seiler, *Lehnsprichwort*, VIII, ch. vii, "Inhaltliche Gruppierung des Sagworts," 24–53.

examples it is interesting to observe that the same model has been used before in other connections; but it is not easy to find Wellerisms fashioned after already existing forms.

Stylistic consideration of Wellerisms may be based on form as well as content. Kalén's interesting observations on Wellerisms from the province of Halland show what can be accomplished in this direction, although it is not clear how far his conclusions are generally applicable.[1] He points out that there are two types of Wellerisms, those in which the allusion requires an indication of the scene, the speaker, or the object to which reference is made, and those in which no additional details are given. An English example of the first kind is *"Neat but not gaudy," said the monkey, as he painted his tail blue,* and of the second kind, *"The case is altered," quoth Plowden.* His article gives an illuminating analysis of the first and more abundant kind. All Wellerisms in which a proper name appears are, he finds, of comparatively recent origin. They have not spread very far and are ordinarily capable of immediate explanation. An older stratum is distinguished by naming the speaker with a pronoun or a title based on sex, age, or a trade. Probably Wellerisms in which an animal speaks are to be assigned to this older stratum. Of course these older Wellerisms can no longer be explained from al-

[1] "Några utbyggda ordstäv," *Folkminnen och Folktankar,* XII (1925), No. 2, 27–38.

lusions to definite individuals or incidents and they
include those sayings which have won wider dissemination. On examining the three subdivisions in which
the allusion is explained by a temporal clause, a relative clause, or a prepositional phrase, Kalén finds that
very curious distinctions can be made. Wellerisms
involving a temporal clause, e. g. *"Much noise and
little wool," said the Devil when he sheared a pig*, are
largely used of women, although men and boys are
occasionally mentioned. Here the speaker is often
designated by age, sex, or trade. In sayings with a
relative clause, e. g. *"The week is beginning well," said
one who was to be hanged on Monday*, we rarely find
any designation of the speaker other than a proper
name or a pronoun, and women are mentioned very
infrequently. Sayings which employ a prepositional
phrase, e. g. *"These are fine cuffs," said the thief of his
handcuffs*, ordinarily refer to a thing and much more
rarely to a person; when the speaker's name is replaced by a pronoun or some other vague designation,
they concern themselves almost exclusively with
things. How these striking differences came about
remains to be discovered. Perhaps similar differences
can be found in Wellerisms from other regions.
Kalén's classification cannot be directly applied to
English and German Wellerisms; but a search for
analogous principles is likely to be fruitful.

Wellerisms which give no accompanying details are
not examined by Kalén. Typical examples are *"God*

help the fool," quoth *Pedley*; *"Backare,"* quoth *Mortimer to his sow*; *" Ei wer möchte das nicht,"* sagte der *Abt von Posen.* These may represent the first stage in the growth of a Wellerism. So long as the allusion is immediately intelligible, — in other words, so long as Pedley is remembered as the court fool, — no explanatory clause or phrase is needed. Just so soon as the point of the witticism is no longer obvious, the time, the speaker, or the thing spoken of must be indicated.

We may perhaps recognize a special group of Wellerisms in those which use already existing proverbs, e. g. *"Every little helps,"* said Mr. *Little and took the six little Littles out to help him saw a pile of wood*; *"Like will to like,"* quoth the *Devil to the collier*; *"To err is human,"* said the *housewife and shook ground pepper in the coffee*; *"Much noise and little wool,"* said the *Devil and sheared a pig* ("Viel Geschrei und wenig Wolle," sagte der Teufel und schor ein Schwein). Obviously the proverb is older than the Wellerism, for part of the humor arises from the presence of a sober proverb in such surroundings.

PROVERBIAL COMPARISONS [1]

Comparisons which we may call proverbial are many and varied. In connection with them, just as with proverbs, questions regarding origin, history,

---

[1] Special collections are not numerous: see Wilstack, *A Dictionary of Similes* (London, 1917); Lean, *Collectanea*, II, 753–895; Woeste, *Die deutschen Mundarten*, V (1858), 57–66; Zingerle, *Die Deutschen Sprich-*

and form arise, but it is often difficult to collect enough examples of a particular comparison to study these questions effectively. Apparently the proverbial comparison offers fewer opportunities for study than the proverb, although it seems probable that something new can be learned by examining variations in taste from age to age. We see that the synonyms for "cold" or "white" differ at different periods, but the variations have not been collected and studied.

Ordinarily literal proverbial comparisons which single out some obvious and familiar quality offer little of interest, e. g. *as old as Methuselah*; *as quiet as a mouse*; *as free as air*; *as dry as a bone*; *as hard as a rock*; *as fat as a pig*; *as heavy as lead*; *as clear as crystal*. Some literal comparisons are amusing in their whimsicality: *cold enough to freeze the tail off a brass monkey*; *as little chance as a snowball in Hell*, or with still further expansion, *as little chance as a celluloid cat chasing an asbestos dog in Hell*. Occasionally we find a proverbial comparison which has been made on the model of another one, e. g. *as clear as mud*. Other proverbial comparisons find a similarity between an ethical quality and an object: *as crooked* ('dishonest') *as a*

---

wörter im Mittelalter (Vienna, 1864); F. Rodríguez Marín, *Mil trescientas comparaciones populares andaluzas* (Seville, 1899). Studies of imagery in individual authors, e. g. Klaeber, *Das Bild bei Chaucer* (Berlin, 1893), often include proverbial comparisons. See also Gabriel Meurier, *La Perle des Similitudes* (Malines, 1583), which contains 866 comparisons with moral applications (cited from Bonser, *Proverb Literature* [London, 1930], p. 127, No. 1061).

pretzel; *as good* ('virtuous') *as gold*; *as green* ('inexperienced') *as grass*.

Some proverbial comparisons offer interesting problems in interpretation: *as cold as sin* (euphemism for Hell?); *as dead as a door nail*; *as deaf as an adder* (implies a mediaeval superstition); *as cool as a cucumber*; *as ignorant as Thompson's colt*. For half a century inquirers in *Notes and Queries* have called for an explanation of *as thrang* ('hurried') *as Throp's wife*, but none has been forthcoming. Although I cannot give an explanation, this clue may lead to one. In the "Flyting of Dunbar and Kennedy" certain persons are named as fit relatives for Kennedy:

> Thy trew kynnismen, Antenor et Eneas,
> Throp thy nere nece, and austern Olibrius.[1]

No one has yet identified Throp. Since the Scotch "nece" may refer to a man, Throp may have had a wife about whom a story was told. *As crazy as Dick's hatband*, which is found in the variant form *As crazy as Dick's hatband which went round nine times and then wodn't tee*, is usually explained as an allusion to Richard Cromwell, Lord Protector of England; but the explanation is far from convincing. *As drunk as a lord* seems still to reflect the manners of old England. We cannot be sure what comparisons are worth the labor of seeking an interpretation: what shall we say of *as busy as a cranberry merchant*; *as*

[1] See Taylor, "Notes on the Wandering Jew," *Modern Language Notes*, XXXIII (1918), 394 ff.

thick ('intimate') *as hops* (perhaps because hops grow thickly); *as poor as Job's turkey* (var. *turkey hen*)?

Some proverbial comparisons have a long history and are widely used in poetry: *as red as blood*; *as white as snow*; *as green as grass*. Comparisons which involve colors can be readily traced through centuries of use.[1] Some variations in taste and meaning appear: *as green as grass* acquires in recent times the added meaning of "ignorant, inexperienced"; *as white as chalk* was once merely a comparison for "white," even for "shining white," while now it is ordinarily used of a dull white without gloss: "His face was as white as chalk." The comparison of green with the clover, which was long a commonplace of mediaeval poetry and later popular verse, is now little used, and *as white as a swan* or *as white as ermine* have perhaps a more poetic or artificial sound today than they once had. *As white as silver* is hardly known today, and *as white as a sheet* applies only to an unnatural pallor. The colloquial comparison *as brown as a berry* is as old as the twelfth century, and although some berries are brown, its appropriateness seems rather doubtful.

1 See I. V. Zingerle, "Farbenvergleiche im Mittelalter," *Germania*, IX (1864), 385–402.

FF COMMUNICATIONS No. 113

AN INDEX TO "THE PROVERB"

BY

ARCHER TAYLOR

HELSINKI 1934
SUOMALAINEN TIEDEAKATEMIA
ACADEMIA SCIENTIARUM FENNICA

225

Printed by
Suomalaisen Kirjallisuuden Seuran Kirjapainon Oy.
Helsinki 1934

TO

RICHARD JENTE

INTRODUCTION.

The following list of proverbs came into existence as the basis of my book, *The Proverb* (Harvard University Press, Cambridge, Mass., 1931). All the proverbs and proverbial phrases there mentioned are here given with indication of the page on which they occur. The proverbs are arranged alphabetically according to the different languages from which they are quoted. For the user's convenience, however, I have inserted in the English list those proverbs, chiefly Arabic and modern Greek, which were cited only in translation. In addition to supplying an index to my book, this list includes a considerable number of references to the parallels to the proverbs, particularly to those in English, German, and Latin. References to proverbs quoted from other languages are ordinarily given in *The Proverb* and are therefore omitted here. References to the proverbs in the Dutch *Proverbia communia sive seriosa* are limited to the number of the proverb in that collection, since Richard Jente's promised edition will provide abundant material for their study. The titles of books cited by the author's name will be found in the appended »List of Books Cited». Collections of proverbs have so increased in numbers that a vast amount of material is now available for use. This *Index* is intended to make accessible the literature on many important and commonly used proverbs and thus to awaken interest in a rich, but neglected field of philological and folkloristic study.

ADDENDA AND CORRIGENDA TO »THE PROVERB».

p. 14, n. 2: Add in third line: Harrebomée (I, p. xli) cites Lennep's reprint of Winschoten. Add at the end of the paragraph: Atlantic Monthly, CL (1932), 383—84.

p. 31 note: Insert comma before »plane» and delete the following comma. Read 204 for 262.

p. 39, line 1: Read »Though» for »When.»

p. 44: Read Plutarch for Pompey. Read Amoris vulnus idem sanat, qui facit.

p. 66, n. 1: Add E. Nicolin, Les expressions figurée d'origine cynégétique en français (Diss., Upsala, 1906).

p. 89: Add M. Franke, Der Stabreim in der neudeutschen Literatur (Diss., Rostock, 1893); O. Hoffmann, Reimformeln im Westgermanischen (Darmstadt, 1885); K. Seitz, Niederdeutsche Alliterationen (»Forschungen» edited by the Verein f. niederdeutsche Sprachforschung, VI [Norden, 1893]); M. A. Schwarz, Alliteration im englischen Kulturleben (Diss., Greifswald, 1923); E. M. Wright, Rustic Speech and Folklore (London, 1913), pp. 124—25; Zingerle, »Die Alliteration bei mittelhochdeutschen Dichtern», Sitzungsberichte der Wiener Akademie, phil.hist. Klasse, XLVII (1864), 103—74.

p. 94: Insert after second sentence in the second paragraph: Such legal proverbs are called brocards.[1]

---

[1] See the writings of Nicolaus Tudeschi; the rules of Olaus Petri, 1552, as cited in Paul's Grundriss[2], II, i, 1173; Herbert Broom, A Selection of Legal Maxims (London, 1845, [5] 1870). The close

p. 97, n. 11: Add: Bolte, Zeitschrift des Vereins f. Volkskunde, XVIII (1908), 300, n. 1; B. Kahle, Ortsneckereien
und allerlei Volkshumor im badischen Oberlande (Freiburg,
1908) and compare the review by Heilig, Hessische Blätter
f. Volkskunde, VII (1908), 191—95; Karg, Zeitschrift des
Vereins f. Volkskunde, XL (1930), 163—69; G. M. Küffner,
Die Deutschen im Sprichwort (Diss., Heidelberg, 1899);
R. Kubitschek, Böhmerwälder Spottbüchlein (Pilsen, before
1930); H. Lienhart, Elsässische Ortsneckereien (Heidelberg,
1927); A. Matschoss, Scherz, Spott und Hohn in der leben-
den Sprache (Berlin, 1930); Müller, Zeitschrift des Vereins f.
Volkskunde, XXIV (1914), 90—94, 183—88; M. Plaut,
Deutsches Land und Volk im Volksmund (Breslau, 1897);
H. Tardel, Bremen im Sprichwort (»Bremische Weihnachts-
blätter», II, Bremen, 1929). English: Northall, English
Folk-Rhymes (London, 1892), p. 4. French: Morawski, Les
diz et proverbes des sages (Paris, 1924), 146—47, no. 14.
Modern Greek: Bonturas, »Neugriechische Spottnamen und
Schimpfwörter», Zeitschrift des Vereins f. Volkskunde, XXIV
(1914), 162—75.

p. 105: Add as a new footnote: Lössl, »Redensarten zur
Nachahmung mundartlicher Eigentümlichkeiten», Unser
Egerland, IX (1905), 12 (as cited in G. Jungbauer, Bibliographie der deutschen Volkskunde in Böhmen, No. 1117)
lists proverbs which mock dialectal peculiarities.

p. 108: Add as a new footnote, line 12: See J. Lewalter
and G. Schläger, Deutsches Kinderlied und Kinderspiel
(Kassel, 1911), p. 373 note on No. 449 and compare passim
Meringer und Mayer, Versprechen und Verlesen (Stuttgart,
1895); K. Wehrhan, Kinderlied und Kinderspiel (Leipzig
1910), p. 22.

relation of the proverbial form to law appears in such a work as
Edmond Wingate, Maximes of Reason; or, the Reason of the Common
Law of England (London, 1658). See F. Stroud, The Judicial Dic-
tionary of Words and Phrases (London, 1891).

p. 109, n. 1: Add: 100 gamle Bunde-regler (= »Norske folkeminne», 1, Kristiania, 1916); E. Kück, Wetterglaube an der Lüneburger Heide (Hamburg, 1915); C. Kassner, Das Wetter und seine Bedeutung für das praktische Leben (Leipzig, ¹1908, ²1918); G. F. Northall, English Folk Rhymes (London, 1892), p. 430; N. G. Polites, Demodeis metrologikai mythoi (Athens, 1880). The curious superstitions associated with certain days and the determining of the weather by the circumstances on particular days need study for their bearings on proverbs; see, as introduction, the forthcoming article »Lostage» in the Handwörterbuch des deutschen Aberglaubens; Olrik, Zeitschrift des Vereins f. Volkskunde, XX (1910), 60 n.; H. Kasserer, Bauernregeln und Lostage (Vienna 1926); Classical Weekly, 1928—31 (see indices).

p. 115: Read »April grode» etc.

p. 127, n. 1: Add: K. Knortz, Der menschliche Körper in Sage, Brauch und Sprichwort (Würzburg, 1909); H. Schlandt, Der menschliche Körper: eine deutsch-magyarische Zusammenstellung von Redensarten und Sprichwörtern, die sich auf dem menschlichen Körper und dessen Teile beziehen (Kronstadt, 1902), J. Köferl, »Der Kopf des Menschen im Aberglauben, in Sprüchen und Redensarten», Unser Egerland, XIV (1910), 33—35 as cited in G. Jungbauer, Bibliographie der deutschen Volkskunde in Böhmen, No. 3588.

p. 103, n. 1: Add: Manacorda, Zeitschrift des Vereins f. Volkskunde, XVIII (1908), 436—41; Notes and Queries, 12th Series viii (1921), 247, 297.»

p. 130, line 8: Read »voorbij.»

p. 132, n. 1: Add: L. T. A. Bouché-Leclercq, Placita Graecorum de Origine Generis Humani (Paris, 1871); McCartney, »Unde Hominum Genus», Classical Journal, XX (1925), 367—8; McCartney, »Folklore Heirlooms», Papers of the Michigan Academy of Science, Arts and Letters, XVI (1931), 109—10; »Kinderherkunft» Handwb. d. dt. Aberglaubens IV 1342—59.

p. 138, line 20: Read »magpie» for »witch.»

p. 140, line 12: Insert: The proverb *Hindsight is better than foresight*, which is current in American oral tradition, means of course that knowledge after the event is fuller than what can be foreseen; a different thought is expressed in the German *Better foresight than hindsight* (Besser Vorsicht als Nachsicht. Wander, V, 1700), which admonishes one to foresee rather than to regret.

p. 144, n. 2: The date of the book by Erasmus should be 1528.

p. 146, Read Quintilian.

p. 147, line 9: Read »de'.»

p. 154, last line: Read »thousand» for »dozen.»

p. 162, line 9: Insert »not» before »rife.»

p. 162, n. 1: Insert J. Rasch, Vier stuck. Nichts wehrt (Munich, 1589) as cited in Bonser-Stephens, No. 1728.

p. 181, line 9: Read: 1st ed., 1644, 2d ed., 1657.

p. 200, n. 2: Add at the end of the first sentence: Schrader, Bilderschmuck[5], p. 511.

p. 201, n. 2: Add in the second paragraph: P., Archiv f. lateinische Lexikographie, III (1886), 62.

p. 204, line 6: Read cantherium.

p. 206, last line: Read: »1, 542 sheets.»

p. 206, n. 2, second sentence: Read: The collectanea of Franck are reputed to be the most extensive ever made, but Seiler (Deutsche Sprichwörterkunde, p. 147) found no trace of them, although the Allgemeine deutsche Biographie says that a Dr. Steiff of Stuttgart inherited the manuscripts.

p. 216, n. 2: Add: Gaster Exempla of the Rabbis 176.

p. 220, n. 1: Add: G. Pitrè, Proverbi, motti e scongiuri (Turin, 1910); G. Pitre, »Voci siciliane di paragone raccolte ed illustrate», Rivista Sicania (Acireale), II (1914); W. Widmer, Volkstümliche Vergleiche im Französischen nach dem Typus »Rouge comme un coq» (Diss., Basel, 1929). A few dissertations and studies which collect comparisons used by

different authors are: F. I. Carpenter, Metaphor and Simile
in the Minor Elizabethan Drama (Chicago, 1893); G. S.
Heise, Gleichnisse bei Shakespere (n. p., n.d.); E. Hüttig,
Der Vergleich im mittelhochdeutschen Heldenepos (Diss.
Halle, 1930); O. Saechtig, Ueber die Bilder und Vergleiche
in den Sprüchen und Liedern Heinrichs von Meissen,
genannt Frauenlob (Diss., Marburg, 1930); F. Sellert, Das
Bild in Pierce the Plowman (Diss., Rostock, 1904); W. Tap-
pert, Bilder und Vergleiche aus dem Orlando Innamorato
(Marburg, 1886); H. Voigt, Metaphern und Gleichnisse in
Shakespeares Dramen (Strassburg, 1904).

ENGLISH.[1]

---

[1] Including proverbs from other languages which are quoted only in English.

Air *see* free.
Air castles *see* castles.
Don't sell **America** short 9,   37
Young **angel**, old devil   16
   Apperson 720.
To be on the side of the **angels** 188
   Benham 118 a.
   Annoy *see* joy.
A soft **answer** turneth away wrath   60
   Aeschylus Prom. 378; Prov. 15: 1; Seiler *Zs. f. dt.*
Phil. XLVII (1916—8) 244 no. 10, XLVIII (1919—20)
82 no. 11.
»Many a thing is made for a penny», said the old wife,
when she saw an **ape** 209
   Tuinman I 322; Harrebomée I 4 = ten Dam *De diet-*
sche Warande IV (1858) 222 nos. 94, 95; Apperson 511;
Lean II 748, 752; Cederschiöld 12; Küffner 273 a—b;
Kok *Danske ordsprog og talemåder fra Sønderjylland*
(Copenhagen 1870) 350. Cf. Gering *Zs. f. dt. Phil.* XLVIII
(1919—20) 314.
To lead **apes** in Hell 191
   Kuhl »Shakespere's 'Lead apes in Hell' and the ballad
of 'The Maid and the Palmer'» *Studies in Philology* XXII
(1925) 453—66; Apperson 13; Lean II 661—2; A. Haas
Die Tiere im pommerschen Sprichworte (1925) no. 32;
Jente 8.
An **apple** a day keeps (var.: drives) the doctor away 124
   Trans. of the Devonshire Assoc. for the Advancement
of Science XIV (1873) 591; Apperson 13.
»We **apples** are swimming», said the horse chestnut
   (rectè: sterquilinum equi) and swam down the stream
   with the apples 209
   Wesselski *Erlesenes* 102—5; Lean II 748, IV 91;
Apperson 14; Tuinman I 112, 349; Harrebomée I 18;
Carstens *Zeitschrift des Vereins f. Volkskunde* XVI

(1906) 306 no. 61; Fitzgerald *Polonius* 51, (ed. S. S. Allen) 40.

April showers bring May flowers 111, 114, 118
    Apperson 15.

They asked the **ass**, »Whither?» He answered, »To fetch
    wood or water». (Arabic) 157
    Altenkirch 33 no. 37; Polites III 328—9; *see* âne.

Ass in a lion's skin 32
    Hyamson 23.
        Ass *see* teeth.
        Attack *see* brunt.

To have an **axe** to grind 190
    Hyamson 27.

»**Backare**», quoth Mortimer to his sow 202, 213, 220
    Lean III 347, 370; Apperson 21; Jente 11.
        Bag *see* sack.
        Bait *see* fish.

To strike a **balance** 191

When **bale** is hest, thenne bote is nest 81
    Skeat 83; Proverbia communia 7.

To **bank** on 189

Two words to a **bargain** 90
    Tilley 715; Apperson 657.

To make the best of a bad **bargain** 191
    Apperson 40.

To get more than one **bargained** for 191
    Hyamson 33.

To **bark** up the wrong tree 189
    Hyamson 34.

Barnaby bright, the longest day and the shortest night 116
    Apperson 27.
        Barndoor *see* horse.

To be caught with his foot off first **base** 189

To be over the **bay** 200

To **be** or not to be 34

Shakespeare, *Hamlet* III i.

Do not sell a **bear** on the United States 37

»I have caught a **bear**.» »Bring it here.» »It won't come.»
»Then come yourself.» »It won't let me go.» (Modern
Greek) 156

Altenkirch 15 no. 10, 27—8 no. 20; Reinsberg-
Düringsfeld *Internationale Titulaturen* I 47; Adalberg
»tatar» 12.

Bear *see* hungry, skin.

»To late y-war», quod **Beautee**, »whan it paste»............ 203

Chaucer *Troilus and Cryseide* II 397—8; Skeat 160;
Haeckel 185.

Early to **bed** and early to rise Makes a man healthy,
wealthy, and wise 124

Büchmann 305; Apperson 173; Lean II 733.

To get out of **bed** with the wrong foot first 186

A. de Cock *Volksgeloof* I 212; Stoett 173.

Beggars cannot be choosers 90

Apperson 34.

Well **begun** is half done... 61

Apperson 674; Bohn 70; Skeat 67; Büchmann 385;
Polites II 510—12; Stoett 184; Seiler *Zs. f. dt. Phil.*
XLVIII (1919—20) 85 no. 49.

To bear the **bell** 196

Haeckel 167; Apperson 30.

To curse with **bell**, book, and candle 188

Apperson 37.

Bell *see* cat.

To hit below the **belt**... 189

Hyamson 42.

To **bet** on the wrong horse 189

When **Billing Hill** puts on its cap, Calverley Mill will
get a slap 120

Apperson 47.

The **bigger** they come, the harder they fall.............. 37

It's an ill **bird** that fouls its own nest 51
 Proverbia communia 677.
A little **bird** told me 131
  Ecclus. 10: 20. A. de Cock *Volksgeloof* I (1920) 112;
Volkskunde XXII (1911) 96—100.
A **bird** in the hand is worth two in the bush 13, 22
 Proverbia communia 135.
To kill two **birds** with one stone 199
 Apperson 340.
The hasty **bitch** bears blind whelps..................... 25, 77
 Aristophanes Pac. 1078; Martin 20, 23 no. 23; Meyer
Byzantinische Zs. III (1894) 402 no. 16; Krumbacher
(1893) 153 no. 16, (1900) 427 no. 35; Wesselski *Poliziano*
p. 190; Altenkirch 17, 345 no. 39; Tilley 39; Lean III 391;
Apperson 289; Seiler *Lehnspr.* V 16—17. Cf. cagna.
Don't **bite** off more than you can chew..................... 12
 Lean III 450; Hyamson 47.
To make two **bites** of a cherry 188
 Lean III 339; Apperson 653; Hyamson 47.
  Bite *see* cur.
  Black *see* Devil, ox, pot.
Out of God's **blessing** into the warm sun 77
 Marvin *Curiosities* 60; Jente 29; Lean II 706, cf.
I 19; Apperson 476; Bond *Athenaeum* 15 Aug. 1903;
P. L. Carver *Modern Language Review* XXV (1930)
478—81.
The **blind** man eats many a fly 77
 Tilley 42; Apperson 55—6; Wander »Blinde» 14,
15, 42.
  Blind *see* bitch, love, blindr (Icelandic).
You can't get **blood** out of a turnip 12
 Apperson 56.
To give him a body **blow**...................................... 189
  Blow *see* horn, hot, wât (German).
To call his **bluff**.. 189

To be in the same **boat**...................................... 190
    Hyamson 55.
To have shot one's **bolt** 189
The nearer the **bone**, the sweeter the meat 21
    Proverbia communia 801.
What's bred in the **bone** will not out of the flesh........ 38
    Tilley 49; Apperson 66.
        Bone *see* dry.
To make no **bones** about it 192
    Apperson 392; Hyamson 57.
        Boot (bote) *see* bale.
Under **boske** shal men weder abide 151
    Skeat 82.
Boys will be boys 130, 138
    Proverbia communia 443. Is this really derived from
I Cor. 13:11: Cum essem parvulus, loquebar ut parvulus,
sapiebam ut parvulus, cogitabam ut parvulus (When I
was a child, I spake as a child, I understood as a child,
I thought as a child)?
Sent a **boy** to mill.................................... 130
Brag is a good dog, but Holdfast a better 142
    Jente 113; Apperson 63.
Bread and cheese 125
    See fromage.
To know which side his **bread** is buttered on 188
    Apperson 64.
Gooid brade (**bread**), botter and sheese is good Halifax
    and good Friese 105
    Küffner 281 a, b (Hazlitt 100, 158); Northall 517—8.
Bread and cheese be two targets against death 125
    Apperson 64; f. LeRoux de Lincy II 206.
        Bread *see* half.
        Bred *see* bone.
When **Bredon Hill** puts on his hat, Ye men of the vale,
    beware of that 121

Apperson 66.

Happy is the **bride** the sun shines on, and happy the
    corpse the rain rains on 72
    Apperson 283; Lean II 591; Jente 36.

»All the women we need are inside», said the **bridegroom**
    and closed the door on the bride (Greek) 203

To burn his **bridges** behind him 198
    Seiler Sprwk. 34; Hyamson p. 55; Wander »Brücke»
28; Stoett 1988.

It's as **broad** as it is long 130
    Hyamson 64.

New **brooms** sweep clean 10, 51, 141
    Proverbia communia 549.

»Who knocked out your eye?» »My **brother.**» »That's why
    the blow went so deep.» (Modern Greek) 157
    Altenkirch 24 no. 4; Polites I 309.

As **brown** as a berry 223
    Zingerle *Germania* IX (1864) 395; Apperson 70.

To be in a **brown** study 192
    Apperson 70.

To bear the **brunt** of the attack 190
    Hyamson 65.
    Brush *see* tarred.

To pass the **buck** 189
    Hyamson 65.

To kick the **bucket** 192
    Apperson 339; Hyamson 208.
      Build *see* sand.

A **bull** in a china shop 31
    Apperson 72.

To take the **bull** by the horns 190
    Apperson 72; Hyamson 336.
      Burn *see* bridges.

To **burst** with envy 186
    Büchmann 399; Seiler *Lehnspr.* V 213.

To beat about the **bush** 189
 Hyamson 38.
  Bush *see* bird, wine.
Business is business 5
 Apperson 73.
As **busy** as a cranberry merchant 222
To look as if **butter** would not melt in his mouth 188
 Lean III 368; Apperson 74; Hyamson 68.
To **buy** for a song 190
 Apperson 587.
To take the **cake** 196
 Aristophanes *Knights* 277, *Thesm.* 94 (cf. B. B.
Rogers *ad loc.*); also colloquial (Pennsylvania).
  Calf *see* cow.
After the **calm** comes a storm 19
 Apperson 604; Polites III 243—5.
  Calverly Mill *see* Billing Hill.
They said to the **camel-bird** (ostrich), »Carry.» It an-
 swered, »I cannot, for I am a bird». They said,
 »Fly». It answered, »I cannot, for I am a camel».
 (Arabic) 156
 Trench p. 18.
Timely crooks that tree that will be a **cammock** 18
 Proverbia communia 698.
The more **camomile** is trodden on, the faster it grows ... 73
 Tilley 68; Jente 44.
The game (var.: flame) is not worth the **candle** 74, 75
 Lean IV 123; Apperson 242; de Cock *Volkskunde* X
(1897—8) 163.
To hold a **candle** to 193
 Lean III 350; Hyamson 72.
  Candle *see* Tace.
  Canoe *see* paddle.
If the **cap** fits, put it on 68
 Apperson 81; cf. Lenschau 38; Hyamson 73.

To make **capital** of 191
  Hyamson 74.
      Card *see* turn.
To lay all the **cards** on the table (var.: to show one's
  cards) 189
  Hyamson 75.
To hold all the **cards** (var.: to have the cards in one's
  hand) 189
  Hyamson 75.
To stack the **cards** 189
A **carpenter** is known by his chips (var.: tools) 15
  Apperson 82.
To put the **cart** before the horse 186
  Bohn 152; Apperson 83; Martin 32 no. 119; Stoett
  1756.
That has nothing to do with the **case** 44
»The **case** is altered», quoth Plowden 215, 218
  Bohn 147; Lean II 749; Apperson 83; Büchmann 118;
  W. Hone *Table Book* II col. 250 (Hackerston's cow);
  Jente 51.
To build **castles** in Spain (var.: air castles) 188
  Seiler *Lehnspr.* V 199—200; Stoett 1444; Quitard
  353 ff.; Winter 120 ff.; Büchmann 411; Apperson 84;
  Haeckel 60; F. Polle *Wie bezeichneten die alten Grie-
  chen den Witz? Ueber Luftschlösserbaukunst* (Leipzig,
  1896).
To bell the **cat** 199
  Baum »The Fable of Belling the Cat» *Modern Lan-
  guage Notes* XXXIV (1919) 462—70; Wesselski *Poli-
  ziano* 93—94 no. 196; Stith Thompson *The Types of the
  Folk-Tale* (FF Communications LXXIV (Helsinki 1927))
  no. 110; Apperson 88; Stoett 1094; *Zeitschrift des Vereins
  f. Volkskunde* XXI (1911) 169; Bolte *Zs. des Vereins f.
  Volkskunde* XXV (1915) 300 no. 13; Borchardt-Wust-

mann 247—8; Hulme 185; Fecunda ratis 709 note.;
Wesselski *Arlotto* II 226 no. 93.
Tobe a **cat's** paw 199
   Hyamson 77; see chestnuts.
When the **cat's** away, the mice will play 13
   Proverbia communia 276.
The **cat** would eat fish but would not wet her feet 30
   Apperson 88; Voigt *Zs. f. dt. Altertum* XXIII (1879)
305 no. 11; Fecunda ratis 336; Skeat 209; Jente 54;
Haeckel 31; Polites III 240—2.
A **cat** may look at a king 42
   Reinsberg-Düringsfeld I 867; Seiler *Lehnspr.* V
86—7; Borchardt-Wustmann 249—50; Apperson 85;
Singer 404 no. 149.
To buy a **cat** in a sack 78
   Stoett 1093; Gittée *Volkskunde* (Ghent) VI (1893)
45—6; compare pig.
First **catch** your hare 79
   Lean II 727, III 464; Hyamson 177; *Notes and
Queries* 8th Ser. VII 233.
As little **chance** as a celluloid cat chasing an asbestos
   dog in Hell 221
As little **chance** as a snowball in Hell 221
To give **chapter** and verse 191
   Hyamson 81.
A stern **chase** is a long chase 14
   Apperson 601; Lean III 405.
Bread and cheese *see* bread.
That's the **cheese** 80
   Hulme 125.
Those who eat **cherries** with great lords shall have their
   eyes dashed out with the stones 30, 74
   Proverbia communia 669. Compare »Eat pease with
the King and cherries with the beggar»: Lean I 490,
II 679.

Cherry *see* bites.

Cheshire born and Cheshire bred, Strong i' th' arm and
weak i' th' head 128
Apperson 93, cf. 398: »Manchester bred: long in the
arms and short in the head»; Northall 9.

Cheshire for men, Berkshire for dogs, Bedfordshire for
naked flesh, and Lincolnshire for bogs 102
Apperson 93.

To pull the **chestnuts** out of the fire 184, 199
Wesselski *Erlesenes* 108—14; Apperson 94; Winter
102; Borchardt-Wustmann 245; Stoett 1089; Harrebomée III 100.

When **Cheviot** ye see put on his cap, Of rain ye'll have a
wee bit drap 121
Apperson 94.

Chew *see* bite.

Don't count your **chickens** before they are hatched 13,   28
Apperson 95.

Chickens come home to roost 10

To cover the well after the **child** is drowned 64

The burnt **child** dreads the fire 13
Skeat 286; Apperson 73; Haeckel 68; Fecunda ratis
106.

Children and fools speak the truth 159
Apperson 96, 225; Suringar *Bebel* 276; Singer 404
no. 156; Lauchert 11; Suringar *Erasmus* 101; Stoett
1145; Krumbacher (1893) 136 no. 7; Meyer *Byzantinische Zeitschrift* III (1894) 401 no. 7; Polites I 472—5.

China shop *see* bull.

Chips *see* carpenter.

There's small **choice** in rotten apples 152
Jente 61.

A green **Christmas**, a white Easter 115
Apperson 98; Frick *Schweizerisches Archiv f. Volkskunde* XXVI (1926) 171; Beirens *Nederlandsch tijd-*

schrift voor Volkskunde XXXIV (1929) 32; Hellmann 161
n. 2; Tuinman II 94; Polites III 534—5.
    Christmas *see* winter.
The nearer the **church,** the farther from God ... 20, 143, 150
    Apperson 438; Skeat 100; Lean II 709; Wander »Kir-
che» 100. Cf. Proverbia communia 798; Stoett 1787;
Mau 4576.
As clear as **crystal** (var.: mud) 221
    Hyamson 88; Apperson 101.
To go like **clockwork** 190
»I'll make one», quoth Kirkham, when he danced in his
    clogs 210
    Bohn 167.
There's nobbut three generations atween **clogs** and clogs   11
    Apperson 102; Lean IV 152.
Clothes make the man 26
    Lenschau 90; Suringar *Erasmus* 236; Harrebomée
III 258; Stoett 1169; Seiler *Zeitschrift f. deutsche Philo-
logie* XLVIII (1919—20) 85 no. 55; Bernstein Catalogue
no. 3877; Seiler *Lehnspr.* I, 79; Otto 476; Jente 9.
Rabener bases a satire on the proverb.
Every **cloud** has a silver lining 111
    Apperson 572.
To heap **coals** on fire on his head 186
    Rom. 12: 20.
Turn your **coat** according to the wind 151
    Apperson 652; *see* Mantel (German).
The **cobbler's** wife is always ill-shod 15
    Apperson 566.
    Cobbler *see* last.
A **cock** is mighty on his own dunghill 13, 90
    Seneca *Apocol.* 7; Otto 752; Skeat 22; Apperson 104;
Suringar *Erasmus* 83; Kock and Petersen II 185; Alten-
kirch 351—2 no. 67; Seiler *Lehnspr.* II 68—9; Zingerle
197; A. de Gubernatis *Zool. Myth.* II 291; *Baudouin de*

Sebourc VI 645; Congreve *The Old Bachelor* II i. Compare *Prov. comm.* 313; *Fecunda ratis* 239 note.

»Pray, good folk, let us not step on each other», said
the **cock** 210
    Defoe *Shortest Way with the Dissenters;* Wesselski
Erlesenes 101—2.

The first **cock** of hay frights the cuckoo away 110
    Apperson 128.

A **cock's** stride etc. 117
    Northall 444; Apperson 652.

To live like a fighting **cock** 189
    Hyamson 142.

To pay him back in his own **coin** 191
    Apperson 487; Hyamson 92.

Cold enough to freeze the tail off a brass monkey 221

As **cold** as sin 222
    Cold *see* days, hot.

To fly false **colors** 188
    Hyamson 93.

A ragged **colt** may make a good horse 13
    Apperson 520; Whittington *Vulgaria* (1520) fol.
XXXV: »Many a ragged colt proued to (be) a good
horse».

»Blow for blow», as **Conan** said to the Devil (Gaelic) ... 213
    Scott *Waverly* ch. XXII.
        Consent *see* silence.
        Contempt *see* familiarity.
        Cook *see* hunger.

Too many **cooks** spoil the broth 142
    Stoett 1224; Apperson 640.

As **cool** as a cucumber 222
    Apperson 113.

To be **corned** 200
        Cornish *see* Tre.
        Corpse *see* bride.

To take the **count** 189
»Every man to his taste», said the farmer and kissed
  the **cow** 210
> Apperson 191; *Trans. of the Devonshire Assoc. for the
> Advancement of Science* LIII (1902) 164.

He that bulls the **cow** must keep the calf 91
> Tilley 123; Apperson 72.

Curst **cows** have short horns 13
> Apperson 118; Jente 81; Lean III, 381.
> Cranberry merchant *see* busy.

As **crazy** as Dick's hatband 222
> *Folk-Lore* XXXVII (1926) 270; Apperson 151; *Notes
> and Queries* 8th Ser. XII 171.

You must learn to **creep** before you can go 13
> Jónsson *Arkiv f. nord. fil.* XXX (1914) 105 no. 223;
> Apperson 214, cf. 665, »walk», 3.

It's ill halting before a **cripple** 13, 152
> Skeat 196; Apperson 280.

To shed **crocodile** tears... 197
> Stoett 1283; de Cock *Volkskunde* VIII (1895—6)
> 9—13, XXII (1911) 233—4 = *Volksgeloof* I 136 no. 343.

To be **crocked** 200
As **crooked** as a pretzel 221
> Crooks *see* cammock.

To **crow** over... 190
> Hyamson 103.

To have a **crow** to pluck with you and a poke to put the
  feathers in 199
> Apperson 124.
> Great cry *see* Geschrei.
> Crystal *see* clear.

An unlicked **cub**... 72
> Peuckert in Bächtold-Stäubli *Handwörterbuch des dt.
> Aberglaubens* I 884 n. 60; Stoett 179; Borchardt-Wust-

mann (1925) 41; de Cock *Volksgeloof* I 96 no. 100.

> Cucumber *see* cool.

The **cuckoo** comes in April, Sings a song in May, Then in
June another tune, And then she flies away 110

> Apperson 127—8.

> Cuckoo *see* cock.

There's many a slip between **cup** and lip 13, 42, 50

> Otto 1035, 1311; *Archiv f. lat. Lexikog.* IV (1887) 346;

Apperson 129; Marvin *Curiosities* 82 —3; Büchmann 201.

A **cur** will bite before he will bark 13

> Apperson 158 (dog).

To **curry** favor 197

> A. Beets »Over eene middeleeuwsche allegorie» *Han-*
> *delingen van het 6de nederlandsche philologencongres* (Lei-
> den 1910) 108 ff.; Lean II 725, III 302; Borchardt-
> Wustmann 369.

> Curse *see* bell.

> Cut loaf *see* slice.

Tell it to the **Danes** 131

»I'll tent thee», quoth Wood, »if I can't rule my **daugh-**
ter, I'll rule my good» 210

> Bohn 46.

Praise the fair **day** at even 26, 178, 179

> Taylor »In the evening praise the day» *Mod. Lang.*
> *Notes* XXXVI (1921) 115—8; Jente 260; Seiler *Sprick.*
> 224; Suringar *Erasmus* 141; Apperson 509—10; Frauen-
> lob Spr. 103, 5 —6; Zingerle 145; Ysengrimus (ed. Voigt)
> III 594.

> Day *see* dog.

As the **days** begin to lengthen, The cold begins to streng-
then 112

> Apperson 136; Northall 461; cf. Beirens *Ndl. tijdschr. v.*
> *volksk.* XXIX (1924) 30—8.

Dead men tell no tales 9

> Apperson 137—8; cf. 158, »dog» 25.

As **dead** as a door nail 222
    Skeat 105; Apperson 137; Stoett 449; Jente 91.
        Dead Indian *see* Indian.
As **deaf** as an adder 222
    Apperson 2, 139.
        Deaf *see* ears.
To be in at the **death** 189
    Hyamson 111.
Better old **debts** than old grudges (Irish) 39
    Proverbia communia 139.
Of ill **debtors** men take oats 90
    Proverbia communia 770.
        Deed *see* thought.
        Deep *see* waters.
The **Devil** is beating his grandmother 70
    Apperson 150; Quitard 304; Grimm *Dt. Myth.*[4] II 842
    ([1]960), III 297; Lehmann »Teufels Grossmutter» *Arch.*
    f. Rel.wiss. VIII (1905) 411—30; Chamberlain *J. Am. Fl.*
    XIII (1900) 278—80; A. Götze »Teufels Grossmutter» *Zs.*
    f. dt. Wortf. VII (1905) 28—35; Tuinman I 308; de Jager
    Taalkundig Magazijn III 122; Harrebomée I 299, II xii,
    III 221; Beirens *Ndl. tijdschr. v. volksk.* XXX (1925)
    32—35; Sprenger van Eijk *Dierenrijk* (Proeven 1839)
    p. 7 no. 16; Thiele *Luthers Sprw.* 299 no. 326; De Cock
    and Teirlinck *Kinderspel* (Gent 1905) VI 218—20; Feil-
    perg *Ordbog* III 454 »sol»; Apperson 150.
»Much noise and little wool», said the **Devil** 219
    See Geschrei.
The **Devil** is not as black as he is painted 165
    Apperson 147; Ström 26; Altenkirch 332 no. 31; Poli-
    tes IV 383—4.
Needs must when the **Devil** drives 70
    Lean IV 55; Apperson 440.
When the **Devil** was sick, the Devil a monk would be;

When the **Devil** was well, the devil a monk was he ...   51
    Lenschau 115; Seiler *Sprick.* 90; Suringar *Bebel* 297;
Apperson 148—9; Quitard 306; Wesselski *Märchen* 200
n. 1; Polites III 571—4; Fecunda ratis 911 ff.; Zingerle
84; Morawski *Les diz et proverbes des sages* 151 no. 18.
He must have a long spoon that would sup with the
Devil   70
    Apperson 143—4; Jente 99; Lean III 485; Haeckel
70.
To be the **Devil's** advocate 188
    Hyamson 114.
       Devil *see* Conan, saint.
To play with loaded **dice** 189
The **die** is cast 44
    Otto 55; Stoett 2244; Seiler *Lehnspr.* V 282; Büch-
mann 437.
A man can **die** but once 8
    Lean III 395.
All men must **die** 8
    Seiler *Lehnspr.* V 249; Jónsson *Arkiv f. nordisk filo-
logi* XXX (1914) 74 no. 67; Jente 105.
Diligence is the mother of good luck 147
    Apperson 152—3; Cervantes *Don Quijote* I ch. xlvi.
After **dinner** rest a while After supper walk a mile 122
    Apperson 3; Quitard 287—8; Plutarch *Natural history*
21; C. Meaux Saint-Marc *L'école de Salerne* p. 79; Nor-
thall 500.
You must eat a peck of **dirt** before you die 124
    Lean IV 205; Bohn 68; Apperson 178.
»Ahem», as Dick Smith said, when he swallowed the
dishcloth 210
    Marvin *Curiosities* 47; Apperson 154.
Disuse is sister to abuse 148
    Lean III 448.
Do as I say and not as I do 131

Lean II 743, III 448; Apperson 154; Quitard 368. Cf.
Matth. 23: 3; Livy 7: 32.

You're the **doctor** 130

    Doctor *see* apple.

A hair of the **dog** that bit you 131

    Apperson 278; Lean II 503; Richter[4] 95; Lauchert 23;
Borchardt-Wustmann 224; Wesselski *Erlesenes* 13—17;
Englert and Bolte »Hundshaare heilen den Hundebiss»
Zs. d. Ver. f. Volksk. XXIX (1919) 44; de Cock *Volks-
geloof* II 14—18 no. 259.

A live **dog** is better than a dead lion 54

    Eccl. 9: 4; Lenschau 104.

Dog eat dog 12

    Cf. Apperson 158.

Every **dog** has his day 27, 75

    Apperson 159; *New English Dictionary* »dog»; Jente
112.

A **dog** in the manger 28, 32

    Apperson 160—1; Seiler *Lehnspr.* II 78.

To beat the **dog** before the lion 196

    Jente 114; Skeat 280; Lean II 729; Apperson 161;
Bolte *Zs. d. Verf. f. Volksk.* XVI (1906) 77—81, XXX—
XXXII (1920—22) 145, XXXVII (1927) 19; Seiler
Lehnspr. V 24—6; Fecunda ratis 497; Morawski *Les diz
et proverbes des sages* p. 113 no. 3; Röhricht *Zs. f. dt.
Phil.* IX (1878) 473—4.

Barking **dogs** never bite 10

    Apperson 157; Stoett 921.

    Dog *see* Brag.

What's **done**'s done 5

    Polites III 664.

      Done *see* well.

      Door *see* sweep.

      Doornail *see* dead.

Don't hit (kick) a man when he is **down** 97

To be **down** but not out 189
You can't keep a good man **down** 169
    Draw *see* straw.
A **drowning** man will catch at a straw 13
    Apperson 166.
As **drunk** as a lord 222
    Apperson 166.
As **dry** as a bone 221
    Apperson 168.
All signs fail in **dry** weather 113
To take to a thing like a **duck** to water 190
To make **ducks** and drakes of his money 193
    Apperson 169.
To be **duck soup** for 192
    Dunghill *see* cock.
»What a **dust** I am raising», quoth the fly on the cart ... 213
    Romulus II 17 (ed. Oesterley 60); Apperson 220;
Cederschiöld 26; Lean II 752.
To throw **dust** in his eyes 196
    Otto 1483; Seiler Lehnspr. V 24; Quitard 610 —11;
Apperson 172; Stoett 2624.
    Dust *see* March.
    Each *see* every.
    Early *see* bed.
    Ears *see* walls.
    Easter *see* Christmas.
Easy come, easy go 61
    Apperson 365; Skeat 261; Lenschau 147; Seiler *Lehn-*
spr. VI 161; Suringar *Bebel* 363; cf. Proverbia communia
466; Stoett 688.
    Eat *see* dirt.
You can't spoil a rotten **egg** 12, 151
Eggs, butter and cheese are good English and good
    Friese 105
You can't unscramble **eggs** 37

Eggs *see* omelettes.

Elbow *see* eye.

To carry (see) it through to the bitter **end** 190
    Hulme 126; *Atlantic Monthly* February (1930).

All things have an **end** 27
    Apperson 8; Lean II 736; Haeckel 148; Zingerle 193.

The **end** justifies the means 41
    Stoett 436; Büchmann 422.

To be at loose **ends** 190

Merry **England** 100
    Hyamson 238.

England is the paradise of women, hell of horses, and
    purgatory of servants 101, 160
    Lean I 11; Apperson 183. Similar in form is Liége
est l'enfer des femmes, le purgatoire des femmes et le
paradis des prêtres (Dejardin p. 41).

He that **England** will win Must with Ireland begin 133
    Apperson 183; Jente 149; Northall 1.
        England *see* hemp.

Enough is enough 5
    Apperson 185.
        Envy *see* burst.

To **err** is human and to forgive divine 25, 37,   61
    Pope *Essay on Criticism* 1. 525; Lenschau 144; Otto
820; Tilley 192; Büchmann 411.

»To **err** is human», said the housewife and shook ground
    pepper in the coffee 220
    Lenschau 144.

To **euchre** 189
        Even *see* day.

Evening red and morning gray Will speed a traveler on
    his way, But evening gray and morning red Will
    pour down rain upon his head 112
    Apperson 186, 526—7; Wood *Folk-Lore* V (1894) 256
no. 178, 257 no. 183; *Folk-Lore* XXXV (1924) 357;

Northall 459; Zingerle 8; *Handwb. d. dt. Aberglaubens* I
col. 57.

Every (var.: each) man for himself and God for us all
(var.: the Devil for all) 26
    Apperson 189; Wood *Folk-Lore* V (1894) 241 no. 51.
      Everything *see* place, waits.

Of two **evils** choose the least 61
    Apperson 654; Haeckel 73; Skeat 161; Harrebomée
III 271—2; Stoett 1304.

He that doeth **evil** hateth the light 54
    Proverbia communia 209.

The **exception** proves the rule 78
    Apperson 194.

A fair **exchange** is no robbery............................. .. 93
    Seiler *Zs. f. dt. Phil.* XLVII (1916—8) 251 no. 85;
Apperson 199.

Experience is the mother of wisdom 147
    Tilley 199; Seiler *Lehnspr.* V 123; Stoett 2474; cf.
Harrebomée I 56 »Bier» 10; Apperson 195.

The master's **eye** makes the horse fat 13, 61
    Proverbia communia 387.

Never rub your **eye** but with your elbow 126
    Apperson 196; Bohn 29—30.

What the **eye** sees not, the heart rues not 51
    Proverbia communia 165, 166.

His **eyes** are bigger than his stomach 130
    Tilley 204; Apperson 195; Borchardt-Wustmann 28;
Stoett 1683; Tuinman I 99.

To have **eyes** in the back of his head 185
    Seiler *Lehnsprichwort* V 103; Apperson 195.

To open his **eyes** 185
    Otto 1276.

      Eyes *see* dust.
      Face *see* nose.
      Fair *see* love.

To lie **fallow** 190
     False *see* colors.
Familiarity breeds contempt 146
     Tilley 211; Apperson 203; Jente 126.
Farewel feldfare 193
     Chaucer *Troilus* III 861; *Romance of the Rose* 5510;
Apperson 204; Haeckel 181; Lean II 672.
     Farmer *see* cow.
As **fat** as a pig 221
     Apperson 205.
To be at **fault** 189
     Favor *see* curry.
To show the white **feather** 189
     Hyamson 140.
     Feather *see* nest.
Good **fences** make good neighbors 149
     See custodia.
The **fewer** the better fare 145
     Apperson 428.

Finders, keepers; losers, weepers 90
Findings, keepings 90
     Northall 335.
To have a **finger** in the pie 190
     Jente 132; Apperson 212.
My little **finger** told me 131
     Winter 126; Wesselski »Der säugende Finger» *Sude-*
tendt. Zs. f. Volksk. I (1928) 12—17 = *Erlesenes* 144
—50; A. de Cock *Volkgeloof* I (1920) 180—3 = *Volks-*
kunde XXIII (1912) 232—5; Quitard 322; Schrader
Bilderschmuck 390; Bächtold-Stäubli *Handwb. d. dt.*
Aberglaubens II 1489—90. Should we compare »to
have it at one's finger's ends»? See Stoett 509; Apperson 212. Cf. Taylor »Finger» *Handwb. d. dt. Märchens* II.
     Finger *see* wind.

Fingers were made before forks 130
    Lean III 464; Apperson 212.
The ner the **fir[e]** the hatter is 21
    Apperson 214; Haeckel 56; Fecunda ratis 378; Seiler
Lehnspr. V 130.
Soft **fire** makes sweet malt 10
    Apperson 585.
      Fire *see* child, North River, removes, smoke.
First come, first served 90
    Apperson 214; Skeat 266; Graf and Dietherr 284; Sei-
ler *Zs. f. dt. Phil.* XLVII (1916—8) 252 no. 105, 387
no. 43; Quitard 342; Harrebomée III 384; Suringar *Eras-
mus* 183; Stoett 1452; Haeckel 79.
Fish or cut bait 10
Fish should swim thrice 125
    Apperson 215; Stoett 2416.
All **fish** are not caught with flies 13
    Apperson 5.
Neither **fish**, flesh, nor good red herring 26
    Jente 135; Tilley 240; Apperson 219; Stoett 2415.
I have other **fish** to fry (and their tails to butter) ... 26, 130
    Apperson 216.
To feel like a **fish** out of water 39, 188
    Lean III 353; Skeat 211; Apperson 216; cf. Stoett
693.
It's good **fishing** in troubled waters......................... 13
    Apperson 217; Lauchert 14; Harrebomée III 359;
Stoett 2529.
It's ill **fishing** before the net 13
    Apperson 217.
»Now we have rowed well», said the **flea**, when the fisher
    drew the boat to land (Lettish) 213
    Meyer *Byzantinische Zs.* III (1894) 400.
»Soth play, quad play», as the **Flemyng** saith 203
    Haeckel 123; Proverbia communia 752.

To run the **gauntlet** 188
    Günther *Deutsche Rechtsaltertümer* 71 n. 102; Hyamson 156; de Cock *Oude gebruiken*² 26 no. 55.
        Generations *see* clogs, shirtsleeves.
Let **George** do it! 9
    Quitard 423.
Them as has **gets** 5
    Cf. Matt. 13: 12, 25: 29; Mk. 4: 25; Lk. 8: 18, 19: 26.
Don't look a **gift-horse** in the mouth 4, 158
    Proverbia communia 480; Stoett 1753.
A whistling **girl** and a crowing hen will come to no good
    end 72
        Apperson 680; Lean III 381; A. de Cock *Volksgeloof*
I 167 = *Volkskunde* XXIII (1912) 148—54; Lewalter
and Schläger *Dt. Kinderlieder* (1911) 285no. 53; Lewy
Zs. d. Verf. f. Volksk. XLI (1931) 58; Northall 295, 506;
de Cock *Vrouwen* 32, 103.
To be an Indian **giver** 192
    Hyamson 197; cf. Apperson 247.
Those who live in **glass** houses should not throw stones 74,
                                                84, 141
        Apperson 248; Marvin *Curiosties* 84—5; Bohn 9.
Compare Covarubbias (1611): El que tiene el tejado de
vidrio, no tire piedras de su vezino.
To **gloss** over 191
To strain at a **gnat** and swallow a camel 59
    Matt. 23: 24; Marvin *Curiosties* 121.
To kick against the **goad** (var.: pricks) 59
    Acts 9: 5; Proverbia communia 686.
God is above all 8
    Proverbia communia 352; Jente 159.
God helps those who help themselves 157
    Proverbia communia 690.
        God *see* blessing, church, every, man, wind.

All is not **gold** that glitters 19, 51, 138
  Proverbia communia 623.
      Gold *see* good.
If you can't be **good**, be careful 9
  Apperson 92.
As **good** as gold 222
  Apperson 256.
Be **good** and you'll be happy 169
      Compare »Be good and leave the rest to Heaven»
W. Combe, *Dr. Syntax*, canto 7.
      Good Indian *see* Indian.
      Good luck *see* diligence.
It is a blind **goose** that knoweth not a fox from a fern-
  bush 129
  Tilley 265; Apperson 266.
Don't kill the **goose** that lays the golden eggs 28
  Marvin *Antiquity* 188 —9; Apperson 266. Cf. Polites
II 604—6.
To cut the **Gordian** knot 186
  Seiler *Lehnspr.* V 180; Büchmann 429; Stoett 1203.
Sour **grapes** 28, 32
  Altenkirch 342—3 no. 27; Apperson 268; Stoett 501.
No **grass** grows where the Turk's horse has trod 83
  Apperson 269; Lean II 715.
To hear the **grass** grow 186
  Suringar *Bebel* 85; Stoett II 556.
As **green** as grass 222, 223
  Zingerle *Germania* IX (1864) 391—3; Apperson 273.
Someone is walking over my **grave** 198
  Stoett 726; Goethe *Faust* 1. 2757; de Cock *Volks-
kunde* XXV (1915) 168 = *Volksgeloof* T 237 no. 249.
To keep his nose to the **grindstone** 190
  Apperson 452.
      Groaning *see* horse.

To break fresh **ground** 190
    Hyamson 171.
To stand one's **ground** 190
    Hyamson 171.
»The water will tell you», said the **guide** when the trave-
    lers asked him how deep the river was (Greek) 203
Better ten **guilty** escape than one innocent person suffer 88
    Lean III 431.
The **hailer** is as bad as the stailer 78, 92
    Apperson 277—8; Lenschau 50; Seiler *Zeitschrift f.*
deutsche Philologie XLV (1913) 252 no. 77; Zingerle 65;
Stoett 890; Northall 521.
      Hair *see* dog.
Half a loaf is better than no bread 13
    Proverbia communia 117.
To be **half seas** over 200
    Hyamson 173.
      Half-done *see* well.
      Halting *see* cripple.
To go at it **hammer** and tongs 190
    Hyamson 174; N.E.D. s.v.
To come under the **hammer** 198
    Stoett 785; N.E.D. s.v.
»St. John, help me.» »Put out your **hand** yourself.»
    (Modern Greek) 157
    Altenkirch 16 no. 11; Polites I 241.
Good **hand**, good hire 145
    Apperson 259.
Don't bite the **hand** that feeds you 12
    Hyamson 47.
Hands off is fair play 97
    Cf. Scott *Old Mortality* c. iv.
To wash one's **hands** of it 186
    Deut. 21: 6; Psalms 26: 6; Matth. 27: 24; Stoett 802.

To **hang** by a thread 186
    Seiler *Lehnspr.* V 127; Stoett 481.
As well be **hanged** for a sheep as a lamb 92
    Apperson 562; Lean III 421.
As **hard** as a rock 221
    Apperson 284 (flint, stone).
      Harder *see* bigger.
To hold (run) with the **hare** and run (hunt) with the
    hounds 189
    Lean III 321; Apperson 541.
      Hare *see* catch.
Haste makes waste 5
    Apperson 288.
He is none of the **Hastings** 141
    Bohn 165; Apperson 288—9.
      Hasty *see* bitch, heads.
Keep that under your **hat**! 131
To bury the **hatchet** 191
    Apperson 289.
Make **hay** while the sun shines 13, 165
    Apperson 291; Wood *Folk-Lore* V (1894) 259 no. 201.
Hazlewoods shake 193
    Chaucer *Troilus* III 890, V 505, 1174.
Heads I win, tails you lose 130
    Apperson 293.
Curled **heads** are hasty 128
    Stoett 755; de Cock *Volkskunde* XXIII (1912) 195
—96 = *Volksgeloof* I 173 no. 165.
Two **heads** are better than one 61
    Apperson 655.
      Hear *see* grass.
To pour out one's **heart** 188
Faint **heart** ne'er won fair lady 35, 135
    Apperson 198; de Cock *Volkskunde* XVIII (1906) 35.
With **heart** and soul 89

Matth. 22: 37; Stoett 853.

> Heart *see* eye.

To be in the seventh **heaven** 197

> Stoett 898.

As **heavy** as lead 221

> Apperson 296; Polites III 37 —8.

>> Hell *see* apes, chance.

>> Helps *see* God.

As long as **Helsby (Hill)** wears a hood, the weather's
never very good 120

> Apperson 297—8.

When **hemp** is spun, England is done 133

> Apperson 183 —4.

>> Hen *see* girl.

To draw a red **herring** across the trail 189

> Hyamson 290; N.E.D.

Hide nor hair 89

> Stoett 977.

>> Himself *see* every man.

Hindsight is better than foresight 140, 143

> Wander IV col. 1700 no. 13 (the reverse); cf. Apperson 470: »One good forewit . . .»

To have him on the **hip** 189

> Apperson 474.

>> Hit *see* down.

To go the whole **hog** 190

> Apperson 249; Benham 455 a.

>> Holdfast *see* Brag.

The vale of **Holmsdale** was never won and never shall... 133

> Apperson 305; Northall 71.

>> Home *see* way; bu, daelt (Icelandic).

By **hook** or crook 193

> Lean III 351; Apperson 308 —9; Hulme 127; Skeat 300.

>> Hope *see* life.

263

Hops *see* thick.

Cf. Apperson 310.
Hyamson 190; Apperson 164.
Seiler *Sprwk.* 234; Stoett 963; cf. Apperson 126;
Elworthy *Horns of Honour* (1900); Sprenger van Eijk
Dierenrijk (1838) 38—39; Quitard 263 ff.; de Cock *Volkskunde* XVIII (1906) 235; *Taal en letteren* III (1893) 50
—2, 118, 156—57; IV (1894) 177—86, 203—16, V (1895)
237—8; J. Moller *Discursus de cornutis et hermaphroditis
eorumque jure* (Berlin 1708); *Germania* XXIX (1884)
59—70; Weigand-Hirt *Dt. Wörterb.* I 891; Bolte *Zs. d. V.
f. Volksk.* XIX (1909) 63—82; Scheftelowitz *Handwör-
terb. d. dt. Aberglaubens* IV col. 327.
Horns *see* cows.

Apperson 275.
Apperson 567.
Notes and Queries 11 Ser. iii, 433, 358, 269; Benham
815 a.
Seiler *Lehnspr.* V 221—2; Suringar *Erasmus* 215;
Harreboméc III 202; cf. Apperson 312.
Apperson 314.
Otto pp. x, 169 note; Seiler *Zs. f. dt. Philol.* XLV
(1913) 275 no. 198, XLVII (1916—8) 253 no. 111; Stoett

1058; Apperson 598—99; Dickson *Valentine and Orson* (New York 1929) 175 n. 40. Cf. Proverbia communia 15.

To bet on the wrong **horse** 189
>   Horse *see* cart, colt, gift horse, steal, three.
>   Hose *see* man.

To blow **hot** and cold.. 186
>   Seiler *Lehnspr.* V 207; Suringar *Erasmus* 63.
>   Hounds *see* hare.

The darkest **hour** is just before dawn 111
>   Apperson 135.

My **house** is my castle.............................. 90,   95
>   Chaisemartin 527—8; Suringar *Erasmus* 99; Apperson 316; Dejardin p. 35; Sir Edward Coke *Reports* xi fol. 82 as cited in D. Murray *Lawyers' Merriments* (Glasgow 1912) 55 n. 1. Cf. the Icelandic *Every man is master at home* (Halr er heima hver, Havamal 36, 3) to which Heusler (*Zs. d. Ver. f. Volksk.* XXV (1915) 111 no. 5) cites only a Gaelic parallel (Henderson *The Norse Influence in Celtic Scotland* p. 269). Cf. Est dictum verum: privata domus valet aurum (Müllenhoff and Scherer II 41 no. 51); Polites IV 626—8; Williams *Law Magazine and Law Review* 4th Ser. XX (1895) 294.

House and home 89
>   Shakespeare 2 Henry IV, ii, 1.
>   Hundred years *see* same.

Hunger is the best cook 142
>   Suringar *Bebel* 202; Lauchert 10; Suringar *Erasmus* 164; cf. Hunger is the best sauce, Apperson 318; Stoett 937.

Hunger breaks stone walls 142
>   Jente 185; Apperson 317—8.

As **hungry** as a bear 185
>   Otto 1836.

To break the **ice** 186
>   Quitard 427; Stoett 992; Apperson 65.

Idleness is the mother of all the vices 147
    Apperson 322; Quitard 570; Harrebomée I 92; Marvin *Curiosities* 263; Polites II 430—33. See ledigheid (Dutch), ennui (French).

Ignorance is the mother of devotion 147
    Apperson 322—3; Lean IV 5.

Ignorance of the law excuses no one 93, 95
    Lean IV 5; Draxe (ed. M. Förster, *Anglia* XLII [1916]) 389 no. 1085.

Where **Ignorance** is bliss, 'tis folly to be wise 143
    T. Gray Ode on . . . Eton College (1747).

As **ignorant** as Thomson's colt 222

Give him an **inch** and he'll take an ell 51
    Seiler *Spruck.* 89; Suringar *Erasmus* 216; Apperson 327.

The only good **Indian** is a dead Indian 10
    Attributed to Gen. Sheridan; cf. Benham 459 b.
      Indian see giver.

Ingratitude is the daughter of Pride...................... 147
    Bohn 107; Apperson 327; Cervantes *Don Quijote* II ch. 1.
      Innocent *see* guilty.
      Invention *see* necessity.

Strike while the **iron** is hot 15, 51
    Proverbia communia 25.

The **Italian** is wise before the deed; the German, in the deed; and the Frenchman, after the deed 101
    Reinsberg-Düringsfeld *Internationale Titulaturen* I 5; Apperson 328; Küffner 44 a—f, 68.

Go to **Jericho!** 196
    Hyamson 203.

The **Jews** spend their money at the Feast of the Passover; the Moors, at weddings; and the Christians, in law-suits 101

Reinsberg-Düringsfeld *Internationale Titulaturen* I 4;
Apperson 333.
To be **jingled** 200
   Job's turkey *see* poor.
After **joy** comes annoy 19
   Tilley 67. Cf. Apperson 3; Polites III 480—2.
To stew in one's own **juice** 190
   Apperson 269—270.
Good **kail** is half the meal 126
   Apperson 259.
The **kettle** reproached the kitchen spoon. »Thou blackee»,
he said, »thou idle babbler». (Arabic) 158
   Burckhardt 435.
    Kettle *see* pot.
    Kick *see* bucket, down, goad.
To fight like **Kilkenny** cats 192
   Hyamson 209; Feilberg *Bidrag s.v.* »hak»; Gering
Zs. f. dt. Philol. XLVIII (1919—20) 315; Jónsson *Arkiv
f. nordisk filologi* XXX (1909) 80.
The **king** can do no wrong 93
   Lean II 713, IV 128.
A hunting **king**, a dancing queen 83
   Lean III 392.
    King *see* cat.
A cunning **knave** needs no broker 15
   Lean II 685; Apperson 121 (*s.v. crafty*), 653; Jente
197.
    Knot *see* Gordian.
Know thyself 4, 38
   Otto 1236; Seiler *Lehnspr.* V 123—4; Jente 200; Eliza
G. Wilkins The *Delphic Maxims in Literature* (Chicago
1929) pp. 8—9 and passim; Büchmann 330; J. Davies in
Arber *An English Garner* V (1882) »Nosce teipsum».
Knowledge is power 34, 37
   Stoett 1124; Büchmann 295; Apperson 347.

To the best of my **knowledge** and belief 90
    Lady *see* heart.
    Lamb *see* hanged, wind.
A shady **lane** breeds mud 12
    Contemporary Stories (1923) p. 81.
    Larks *see* lovers, sky.
Shoemaker (cobbler), stick to your **last** 15,   41
    Otto 462; Seiler *Lehnspr.* V 240; Lauchert 13; Suringar *Erasmus* 142; Harrebomée III 277—8; Stoett 2012; Jente 280.
Better **late** than never 61
    Büchmann 391; Harrebomée III 273; Apperson 44; Haeckel 76.
Laugh and grow fat 126
    Apperson 351—2.
    Laughter *see* sorrow.
    Law *see* necessity.
    Lead *see* heavy.
    Lead *see* horse.
To take a **leaf** out of his book 191
    Hyamson 218.
To turn over a new **leaf** 191
    Heywood (ed. Farmer) I, 64; Apperson 652.
To read a **lecture** to 191
    Legs *see* lies.
Marry in **Lent**; you'll live to repent 73
    Marvin *Curiosities* 181; Apperson 404.
To **lick** into shape 72
    Hyamson 221—222.
    Lick *see* cub.
To put the **lid** on 190
Lies have short (var.: long) legs 142
    Singer 407 no. 175; Wander III 257 (Lüge 117); *Fecunda ratis* 157; Apperson 362.
While there's **life**, there's hope 61, 154

Apperson 364; Stoett 1373; Polites II 486.
>   Light *see* evil.
Like will to like 60
>   Proverbia communia 365.
»**Like** will to like», quoth the Devil to the collier 220
>   Apperson 367—8; Lean II 747.
To be in the **limelight** 190
To fall into **line** 190
To read between the **lines** 191
To get the **lion's** share 186
>   Seiler *Lehnspr.* V 199; Stoett 9.
>   Lion *see* dog.
>   Lip *see* cup.
To be **lit** (up) 200
»Every **little** helps», said Mr. **Little** and took the six little
>   Little's out to help him saw a pile of wood 220
He was born at **Little Wittham** 141
>   Apperson 373.
Live and learn 5, 152
>   Bohn 113; Suringar *Erasmus* 43; Apperson 375.
>   Loaf *see* half, slice.
Look before you leap 13
>   Apperson 380.
>   Lord see drunk.
Cut your **losses** and let your profits run 9
>   Lean III 445.
You never **lost** money taking a profit 9
>   Benham 817 a.
Love 'em and leave 'em 36
Love is blind 61
>   Otto 99; Apperson 384; Haeckel 2; Stoett 1394;
Jente 209; de Cock *Vrouwen* 110 no. 1.
Love cures the very wound it makes 44
>   Publilius Syrus (ed. Spengel) no. 31; Otto 101.
Love me little, love me long 165

All's fair in **love** and war 93
  Apperson 384.
    Love *see* pity.
Lovers live by love as larks live by leeks 75
  Apperson 387; Lean II 721.
Lucy light, the shortest day and the longest night 116, 119
  Bohn 38; Apperson 388; Northall 455; Quitard 508;
Bernstein catalogue 2578; Bezema *De nieuwe taalgids*
XX (1926) 310; Vercouille *ibid.* XXI (1927) 41—42;
Jungbauer *Handwb. d. dt. Abergl.* V col. 841, 1443. Cf.
passim M. Höfler *Archiv f. Rel.wiss.* IX (1906) 253
—61; Stickelberg *ibid.* XIII (1910) 333—43.
To leave one in the **lurch** 192
  Apperson 358. Cf. Stoett 2161.
Mackerel sky, mackerel sky, Never long wet, never long
  dry 111, 118
  Apperson 389; Northall 459.
Mackerel sky and mare's tails Make lofty ships to carry
  low sails 121
    Dunwoody 9; Apperson 103; *Folk-Lore* XXXV
(1924) 357.
He is one of the **McTak's**, not one of the McGie's 139
    Madge Whitworth *see* mare.
    Malt *see* fire.
A **man** is a man still, if he hath a hose on his head 68
  Apperson 394.
Man proposes, but God disposes 40, 55, 58, 143, 153
    Apperson 397; Skeat 113; O'Rahilly 328; Seiler *Lehn-
spr.* V 205; K. L. Roberts in Hoyt's *New. Clyclopedia
of Practical Quotations* (1927) p. 317; Harrebomée I 241;
Stoett 2578; Cervantes *Don Quijote* II ch. 1 v; Reins-
berg-Düringsfeld *Sprichwörter* II 56—57 no. 94; K.
Sethe *Nachrichten d. Ges. d. Wiss.* (Göttingen), phil.-
hist. Kl. (1925), 141—7.
    Man *see,* clothes, die, drown, team, chorea (Latin).

Seiler *Lehnspr.* VIII 10—11, *Spruck.* 29, 85; Müllenhoff and Scherer I 41 no. 49; Apperson 636; *Zs. f. dt.
Alt.* LXIV (1927) 177; ten Dam *De dietsche Warande* IV
(1858) 253 no. 604; Lean II 743; Fecunda ratis 727.

A hot **May** makes a fat churchyard 126
    Apperson 407.

Marry in **May**, you'll rue it for aye 73
    Otto 1011; Seiler *Zeitschrift f. den deutschen Unter-
richt* XXXI (1917) 17 n. 1; Apperson 408; Tuinman II
247. See J. G. Frazer *Publii Ovidii Nasonis Fastorum
Libri Sex* (1929) V (Index) s.v. »May»; H. Bächtold
»Ueber die Maihochzeiten» *Sonntagsbl. d. Basler Nachrichten* (1912) no. 19 (cf. *Zs, d. Ver. f. Volksk.* XXIII
[1913] 108); Esser »Das Heiraten im Mai» *Zs. d. Ver. f.
rhein. u. westf. Volksk.* V (1908) 46—9; Gaidoz »Le
mariage en mai» *Mélusine* VII (1894—5) 105—11.

    May *see* April.
    Meal *see* kail.
    Means *see* end.
    Men *see* many.
    Methusaleh *see* old.
    Mice *see* cat.

Many a **mickle** makes a muckle 140
    Proverbia communia 760.

»How sweet the **milk** is.» »Where did you see it?» »My
    uncle saw another man drinking it on the other side
    of the river. (Modern Greek) 156
    Polites III 156, 171; D. H. Sanders *Das Volksleben
der Griechen* (Mannheim 1844) 231 no. 127.

Milk before wine, I wish't were mine; Milk taken after
    Is poison's daughter 123
    Lean II 678—9, IV 49; Harrebomée III 293; Leroux
de Lincy II 199; Quitard 696; cf. the Spanish »Dexo la
lache al vino», »Bien seas venido, amigo».

To put him through the **mill** 190

Hyamson 240.

The **miller** has a golden thumb 105
    Apperson 417; Lean II 684.
        Mine *see* yours.

Misery acquaints a man with strange bedfellows 20
    Jente 236; Apperson 418.

Misery loves company 142
    Benham 659 b.

Misfortunes never come singly 169
    Apperson 419.

A **miss** is as good as a mile 13,   79
    Apperson 419; Lean II 666.

Mistakes will happen 5,   6
    Cf. »Accidents will happen», Apperson 1.

To give him the **mitten** 197
    New English Dictionary *s.v.* »mitten».

Money talks 9
    Apperson 423.

Money makes the mare go 12
    Apperson 422.

No **money,** no Swiss 84
    Apperson 449; Marvin *Curiosities* 80; Quitard 657;
    Stoett 646; Borchardt-Wustmann 152; Harrebomée I
    218; Krebs II 72 —73; Polites II 534—5.

(The love of) **money** is the root of all evil 55
    Lenschau 120; Haeckel 38; Stoett 696.

Yo 'pays yo' **money** and yo' takes yo' choice 194
        Money *see* ducks, lost, time.

»Neat but not gaudy», said the **monkey** as he painted his
    tail blue 210, 218
    Marvin *Curiosities* 49 (Devil); Apperson 438.

The **more** he has, the more he wants 56, 143
    Lenschau 121; Apperson 433.

The **more** the merrier 145
    Apperson 428.

Morning *see* Morgen (German).

Mouth *see* gift-horse, spoon.

To pass **muster** 190

Hyamson 247.

For the want of a **nail** the shoe was lost; for the want of
a shoe the horse was lost; for the want of a horse the
rider was lost; for the want of a rider the battle was
lost; and all for the want of a horseshoe nail 31

Taylor »Formelmärchen» § 5 *Handwb. d. dt. Märchens* (forthcoming); Aarne-Thompson no. 2039; Müllenhoff and Scherer I 196 no. 5; Bolte and Polivka *Anmerkungen* III 335—7.

To hit the **nail** on the head 190

Stoett 2123; Apperson 435.

To pay on the **nail** 197

Fehr *Archiv f. d. Studium d. neuer. Spr* CXLII (1921)
262—4; Apperson 435.

To work like a **nailer** 190

Nearer *see* bone, church.

Neat *see* monkey.

Necessity is the mother of invention 145, 148

Otto 1358; Apperson 439; cf. »poverty is the mother
of arts» (Apperson 508).

Necessity knows no law 91, 152, 171

L. Günther *Dt. Rechtsaltertümer* 49; Seiler *Zs. f. dt.
Phil.* XLVIII (1919—20) 83 no. 30; Otto 1216; Quitard
549; Lean II 695; Haeckel 95; Apperson 438; Skeat 231;
Stoett 1641; Polites II 181—5; Sheldon *Studies in Phil.*
XV (1918) 5.

»Nay, stay», quoth Stringer when his **neck** was in the
halter 210

Marvin *Curiosities* 50.

To look for a **needle** in a haystack 190

Apperson 440.

Nene and Welland Shall drown all Holland 133

Apperson 441.

To feather one's nest 190
    Apperson 207.
        Nest *see* bird.
        Net *see* fishing.
        Never *see* late.

Don't take any wooden **nickels** 12

Night is the mother of counsel 147
    Apperson 445; Wander »Nacht» 38; *see* notte (Italian).

To have him in the **nine-hole** 189

To set the **North River** on fire 188
    Apperson 622; *Notes and Queries* Series 8th Ser. VII
69; *Reader's Digest* (March 1930) p. 1051.

When the black fleet of **Norway** is come and gone, Eng-
    land, build houses of lime and stone, For afterwards
    you shall have none 133
    Apperson 184; Northall 3.

Don't cut off your **nose** to spite your face 12
    Apperson 131; Stoett 1631.

Nothing venture, nothing win 143
    Apperson 454; Stoett 2503.

To put in an **oar** 190
    Apperson 461.

To feel his **oats** 190
    Borchardt-Wustmann 172; Stoett 369; Apperson 515
(»provender pricks him»); Lean III 333.
        Oats *see* debtors.

To pour **oil** on troubled waters 190
    Apperson 463.

As old as **Methuselah** 221
    Stoett 1734.

You can't make **omelettes** without breaking eggs 37
    Büchmann 477; Apperson 468; Polites II 595—6.

One boy's a boy, two boys is half a boy, three boys is no
   boy at all 12
      One man *see* team.
      Open *see* eyes.
      Out *see* down.
The black **ox** hath not trod on her foot 77
      Apperson 52; Tilley 41; Marvin *Curiosities* 61; Polites
III 200—1 no. 45; Schoppe *Mitt. d. schles Ges. f. Vk.*
XXIX (1928) 300; Wander II 1687 »Kuh» *521, *595;
III 1108 »Ochs» *350, *360, *361.
To mind your **P's** and Q's 194
      Lean III 320; *Atlantic Monthly*, Nov. 1929, Feb.
1930; Appersson 481.
Paddle your own canoe 12
      Jente *Aserican Speech* VII 346.
To **paint** the town red 192
      Crane »Painting the town red» *Scientifis Monthly*
XVIII (1924) 605—15.
Children are found in the **parsley** bed 132
      Apperson 483.
Parsley fried will bring a man to his saddle and a
   woman to her grave 127
      Bohn 30; Apperson 483; Harrebomée I xvi, 6 »aarde»
15.
To **pass** out 200
      Pass *see* buck.
It **pays** to advertise 12
»All's well that ends well», said the **peacock** when he
   looked at his tail 210
      Apperson 9.
To cast **pearls** before swine 30,186
      Matth. 7: 6; Suringar *Erasmus* 198; Stoett 1761;
Borchardt-Wustmann 360; Bolte *Zs. d. Ver. f. Volksk.*
XXV (1915) 301 no. 29; Apperson 488; Jente 255.
Cf. »roozen» (Dutch).

Pedley *see* fool.

To **pipe** in an ivy leefe 193
    Chaucer *Troilus* V 1434; *Knight's Tale* 980; Haeckel
189; Apperson 497; Skeat 204.
Pity is akin to love 147
    Apperson 499.
A **place** for everything and everything in its place 8
    Apperson 499.
To walk the **plank** 189
    Lean III 356.
      Plowden *see* case.
Politics make strange bedfellows 12, 20
    Cf. »poverty».
As **poor** as Job's turkey 223
    Wilstack *Dictionary of Similes* (1917) 298.
Possession is nine (var.: eleven) points of the law 94
    Bohn 125; Apperson 507.
To be left at the **post** 189
    N. E. D.
      Post *see* pillar.
The **pot** calls the kettle black 13, 158, 170
    Lean IV 127, 135; Apperson 507; Harrebomée III
223; Lauchert 32; Stoett 1870.
The **pot** goes so often to the well (water, stream) that it
    comes home broken 24
    Proverbia communia 42.
      Pottage *see* weed.
      Pour *see* heart.
Poverty makes strange bedfellows 20
    Apperson 508—9; Jente 236.
      Praise *see* day.
      Preach *see* ears.
      Pretzel *see* crooked.
      Prick *see* thorn.
Pride goes before a fall 55
    Müllenhoff and Scherer II (1892) 139 no. 24; Len-

Seiler *Lehnspr.* V 225; cf. Apperson 524.

The **raven** said to the rook, »Stand away, black coat» 158
Apperson 525.

Read 'em and weep 12

No **receiver**, no thief 92
Apperson 525; Lean IV 63, 152; cf. hailer.

As **red** as blood 223
Zingerle *Germania* IX (1864) 398—9; cf. Wilstack
315; Apperson 526.

Red *see* paint.

To be caught **redhanded** 188
Hyamson 291.

Verify your **references** 37, 38
Lean III 416; Benham 441 a.

Three **removes** are worse than a fire 37, 175
Borchardt-Wustmann 3; Quitard 294; Apperson 629;
Büchmann 307; Stoett 2363.

Right wrongs no man 88
Trench 9 (ed. A. S. Palmer, 8); Apperson 532.

To **ring** true 191
Hyamson 294; N.E.D.

To read him the **Riot Act** 192
Compare »iemand metten lesen» (Stoett 1510 cf.
1081); »Kapitel lesen» (Borchardt-Wustmann 240); »Le-
viten lesen» (Schrader *Bilderschmuck* 401 no. 81).

It's a long **road** that has no turn 13
Apperson 379.

To rule the **roast** 190
Apperson 540; N. E. D. »roast» n. 1 b; G. Harvey's
Letter-Book (ed. Scott) p. 51; Hazlitt *Early Eng. Pop.
Poetry* IV 65; Watson (ed. Arber) p. 82; Gascoigne (ed.
Hazlitt) I 53; Earle *Microcosmographie* 25.

Rob *see* Peter.

Robbery *see* exchange.

Rock *see* hard.

Spare the **rod** and spoil the child 143
    Apperson 592 —3; Seiler *Zs. f. dt. Phil.* XLVIII (1919
—20) 82 no. 10, 85 no. 51.
To have a **rod** in pickle 192
    Apperson 536.
        Rolling *see* stone.
When in **Rome**, do as the Romans do 40
    Tilley 522 (St. Augustine *Letters* 36, 32); Apperson
537.
Rome was not built in a day 25, 51
    Proverbia communia 152.
To rule the **roost** 190
    Cf. »roast».
Root, hog, or die 90
        Rule *see* exception.
Rum, Romanism, and Rebellion 85
    Bartlett *Quotations* (1898) 679.
To be out of the **running** 189
    N. E. D. »running» 2 e.
To give him the **sack** (in England, bag) 192
    Apperson 23. An apprentice carries his belongings in
a sack.
No sooner **said** than done 61
    Seiler *Lehnsprichwort* V 232; Apperson 543.
To **sail** close to the wind 190
    Hyamson 341; N.E.D.
Young **saint**, old devil 16, 17, 19, 143, 144
    Apperson 720; Lenschau 20; Seiler *Zs. f. dt. Phil.*
XLVII (1916—8) 249 no. 68; Kock and Petersen II 296;
Harrebomée III 172—3.
To eat **salt** with 59
    Polites II 299 –303; cf. I 436—40.
It will be all the **same** in a hundred years 169
    Apperson 7.
To build on **sand** 185

Matth. 7: 26; cf. Apperson 71.
    Saved *see* penny.
    Say *see* do.
To turn the scales 191
    Hyamson 306.
To throw on the scrapheap 190
    N.E.D.
To have a screw loose 190
    Hyamson 309.
To put the screws on 188
    L. Günther *Deutsche Rechtsaltertümer* 71 n. 104;
Stoett 513; de Cock *Oude gebruiken*² 79 no. 164.
Seeing is believing 8
    Apperson 556.
    Sell *see* America.
    Served *see* first.
Service is no heritage 93
    Proverbia communia 388.
    Shame *see* pride.
    Shape *see* way.
    Share *see* lion.
To cast sheep's eyes on 192
    Apperson 563.
To lay on the shelf 190
    Hyamson 313.
    Sheep *see* hanged.
Shibboleth 108
    Judges 12: 6; Stoett 1992.
Three generations from shirtsleeves to shirtsleeves 11
    Cf. Apperson 102; Lean IV 152.
    Shod *see* cobbler.
The wearer knows best where the shoe wrings (var.:
    pinches) him 5
    Proverbia communia 337.
The shoe will hold with the sole 14

Apperson 565.

Shoemaker *see* last.

To talk **shop** 191

Hyamson 315.

To give the **show** away 191

Sight *see* rain.

Silence gives consent 93, 95

Tilley 560; Apperson 571; Chaisemartin 256 —7; Büch-
mann 416; W. Girardet *Die Bedeutung des Schweigens bei
Vertragsschlüssen* (Diss. Marburg 1927) p. 24; Williams
Law Magazine and Law Review 4th Ser. XX (1895) 289;
Stoett 2688.

Sin *see* cold.

It's **six** of one and half a dozen of the other 130

Apperson 575.

To be at **sixes** and sevens 192

Skeat 190; Jente 285; Lean III 306; Apperson 575;
Haeckel 175; Gomme, *The Gentleman's Magazine Library* 335. Cf. Stoett 2393.

That's no **skin** off my elbow 130

To sell the **skin** before you have caught the bear 187

Wesselski *Erlesenes* 88—97.

Every man must **skin** his own skunk 12

If the **sky** falls, we shall have larks 74, 77

Seiler *Sprw.* 85, *Zs. f. dt. Phil.* XLV (1913) 254 no.
84, XLVII (1916—8) 385 no. 19, *Lehnspr.* V 168; cf.
Otto 286; Proverbia communia 737 —740; Apperson 576.

Sleep is the brother of death 145

Seiler *Lehnspr.* V 237; Harrebomée II 270.

Anhour's **sleep** before midnight is worth two after 124

Bohn 28; Apperson 577.

Six hours **sleep** for a man, seven for a woman, and eight

for a fool 124

Lean IV 95; Apperson 577.

Sleeve *see* ace.

You never miss a slice from a cut loaf 12, 168
     Apperson 565; Jente 279.
         Slip *see* cup.
         Slow *see* steady.
There is no **smoke** without fire (var.: Where there's
     smoke, 13, 149 there's fire) 13, 149
     Otto 848; Apperson 582; Altenkirch 339 no. 14.
A **smoke**, a storme, and a contentious wife etc. 161
         Smoke *see* pipe.
A **snake** in the grass 64
     Seiler *Lehnsprichwort* V 237; Apperson 583; Harrebo-
mée III 284; Stoett 51; Otto p.; Jente 291. Van Duyse
(*Belgisch Museum* V (1841) 197) thinks the phrase is
derived from Gen. 3.
         Snowball *see* chance.
To be up to **snuff** 192
     Hyamson 321.
         Soft *see* answer, fire.
         Song *see* buy.
To touch a sore **spot** 185
     Otto 1810; Seiler *Lehnspr.* V 282; Stoett 2399, 2631.
Sorrow is laughter's daughter 148
     Lean IV 98.
         Sour *see* grapes.
To be **soused** 200
The still **sow** eats up all the draff 13
     Proverbia communia 464.
         Sow *see* Backare.
To call a **spade** a spade 192
     Lean III 292; Apperson 592. Cf. »gatta» (Italian).
To put a **spoke** in his wheel 190, 195
     Lean III 338; Apperson 597; L. P. Smith 244—5;
Stoett 2108; Harrebomée II 282. It is illustrated in
Breughel's painting (see *The Proverb* p. 182).
To throw up the **sponge** 189

Hyamson 325.

To be born with a silver **spoon** in his mouth 198
    Apperson 572.
        Spoon *see* Devil.
        Spur *see* horse.

To have little (var.: nothing) at **stake** 189
    N.E.D. stake *see* throw.

To be born under a lucky **star** 197
    Stoett 670; Hyamson 327.
        Stay *see* neck.

Steady and slow go far in a day 9,   13
    Compare: Soft and fair goes far (Apperson 585;
    Polites I 141—4).

Better **steal** a horse than stand by and look on   92
    Lean III 431; Apperson 601.

To blow off **steam** 190
To stand **steel** 189
To **steer** clear of 190
Watch your **step** 10
To **step** on it 190
        Stern chase *see* chase.
        Stick *see* tarred.
        Still *see* waters.

A **stitch** in time saves nine 14
    Apperson 603; Wood *Folk-Lore* V (1894) 254 no. 163.
        Stomach *see* eyes.

A rolling **stone** gathers no moss   44
    Skeat 103; Martin 31 no. 103; Quitard 545; Alten-
    kirch 342 no. 25; Apperson 537; Suringar *Erasmus* 202;
    Fecunda ratis 182; Stoett 2164; Publius Syrus 524 (Bart-
    lett *Quotations* [1898] 711); Apostolius (ed. 1653) X 72.

To sit between two **stools** 170, 186
    Seiler *Zs. f. dt. Phil.* XLVIII (1919—20) 88 no. 8;
    Bolte *Zs. d. Ver. f. Volksk.* XXV (1915) 300 no. 10; Bor-

chardt-Wustmann 468; Wood *Folk-Lore* V (1894) 238 no.
23; Stoett 2178; Fecunda ratis 175.

The **stork** 132
> *Handwörterbuch des deutschen Aberglaubens* I col.
1010; *Schweizer Volkskunde* III (1913) 77.
>> Storm *see* calm.

To draw the short **straw** 189
> Richter 117; Stoett 543.
>> Straw *see* drowning.

To have two **strikes** on him 189
> Strike *see* iron.
> Sun *see* blessing, bride, hay.

A **Sunday** journey is not good (Irish) 71
> O'Rahilly 280.
>> Supper *see* dinner.

One **swallow** does not make a summer 19, 29, 61
> Apperson 612; Wood *Folk-Lore* V (1894) 257 no. 188;
Seiler *Lehnsprichwort* V 241; Martin 24 no. 25; Lenschau
Anhang 2; Büchmann 334; Reinsberg-Düringsfeld I no.
377; Krumbacher 206 no. 83; Harrebomée II 146, III
415; Wander IV 412 no. 12; Stoett 1265; Aristotle Eth.
1. 7. 15.

Sweep in front of your own door 14
> Apperson 613; Stoett 1836.
>> Swine *see* pearls.
>> Swiss *see* money.
>> Sword *see* three.

Tace is Latin for candle 75
> Apperson 616; Lean II 697; Hazlitt 398; Benham
135ᵃ und note.

To turn **tail** 189
> Hyamson 336.

»Mair haste, the less speed», quo' the wee **tailor** to the
> long thread (Gaelic) 213
> Marvin *Curiosities* 35.

It takes nine **tailors** to make a man 105
 Apperson 446.

The **tailor** cuts three sleeves for every woman's gown ... 105
 Apperson 616; Feilberg *Bidrag* III 326 »skrædder».
 Tails *see* heads.

Take while the taking is good 130
 Tales *see* dead men.

A **taleteller** is worse than a thief 97
 Lean III 405; Apperson 619.

To be **tarred** with the same stick (var.: brush) ... 188, 190
 Hyamson 337.

One man does not make a **team** 19, 20

To be all **teed** up 200

You never can **tell** till you've tried 8, 151
 Test *see* acid.

As **thick** as hops 223
 Apperson 623.

Set a **thief** to catch a thief 9
 Apperson 624.
  Thief *see* hailer, receiver, taleteller.
  Things *see* end, friends.

To be a **thorn** in the flesh 185
 Numbers 33: 55; Stoett 468.

It pricketh betimes that will be a sharp **thorn** 18
 Lean III 452; Apperson 511; Jente 313.

The **thought** is father (var.: parent of) to the deed 148
 Attributed to Carlyle; cf. Wood *Dict. of Quotations*
(1912) 457.

As **thrang** as Throp's wife 222
 Apperson 631; *Notes and Queries* 8th Ser. i, 12, 9th
Ser. v, 415, 526.

To hang by a **thread** 186
 Seiler *Lehnspr.* V 127; Stoett 481.

Three things are thrown away in a bowling green, namely,
 time, money, and oaths 161

Apperson 629; Scott *Fortunes of Nigel* ch. xii.

Three things drive a man out of his house: smoke, rain,
and a scolding wife .... 40, 50, 58, 160, 161, 163.

Apperson 582, 629—30; Altenkirch 331 no. 29; Lauchert 6, 16; Polites III 457—8, IV 56—8, 225—6; O'Rahilly 263; [London] *Times Literary Supplement* Apr. 24,
1930; A. de Cock *Vrouwen* (1911) 57; R. Köhler *Kleinere
Schriften* II 127; Taylor »Sunt tria damna domus» *Hessische Blätter f. Volksk.* XXIV(1925) 139—46; Jente 290.

Three things are insatiable, priests, monkes, and the sea 162
Apperson 629.

There be **three** things that never comes to no good:
Christmas pigs, Michelmas fowls, and parson's daugh-
ters 161
Apperson 630.

Three things a man lendeth not rife, His horse, his
fighting sword, his wife 162
Apperson 360; Harrebomée III 125; Polites I
589—92.

To **stake** everything on one throw 189
N. E. D.

No **tickee,** no washee 11

There is a **time** for everything 6
Proverbia communia 63.

Time and tide wait for no man............................ 159
Apperson 634.

Time is money
Apperson 634; Büchmann 351; Stoett 647.

Toad *see* masters.

Either the **tod** (fox) or the bracken bush.................. 129
Tilley 265; Apperson 233.

The **tongue** breaketh bone, though itself have none 58
Apperson 638; Seiler *Lehnspr.* V 286; Polites IV
31—33.

A man gave another an ass (and perhaps a horse) and
  he looked at its **teeth** .... (modern Greek) 158
  Krumbacher (1893) 23.
Quickly **too'd** (i.e. toothed) and quickly go, Quickly will
  thy mother have moe 126
  Apperson 588; Northall 497.
To put the finishing **touches** to a thing 190
To kick over the **traces** 190
  Hyamson 346.
       Trail *see* herring.
To fall into a **trap** 189
By **Tre**, Pol and Pen, you shall know the Cornish men ... 106
  Apperson 645; Bohn 200; Lean I 49; Northall 12.
The **tree** is known by its fruit 123
  Proverbia communia 299.
       Tree *see* cammock.
Truth is the daughter of time 147
  Apperson 650; Suringar *Bebel* 134; Hulme 22; *see*
»veritas» (Latin).
Truth will out 142
  Jente 327; Apperson 651.
I'll **try** anything once 168
       Try *see* tell.
Every **tub** must stand on its own bottom 13
  Apperson 193.
To change one's **tune** 190
  Hyamson 349.
       Turk *see* grass.
To risk (stake) everything on the **turn** of a card 189
       Turn *see* road.
It's **twenty** minutes past 130
       Turnip *see* blood.
       Two *see* tveir (Icelandic).
       Unlicked *see* cub.
Uphill spare me, / Downhill ware (var.: forbear) me,

Plain way (var.: level ground) spare me not, Nor let
me drink when I am hot 127
      Bohn 549; Northall 504; variants from oral tradition.
            Venture *see* nothing.
            Verify *see* references.
Vinegar catches no flies 10
      Wander I, 899 Essig no. 16. Cf. Apperson 220.
To be full of **vinegar** 185
      Otto 9; *Archiv f. lateinische Lexikographie* IV (1887)
353; Wander »Grütze» 17.
To nurse a **viper** in one's breast 31
      Otto 1903; Apperson 663.
To make a **virtue** of necessity 186
      Borchardt-Wustmann 345; Haeckel 96; Stoett 1644;
Polites II 190—92; Jente 245; Apperson 663.
Everything comes to him who **waits** 9
      Lean III 415; Longfellow *Tales of a Wayside Inn*,
»Student's Tale,» last line.
            Walk *see* plank.
To give him his **walking papers** 197
      Cf. »Iemand sijn pasport geven» (Stoett 1783).
            Wall *see* weakest.
Walls have ears 142
      Jente 331; Apperson 665—6; Singer 66; Stoett 1581;
cf. Suringar *Bebel* 102.
            Walls *see* hunger.
To go on the **warpath** 191
      N. E. D.
It will all come out in the **wash** 169
      Compare *Todo saldra en la colada* (Cervantes *Don
Quijote* I c. xx, xxii, II c. xxxvi).
            Wash *see* hands.
            Waste *see* haste.
»If this be human, it's light», as the **waterhorse** said
(Gaelic) 213

Still **waters** run deep 141
    Apperson 602; Altenkirch 328 no. 19; Stoett 2531.
      Waters *see* fishing.
The longest **way** round is the shortest way home 143
    Proverbia communia 321.
In any **way**, shape, or manner (var.: form) 90
The **weakest** goes to the wall 75
    Apperson 671; Lean IV 211; *Atlantic Monthly*
CXLIV (1929) 710; Jente 336; Tilley 674. Cf. Apperson
363. »Lie» 6.
One ill **weed** marreth a whole pot of pottage 13, 170
    Tilley 96; Apperson 429, 471; Polites II 200—3. Cf.
Proverbia communia 329; »peor» (Spanish); Lean IV 132;
Suringar *Bebel* 66; Suringar *Zs. f. dt. Phil.* XLVII
(1916—8) 385 no 20.
If you want a thing **well done**, do it yourself 6, 8
    Hazlitt 253.
      Well *see* begun, peacock.
To go **West** 192
    Hyamson 358.
To put one's shoulder to the **wheel** 190
    Hyamson 315.
To hold the **whiphand** 189
    Hyamson 358.
To **whistle** for 196
    N. E. D.
      Whistling *see* girl.
As **white** as chalk, ermine, a sheet, silver, snow, a swan 223
    Wilstack 470—4; Zingerle *Germania* IX (1864) 387—
90; Polites II 558—9.
»Give her her will or she will burst», quoth the good man,
    when his **wife** was dinging him 217
    Lean II 744.
      Wife *see* cobbler.
Where there's a **will**, there's a way 149

Apperson 687.

God tempers the **wind** to the shorn lamb 37
    Lean III 474, IV 254; Apperson 253.

When the **wind** in in the east, It is good for neither man
    nor beast 111
    Apperson 691; Northall 468—9.

To sow the **wind** and reap the whirlwind 60
    Hosea 8:7; Otto *Archiv f. lat. Lex.* VI (1889) 12.
        Wind *see* sail.

To **wind** him around your little finger 188
    Hyamson 143; Stoett 2409.

To be three sheets in the **wind** 200
    Hyamson 313.

Good **wine** needs no bush 67
    Jente 350; Tilley 686; Apperson 264; Stoett 2572;
Suringar *Erasmus* 237; Bolton »The Vintner's Bush»
Journal of American Folk-lore XV (1902) 40-44; Bolte's
note (p. 200 n. 2) to Andrea »Der grüne Wirtshauskranz»
Zeitschrift des Vereins f. Volkskunde XVII (1907) 195ff.

To clip his **wings** 190
    Hyamson 361.

A green **winter** (war.: Christmas) makes a fat churchyard 126
    Apperson 98.

A live **wire** 190
        Wisdom *see* experience.
        Wit *see* head.

My **withers** are unwrung 131
    Shakespere *Hamlet* III ii 252; Jente 93.

They brought the **wolf** to school and read »A, B, C» to
    him; but he said, »Lamb, she-goat, kid.» (Arabic)... 156
    Altenkirch 322 no. 4; Krumbacher 211 no. 95.
Compare In discendo lupus nimis affirmans ait »Agnus»
(Müllenhoff and Scherer I 62 no. 85; Wadstein *Bidrag
til kännedom om de svenska landsmålen och svenskt folk-
liv* XI (1895 —8) no. 6 p. 63; Kock and Petersen II 370).

A **woman,** a dog, a walnut tree, The more they are bea-
ten, the better they be 73
Tilley 578; Reinsberg-Düringsfeld *Spriv.* II 176 no.
314; Lauchert 16; Northall 515—6; Apperson 703.
»Farewell, dear light», said the lustful old **woman** as she
undressed and put out the light (Greek) 203
His **word** is as good as his bond 93
Apperson 710.
Words *see* bargain.
Those who will not **work** shall not eat 90
Marvin *Curiosities* 134; Apperson 711; Stoett 2557.
Work *see* nailer.
The **worst** is yet to come 169
Cf. Singer 393 no. 33.
Wrath *see* answer.
Two **wrongs** don't make a right 88
Apperson 657.
A **year** and a day 89
Richter 97; Stoett 1006; *Woordenboek d. ndl. Taal*
VII (1913) col. 39.
What **your's** is mine and what's mine is my own 130
Jente 234; Tilley 445; Lean II 752.

BOHEMIAN

Když **ovce** pošly i kozy ke čti přišli 155
Tři a třicet etc. 108
Strč brk etc. 108

DANISH.

»De' er ein Dag forseint», sa **Enkjan,** daa Drengen friade
till henne i Gravölet (ho hadde lovat han, so gjorde
Likkistan) 216
Cederschiöld 13.
Jo nærmere **kirken,** jo senere dertil 21
Mau 4576; Wander »Kirche» 99.

DUTCH

Weten wel waer **Abraham** de mostaerd haelt 195
 See Barthel (German).

Acht is meer dan duizend 154
 Stoett 45.

Men nighet den **boom**, daer men die bate af havet 76
 Proverbia communia 486.

»Kwaad gezelschap», zei de **dief**, en hij ging tusschen den
 beul en eenen monnik naar de galg 217
 Harrebomée I 51.

De **dominé** gaat voorbij 130
 Stoett 443; *see* Engel, Leutnant. Cf. de Cock *Oude*
*gebruiken*² 273 no. 507.

Op **Driekoningendag** zijn de dagen een hanengekraai
 gelongen 117
 Beirens *Nederlandsch tijdschrift voor volkskunde*
XXIX (1924) 35—36.

De **gekken** grijsen niet, maar de ezels worden grijs ge-
 boren 128
 Hentig *Archiv f. Kriminologie* LXXX (1927) 138.
 Gent *see* Keulen.

God es boven al 8
 Proverbia communia 352; *see* God.

God wolts is alder bede moeder 148
 Proverbia communia 354.

Keulen (war.: Gent) en Aken zijn niet in eed dag gebouwd 25
 Proverbia communia 152; *see* »Rome».

»Geeft tijd», zei **Koekkenbakker** 214
 Harrebomée I 28 »bakker»; III 114; Tuinman I
64—5.

»Alles met matn», zei de **kleermaker** (var.: snijder), en
 hij sloeg zijn vrouw met de el 159

Harrebomée I 10 (*s. v.* achterste); Hesseling *De Gids* LXVI, pt. 4 (1902) 94; de Cock *Vrouwen* 253.

Ledigheid is hongers moeder en van dieverij een broeder. 147
Harrebomée I 92; Marvin *Curiosities* 263; Polites II 430—3.

De **mensch** wikt, maar God beschikt 154
Harrebomée I 241.

Niet is voor die oogen goed, maer quaad voor de tanden 80
See nichts.

Iemand zijn **pasport** geven 197
Stoett 1783; oe Cook *Vrouwen* 135 no 259.

Zoo nader den **paeus,** so quader kersten 21
Proverbia communia 798; Stoett 1787.

Die **quade** schuwet dat licht als die duvel dat cruce 54
Proverbia communia 209; *see* evil.

Als 't **regent** en de zon schijnt, dan is het kermis in de hel 71
See Devil.

Als het **regent** en de zon schijnt, bakken de heksen pannekoeken 71
See Devil.

Roozen strooien voor de varkens 186
See pearls.

Er is eene **spaak** in het wiel gestoken 195
Stoett 2108; *see* spoke.

Op St. **Thomas** lengen de dagen 116
Beirens *Ndl. tijdschr. v. uolksk.* XXIX (1924) 32.

Voorzichtigheid is de moeder der wijsheid 148
Stoett 2474.

Zijn niet alle **vrienden,** die hem toelachen 19
Proverbia communia 721.

FRENCH

Amour et mort, rien n'est plus fort 153
See amor.

L'âne convié aux noces eau ou bois y doit aporter 157

LeRoux de Lincy I 139, II 342; *see* ass (Arabic).

»**L'appetit** vient en mangeant», dit Angestrom, »et la soif en buvant.» 211
   Rabelais *Garguantua* I ch. v; LeRoux de Lincy II 185; Büchmann 270.

Ce n'est plus le temps, que **Berthe** filoit 155
   See »Bertha» (German).
      Beurre *see* pain.

Chair fait chair, poisson poison 124

Un **chien** regarde bien un éveque.......................... 43
   Quitard 224; *see* cat.

La **défiance** est mère de sûrété 148

Le **diable** marie sa fille 70
   See Devil.

Disne honnestement et soupe sobrement, Dors en haut et vivras longuement 126

L'ennui est mère de toutes les vices 147
   Quitard 570; Apperson 322; cf. »Trunkenheit ist die Mueter aller Sünden» *Niemand und Jemand* (Graz 1608) in W. Flemming *Dae Schauspiel der Wanderbühne* (Leipzig 1931) 83 line 17; Polites II 430—3.

L'état c'est moi 39

Filer à l'anglaise 192
   Gottschalk 428.

La belle **France** 100

Fromage et pain est médécine au sain 125
   LeRoux de Lincy II 197.

Cil qui mange du **fromage,** Sil ne le fait, il enrage 125
      Fromage *see* pain.

Laissez faire à **George,** il est homme d'âge 9
   Quitard 423; LeRoux de Lincy II 3.

Lait sur vin est venin, Vin sur lait est souhait 123
   LeRoux de Lincy II 199; Quitard 696.

A la saincte **Luce,** Le jour croist le saut d'une puce 117
   Le Roux de Lincy I 12.

Mort *see* amour.

Les **morts** ont toujours tort 152
  LeRoux de Lincy II 333.

Un **oeuf** n'est rien, deux font grand bien, Trois est assez,
  quatre est trop, Cinq donnent la mort 124

Mieux vaut en paix un **oeuf**, qu'en guerre un boeuf 152
  See Ei.

Pain et beurre et bon fromage Contre la mort est le vray
  targe 125
      Pain *see* fromage, bread.
      Paix *see* oeuf.

Poisson sans boisson est poison 125
  Poisson *see* chair.

»Oh! Oh!» dit le **portugais** 211
  A. van Gennep *Mercure de France* CLXXVIII (1925)
  79.

Faire **promener** 197
      Salade *see* vin.
      Sûreté *see* défiance.
      Temps *see* Berthe.

»Faut pas cracher sur la **vendange**», dit le paysan 211
      Vice *see* ennui.

Qui *vin* ne boit après salade Est en danger d'être malade 126
      Vin *see* lait.
      Vivre *see* disner.

GERMAN

  Abend *see* morgen, Tag.

Wo der **Abt** Würfel auslegt, ist's dem Konvent erlaubt
zu spielen 78
  Proverbia communia 101.

»Ei, wer mochte das nicht», sagte der **Abt** von Posen ... 220
      Seiler *Lehnspr.* VIII 15; Harrebomée III p. xcix.

Auch rote **Äpfel** sind wurmstichig 32
      Skeat 284; Wander »Äpfel» 6; Kopp *Ein Sträusschen*

Bier *see* Wein.

Borghard ist Lehnhards Knecht 142
    Wander I 433.
    Braut *see* Glück.

Seine Schiffe hinter sich **brennen** 198
    See bridges.
        Nä, nich und jawol
        Is *Brôkmer* Prôtcoll.
        Nee, niet und jawall.
        Seggen de Krummhörners all 105
    J. F. de Vries and T. Focken *Ostfriesland* (Emden
1881) 161.

Ich bin **dein**, Du bist mein 90
    Bolte and Polívka *Anmerkungen* II 58; *Anzeiger f.*
deutsches Altertum VI (1880) 151, XVII (1891) 343, XIX
(1893) 94; *Alemannia* IX (1881) 55; *Zeitschrift des
Vereins f. Volkskunde* IV (1894) 13, XXVI (1916) 411;
Winterfeld *Archiv f. das Studium der neueren Sprachen*
CXIV (1905) 297; *Hessische Blätter f. Volkskunde* II (1903)
170; *Zeitschrift f. den deutschen Unterricht* XXV (1911)
239; Euling *Das Priamel* (Germanistische Abhandlungen
XXV) 29; Hildebrand *Materialien zur Geschichte des deut-
schen Volksliedes* I (*Zeitschrift f. den deutschen Unterricht,
Ergänzungsheft V*) 130; Weinhold *Die deutschen Frauen*
I 136; Koegel *Literaturgeschichte* I ii 387; Krainz *Mythen*
343 no. 265; Szklarek *Ungarische Märchen* II 285;
Schiller *Wallenstein: Piccolomini* III vi; Flemming *Schauspiel der Wanderbühne* (Leipzig, 1931) 275 (*Der Jude von
Venetien* V ix). Compare the Roman marriage formula,
»Ubi tu Gaius, ego semper Gaia» (Wordsworth *Fragments and specimens of early Latin* p. 5 n. 1; Plutarch c.
xxx; Gummere *Germanic origins* 158; Burton *Anatomy of
melancholy* Part III sec. ii subsec. 2).

Deutsche Treue 100

Die kleinen **Diebe** hängt man, die grossen lässt man
    laufen 62, 153
    Proverbia communia 274.
Drückeberger 141
    Borchardt-Wustmann 94.
Ehestand, Wehestand 153
    Wander »Ehestand» 19.
        Ehre *see* Feind.
Besser ein **Ei** im Frieden als ein Ochs im Kriege 152
    Polites IV 156—60.
        Ein *see* Mann.
Ein **Engel** flog durchs Zimmer 129
    Schweizer Volkskunde IV (1914) 95; *Grenzboten*
    LXIII 532—7; R. Koehler *Kl. Schriften* III (Berlin
    1900) 542—3 = *Germania* X (1865) 245—6; cf. domi-
    nie (Stoett 443).
Junger **Engel**, alter Teufel 16
    Lenschau 20.
Erbfeind 99
    Behrend »Im Kampfe mit dem Erbfeind» *Zeitschrift
    des Vereins f. Volkskunde* XXV (1915) 6—17, XXVI
    (1916) 72—76.
Es ist nichts so **fein** gesponnen, Es kommt doch endlich
    an die Sonnen 82
    Seiler *Zeitschrift f. deutsche Philologie* XLVII
    (1916—8) 245 no. 24; Lauchert 7—8.
Viel **Feind**, viel Ehr 144
    Heusler *Altgermanische Dichtung* (Handbuch der Li-
    teraturwissenschaft [Berlin 1923]) p. 68; Suringar, *Bebel*
    62.
Mein kleiner **Finger** hat es mir gesagt 131
    See Finger.
Flederwische feilhalten 192
    Borchardt-Wustmann 129—30.
Flöten gehen 196

Weise »In die Wicken gehen, flöten gehen und ver-
wandtes» *Zeitschrift f. hochdeutsche Mundarten* III (1902)
211—7; Stoett 573—4; Michels *Tijdschrift roor taal en
letteren* XI 85; Haupt *Am. Journal of Phil.* XLIII (1922)
241—3; de Vooys *De nieuwe taalgids* XXIV (1930) 47.
1911 ein **Flutjahr**, 1912 ein Blutjahr 133
     Frauen *see* Tag.
Twischen Paschen un Pingsten **fryen** die Unseligen ... 73
     Wander III 1187; see May.
Das ist ihm ein gefundenes **Fressen** 192
Es sind nicht alle **Freunde,** die einen anlachen 19
     Proverbia communia 721.
     Freunde *see* Wege.
In **Freeslauhn (Friesland)** itet man Brugge, gungt up
    Mühlen uhn hailt di Schaipen in di Sack 106
     Küffner 280 a-b.
     Fuchs *see* Barbati.
Eine jute jebratene **Jans (Gans)** ist eine jute Jabe
    Jottes 107
Fleugt ein **ganss** vber mer, so komt ein gagag wieder
    her 64
     Seiler *Zs. f. dt. Phil.* XLVIII (1919—20) 86 no. 59;
    Lehnspr. VI 20; cf. animus (Latin), Proverbia com-
    munia 482, 483, 484.
Kein **Geld**, kein Schweizer 84
     See money.
Viel **Geschrei** und wenig Ei 25
     Quoted from Abraham à Santa Clara; see Neubauer
    Zeitschrift des Vereins f. Volkskunde XIII (1903) 432.
Viel **Geschrei** und wenig Milch 25
     Neubauer *Zeitschrift des Vereins f. Volkskunde* XIII
    (1903) 432—4 (quoting Grimm *Deutsches Wörterbuch*
    »Geschrei»).
»Viel **Geschrei** und wenig Wolle», sagte der Teufel und
    schor sein Schwein 25, 219, 220

Richter 61; Neubauer *Zeitschrift des Vereins f.
Volkskunde* XIII (1903) 432—4; Borchardt-Wustmann
153—4; Apperson 432; Harrebomée I 156; Cederschiöld
31; Lean II 663, 744; Stoett 662; Gosson *School of Abuse*
(ed. Arber) 28; Green *Alphonsus* (ed. Collins) I 81; Seiler
Lehnspr. V. 23; Sparmberg *Zs. f. dt. Phil.* XLV (1913)
68; Dähnhardt *Natursagen* III 10; *Trans. of the Devonshire Assoc. for the Advancement of Science* XXX (1899)
325.

armen Judas zang geleerd» (van Duyse *Belgisch Museum*
V [1841] 455) seems to imply a misunderstanding, and
van Duyse's note is beside the point. Cf. *Zs. f dt. Wort-
forsch.* I (1901) 72.

Jung gefrait (gefreit), alt geklait (geklagt)................. 17
 Lenschau 20.

Jung gefreit, alt gereut 17, 18

Jung gefreut, alt gereut 17

Jung gewohnt, alt getan 17
 Lauchert 10.

Darf doch die **Katze** den Kaiser ansehen................. 42
 See cat.

Augen auf, **Kauf** ist Kauf 92
 Osenbrüggen *Die deutschen Rechtssprichwörter* 18.

Ein **Kaufmann** ist kein Schenkmann 139

Mit grossen Herren ist nicht gut **Kirschen** essen 30, 74
 See cherries.

Kleider machen Leute und Lumpen machen Leuss 26
 Lenschau 90; Seiler *Zeitschrift f. deutsche Philologie*
XLVIII (1919—20) 85 no. 55; *see* also clothes.

Kleider machen Leute und Pfaffen machen Bräute 26
 See the preceding.

Kleider machen Leute, Schuhe den Soldaten 27
 See the preceding.

Bis an't **Kni** is't fri 94
 Wander II 1430.

Es sind nicht alle **Köche**, die lange Messer tragen ... 18, 19
 Stoett 1223; Bernstein catalogue no. 3877.

Einen **Korb** bekommen (kriegen) 197
 Richter 114; Borchardt-Wustmann 266—7; Lauchert
24; Stoett 1248; J. W. Spargo *Virgil the Necromancer*
(1934) p. 184; C. R. Baskervill *The Elizabethan Jig* (1929)
261 n. 4; de Cock *Vrouwen* 135—6 no. 260—61.

Unter dem **Krummstab** ist gut wohnen 84
 Wander II 1649; Der Marner (ed. P. Strauch, 1876)
186.

Einen **Kuss** in Ehren kann niemand wehren 93,   94
  Winter 56; S(track) *Hessische Blätter f. Volkskunde* II
(1903) 175; Kopp *Euphorion* IX (1902) 286; Pistorius
Thesaurus paroemiarum (1716) I cent. 5 no. 25; Eisenhart *Grundsätze der deutschen Rechte* ([1] 1759) 445, [2] 1792
495.

Land und Leute   89
  Wander II 1774 no. 261.

Ein **Leutnant** bezahlt seine Schulden   130
    Liegen *see* Bärenhaut.
    Löwen *see* Hund.

Sankt **Luzen** macht den Tag stutzen   116
  Hellmann *Sitzungsberichte der Berliner Akademie,
phil.-hist. Klasse* 1923, p. 149; Bohn 38; Quitard 508.
Cf. Op St. Thomas lengen de dagen (Beirens *Nederlandsch tijdschr. voor volkskunde* XXIX [1924] 32).

Wes der **Magen** voll ist, läuft das Maul über   59
  Fischer *Schwäbisches Wörterbuch* IV (1914) 1388.

In **Maien** gehen Huren und Buben zur Kirche   73
  Wander III 346 no. 53; *see* also May.

Ein **Mann**, ein Wort   93
  Harrebomée III 288; Lauchert 15; Brunner, Wiener
Sitz.-ber. 57 (1867) 671; Stoett 1464.

Ein **Mann**, kein Mann 90,   93
  See testis.

Mann und Maus   89
  Stoett 1465.

Den **Mantel** nach dem Winde hängen 63, 151
  Proverbia communia 507.

Der **Mensch** denkt und Gott lenkt 56, 154
  See man.

Einen **Metzergang** machen...............................   195
  Schweizer Volkskunde XVII (1927) 21.

Mitgefangen, mitgehangen   92

Lenschau 51; Chaisemartin 489—91; Meissner *Sude-
tendt. Zs. f. Volkskunde* I (1928) 182.

Mitgegangen, mitgefangen, mitgehangen 92
    Wander III 678.

Mitgehanga, mitgefanga. 93

Möck, Mock und Uhl retteten Rottweil 85
    Seiler *Sprwk.* 31; Wander III 688.
        Reuen *see* jung.

Morgen rot, abend tot 119
    Cf. Harrebomée III 111, 166—7; Hildebrandsson
Antiqvarisk tidskrift för Sverige VII, 2, 17.
        Morgen *see* heute.

Morgenstunde hat Gold im Munde 48, 49, 69, 152
    Jente »Morgenstunde hat Gold im Munde» *Publica-
tions of the Modern Language Association of America*
XLII (1927) 865—72; Stoett 1555; *Taal en letteren* XIII
(1903) 370, 575.
        Most *see* Barthel.
        Mund *see* Herz.

Junge **Musikanten,** alte Beddellüde 16
    Lenschau 20; Wander III 787 no. 7.
        Nachrat *see* Vorrat.
        Name *see* Kind.

Narren soll man mit Kolben lausen 57
    Suringar *Bebel* 189; Lenschau 39; Seiler *Zeitschrift f.
deutsche Philologie* XLVII (1916—8) 245 no. 27; Richter
113; Zingerle 107; Lauchert 12; Zingerle *Germania* VII
(1862) 256.

Lange **Nase,** spitzes Kinn, Da sitzt der Teufel leibhaft
    drin 128
        Hentig *Archiv f. Kriminologie* LXXX (1927) 140;
Handwb. d. dt, Abergl. III col. 1251.

Was ein **Nessel** werden soll brennt beizeiten 18
    Seiler *Zeitschrift f. deutsche Philologie* XLVII (1916

—8) 251 no. 91; Tilley 91; Jente 313; Lenschau 6; Seiler *Sprwk.* 88; Polites I 258—60.

Nichts ist gut (var.: in) die Augen 79
  Seiler *Sprwk.* 118; Wander III 1017; Thiele *Luthers Sprichwörter* 43;Tuinman I 71; Kock and Petersen II 253.

Niederohme — Dreacksome, Habach — hat Kartoffel-
  saat, Ermerod — der Bär brummt, Elperod — die
  Kaffeestadt 101
  Schulte *Hessische Blätter f. Volkskunde* IV (1905) 147.

Nimmweg, Reissweg und Unrecht 140
  Wander III 1036.

Not kennt kein Gebot 152
  See necessity.

Nürnberger Witz, Strassburger Geschütz, Venetier
  Macht, Augsburger Pracht, Ulmer Geld, Wer dieses
  hätte, wäre reich in dieser Welt 103
  Uhl *Priamel* 421; Canzler u. Meissner *Für altere Literatur u. neuere Lit.* II (1784) 22 f. (Drittes Stück); Wesselski *Arlotto* II 228; Keil *Die deutschen Stammbücher*
  (Berlin 1893) 41—42.

Der **Ochse** fällt nicht vom ersten Streiche 20
  Lenschau 10.
      Paschen *see* freien.

Ein jeder **Pfaff** lobt sein Heiligtum 68
  Seiler *Sprwk.* 96; *Romulus* (ed. Oesterley) app. 36;
  Wander III 1228 no. 97.

Herr **Pfennig** geht voran 142
  Müllenhoff and Scherer *Denkmäler* II 141 no. 70;
  G. Rothe *Die Gedichte des Reimar von Zweter* (Leipzig
  1887) 589 (note on 61, 7); [Nuremberg] *Festschrift zur
  vierhundersten Geburtsfeier* (Nürnberg 1894) 179; R.
  Koch *Klagen mittelalterlicher Didaktiker* (Diss.; Göttin-
  gen 1931) 36—39; Oppenheim *Naturgefühl bei den frühen
  Meistersingern* (1930) 21.

Von **Pontius** zu Pilatus schicken 196

Borchardt-Wustmann 379; Stoett 1857, II 561; van
Duyse *Belgisch Museum* V (1841) 196; Polites II 377—8.

De **Preussen** hcbbet twei mâgen un kein harte 106
  Küffner 331.

Aus dem **Regen** in die Traufe 158
  Jente *Pub. Mod. Lang. Assoc.* XLVIII (1933)
  31—33; Stoett 1920.

Wenn es **regnet**, wird es nass 7,   33
  Seiler *Zs. f. dt. Phil.* XLVII (116—8) 253 no. 112;
  Lewalter and Schläger *Dt. Kinderlied* (1911) 285 no. 51;
  Müllenhoff and Scherer II 135 no. 9; Singer 410 no. 210;
  Festschrift zum 25. Jubiläum . . . Lemke (Stettin 1898),
  cf. Zs. d. Ver. f. Volksk. IX (1899) 103, XVII (1907)
  271 no. 12; F. Schwarz *A Soporoni Német Gyermekdal*
  (»Német philologiai dolgozatok» VII [Budapest 1913])
  50—51 no. 123.

»Es ist schlecht Wasser», sagte der **Reiher** und konnte
  nicht schwimmen 205
  Proverbia communia 664.

Der **Riese** Ragi auf dem Rathaus zu Bremen 107

Junger **Ritter**, alter Bettler 16
  Lenschau 20.

Reiner **Roggen**, Bremer Brot 107

Rotbart nie gut ward 70, 71, 128
  Lenschau Anhang 9; Suringar *Bebel* 36, 54; Baum
  »Judas' Red Hair» *Journ alof English and Germanic Philology* XXI (1922) 520—29; Apperson 527; de Cock
  Volkskunde XVIII (1906) 234—35, XXIII (1912) 143—
  44; *Volksgeloof* I 157—60; *Handwb. d. dt. Abergl.* III
  col. 1251.

Ein **roth bart** vnd bärtig Weib grüez von weitem 71
  See Rotbart.

Hüt dich dich eim **roten** Walhen, weissen Frantzosen
  und schwartzen Teutschzen 71
  Küffner 222 a, b, Suringar *Bebel* 45.

Im **Sack** kaufen 187
> Wander III 1821; *see* pig.

Sauf oder lauf 154
> Seiler *Lehnsprichwort* V 233; Suringar *Erasmus* 24;
Otto 253; Wander »saufen» 21.

> Schenkmann *see* Kaufmann.

Er stammt nicht aus **Schenkendorf**, sondern aus Greifswald 140
> Terner 30; Wander IV 144.

Schiffe hinter sich brennen 198
> *See* bridges.

> Schlagen *see* Hund.

Schlauberger (Schlaumeier) 141
> Wander IV 228.

Ein **Schwabe** hat kein Herz aber zwei Magen 106
> Küffner 380; cf. »Preusse».

Im **Schwabenalter** stehen 195
> *Schweizer Volkskunde* XVI (1926) 39—40.

> Schwarz *see* rot.

> Schweizer *see* Geld, money.

Junge **Soldaten**, alte Bettler 16
> Lenschau 20.

Junge **Späler** (Spieler), ole Bedler 16
> Lenschau 20.

Anna sass auf einem spitzen **Stein** 107

Der **Storch** hat der Mutter ins Bein gebissen 132
> *Schweizer Volkskunde* III (1913) 77.

> Streich *see* Baum, Ochs.

Mancher in den **Strick** selbst fällt, den andern hat gestellt 60
> Lenschau 108; Schulze p. 95; Otto 917; Otto *Archiv*
f. lateinische Lexikographie VI (1889) 19—20; Niewöh-
ner *Zeitschrift für deutsches Altertum* LXV (1928) 74;
Stoett 1299. Cf. Polites I 561—6.

»Das ist scharfer **Tabak**», sagte der Teufel 215
> Reuter *Werke* (ed. Seelmann) I 404—5; Borchardt-

Wustmann 469; Feilberg *Bidrag til en ordbog over jyske almuesmål* s.v. »tobak»; M. Busch *Deutscher Volkshumor*[2] (Leipzig 1877) p. 239 no. 3.

Man soll den **Tag** nicht vor dem Abend loben 151
   See day.

Schöne **Tage** soll man abends loben, schöne Frauen morgens 26, 178
   See day.

Die gebratenen **Tauben** fliegen niemand in den Mund ... 28
   Nahum 3: 12; Büchmann 91; Borchardt-Wustmann 471; Stoett 523.

Wo der **Teufel** nicht hinkommen kann, schickt er ein altes Weib (var.: seine Grossmutter) 24, 70
   Proverbia communia 161.

»Virtus in medio», sagte der **Teufel** und setzte sich zwischen zwei Priester 207, 217
   Seiler *Spricw.* 26; Seiler *Lehnsprichwort* VIII 16; cf.
Harrebomée I 166 = ten Dam *De dietsche Warande* IV (1858) 248 no. 509.
      Teufel *see* Engel, Geschrei.

Gegen den **Tod** ist kein Kraut gewachsen 123
   Harrebomée III 166; Stoett II 523 n. 1; *Fecunda ratis* I 725; Lauchert 14; de Cock *Volksgeloof* II 42—4 no. 290; *see* mors.

Ein **tôre** naeme des gouches sanc für den süezen harfen klanc 30
   Seiler *Spricw.* 29; Wesselski *Bebels Schwänke* II 36, 126 no. 81.
      Tot *see* morgen, rot.

Die **Toten** haben immer unrecht 152
   Wander IV 1254, no. 31.
      Traufe *see* Regen.

Trauwohl reitet das Pferd weg................................ 142
   Seiler *Spricw.* 157 n. 1; Suringar *Bebel* 304; Suringar *Erasmus* 79; Müllenhoff and Scherer *Denkmäler*[3] II 141 no. 70.

Das **Volk** dichtet   41
Voll, toll   144
    Wander IV 1682—3.
Vorrat ist besser als Nachrat   140
    Wander IV 1696.
Vorsicht ist die Mutter der Porzellankiste   148
    Wander IV 1700.
Alt **weg** und alt freundt soll man behalten   8
    Müllenhoff and Scherer II 138—9 no. 21; Seiler *Zs.*
f. dt. Phil. XLVII (1916—8) 387 no. 49; Kock and Peter-
sen II 262; Fecunda ratis 190.
So iz **wat** (weht), so uuagôt iz   8
    Müllenhoff and Scherer II 135 no. 10.
Wer nicht liebt **Wein**, Weib und Gesang, Der bliebt ein
    Narr sein Lebelang   39
    Büchmann 99.
Wein auf Bier, das rat ich dir; Bier auf Wein, lass das
    sein   123
    Wander V 105.
      Woche *see* Montag.
Ein **Wort**, kein Wort   93
    Chaisemartin 467—8; *see* testis.
Würden, Bürden   62
    Seiler *Zs. f. dt. Phil.* XLVIII (1919—20) 83 no. 27.
      Würfel *see* Abt.
      Wurmstichig *see* Apfel.
      Zeit *see* Bertha (German).
Zwêne sint eines her (M.H.G.) 7, 155
    Proverbia communia 703.
Auf keinen grünen **Zweig** kömmen   195
    Seiler *Spruck.* 235; Wesselski *Märchen* (Berlin 1925)
2111 n. 1; Günther *Dt. Rechtsaltertümer in uns. heuti-*
gen Spr. 39, 126 n.; Günther *Rect h u. Spr.* 117 f., 142;
Zingerle 60; Lauchert 31; Burdach *Ackermann aus Böh-*
men I (1917) 185 ff. (note on ch. 3: 15), cf. p. 191.

GREEK

Aix (var.: Ois) tēn makhairan 29
See also Fecunda ratis I 476; Böhtlingk Berichte üb.
d. Verh. d. k. sächs. Ges., phil.-hist. Kl. XLVII (1895)
1—15.
Gnōthi seauton 4, 38
See know.
Hoi megaloi **kleptai** ton mikron apagousi 62
See Dieb.
E pīthi ē apithi 154
See sauf.
Synalizomenos 59
Khrēmat' anēr 144
Attributed to Alcaeus; cf. Erasmus (1528) p. 563;
Burckhardt[2] p. 198 no. 680.
Kapoiou **kharisan** gomari kai to tērae 's ta dontia 158

ICELANDIC

Blindr er betri, en brendr sé 7
Bú er betra, þótt lítit sé 7
Dælt er heima hvat 7
At kveldi skal **dag** leyfa 150, 179
Verðr **eik** at fága, er undir skal búa 76
Gnyðia mundu nu **grisir**, ef þeir visse, hvat enn gamle
Eyldi 36
Halr er heima hver 90
»Opt verdr slíkt á sæ», kvad **selr**, var skotinn í auga ... 212
Tveir ro eins heriar 7
Heusler *Zeitschrift des Vereins f. Volkskunde* XXV
(1915) 114 no. 29; *see* zwei.

ITALIAN

Disputar dell' ombra dell' **asino** 185
Cagna frettolosa fa catellini ciechi 25
Wesselski *Poliziano* 190; Tilley 39; Altenkirch 17
no. 2; Lean III 391; Polites III 108; cf. bitch.

La **discrezione** è la madre degli asini 147
»Adagio», disse il **Fibbia** 211
    Wesselski *Poliziano* 216 no. 395.
La **donna** di buona razzia fa sempre la prima figliata
    femina 72
Un bel **fuggir** salva la vita ancora 37
Chiamar **gatta** gatta.. 192
    Wesselski *Poliziano* 213—4; Quitard 213; Winter 94.
Gatta frettolosa fa i gattini acerbi 25
    See cagna.
Un bel **morir** tutta la vita onora 36
La **notte** è madre de' pensieri................................ 147
    Wesselski *Poliziano* 223; *see* night.
»Saran quest' anno di molte pere», dicera **l'orso**, perchè
    n'harebbe volute 211
    Wesselski *Poliziano* 220.
Le **parole** son femine, e fatti som maschi 154
»Io non son **Pecorella** che perde il buccone per dire Umbè»   32
    Wesselski *Poliziano* 103 no. 209.
Non mi morse mai **scorpione,** che io non mi medicasse
    col suo olio 73
Tre cose inanimate sono più ferme che l'altre nel loro
    uso: il sospetto, il vento e la lealtà: il primo mai non
    entra in luogo, d'onde poi si parte, l'altro mai non
    entra, d'onde non vegga l'uscita, l'altra, d'onde un
    tratto si parte, mai non vi ritorna 162
Tutto fanno, niente sanno; Niente sanno, tutto fanno ... 100
»Pongli mente alli mani, e non a gli occhi», disse **l'ucel-**
    lino 32
    Wesselski *Poliziano* 236 no. 409.

LATIN

    Abire *see* bibere.
Actio est filia obligationis 147
    C. Thuriet *Proverbes judiciaires* 47 no. 144.
    Actus *see* exitus.

Aesop *see* asinus.

Alea jacta est 44
 See die.

Ubi **amici,** esse ibidem opes 148
 Otto 88; Suringar *Erasmus* 232.

Vitrei **amici** vitro sunt donandi 68
 Müllenhoff and Scherer II 137 no. 7; Singer 410
no. 217; *see* gläserner Ring.

Fortis ut mors dilectio **(amor)** 153
 Quitard 49.

Amore, more, ore, re firmantur **amicitiae** 154

Amoris vulnus idem sanat, qui facit 44
 Otto 101.

Nihil enim ad **Andromachen** 44
 Otto 106.

Qui tenet **anguillam** per caudem non habet illam ... 46, 47
 Altenkirch *Archiv f. slavische Philologie* XXX (1909)
349 no. 57; Müllenhoff and Scherer II 148 no. 192; Suringar *Erasmus* 54; Stoett 7; *Fecunda ratis* p. lxiv; Voigt
Ysengrimus I 334; Werner Q 140; de Cock *Vouwen* 127
no. 186.

Arbor per primum quaevis non corruit ictum 138
 Proverbia communia 200; *see* Baum.

Fructibus ipsa suis, quae sit, dignoscitur **arbor** 123
 Luke 6: 44; Matthew 7: 16; *Owl and Nightingale* (ed.
Atkins) 1, 135; C. Meaux Saint-Marc 179; Stoett 299.

Asinus de Aesopi puteo 29, 129
 Otto 185.

Asinus in tegulis 29
 Otto 186; Rose »Asinus in tegulis» *Folk-Lore* XXXIII
(1922) 34—56.

Auctoritas pontificis; sapientia regis (sc. Neapolis);
 potentia Venetorum; armia Mediolanensium; aurum
 Florentinum 103
 Wesselski *Arlotto* II 228 no. 94.

Auri natura non sunt splendentia plura 138
  Proverbia communia 623; *see* gold.
Campus habet oculos, silva **aures** 142
  See walls.
Aurora Musis amica 48
  See Morgenstunde.
Aurora, quid est aurum in ore 49
  See Morgenstunde.
Austria erit in orbe ultima 133
  Wander III 1159.
Crudelitatis mater **avaritia** est 146
  Otto 229.
Una **avis** in laqueo plus valet octo vagis 23
Caelum, non **animum** mutant, qui trans mare currunt 63
  Hor. Ep. 1. 11. 27; Otto 285.
Aut **bibat** aut abeat 154
  See sauf.
»Non nostrum», inquit, »onus», **bos** clitellas 204
  Otto 262.
Clitellae **bovi** sunt impositae, plane non est nostrum
  onus 31, 204
  Otto 262.
Luscus praefertur **caeco**, sic undique fertur 138
  Skeat 71; Kemble *Salomon and Saturnus* (1848)
p. 281.
Tanto plus **calidum**, quanto vicinius igni 21
  Fecunda ratis 378; *see* fire.
    Campus *see* oculus.
»Minime, sis» inquit, »**cantherium** in fossa» 204
  Livy 23: 40; Otto 336.
    Cauda *see* anguilla.
Caute, si non caste 9
  Apperson 92.
Certa amittimus, dum incerta petimus 28
  Otto 375.

Unus homo non facit **choream** 19
    Suringar *Bebel* 325; Lenschau Anhang 2; de Cock
Vrouwen 99 no. 33.
Non omnes, qui habent **citharam**, sunt citharoedi 18
    Seiler *Zeitschrift f. deutsche Philologie* XLVII (1916
—8) 389 no. 75.
Impransus non qui **civem** dinosceret hostes.............. 78
    Otto 391.
        Clamor *see* fur.
»Hercle hoc plus negoti est», inquit **coctio**, sex aediles
    viderat 203
    Otto 403; Seiler *Lehnsprichwort* VIII 7.
Post **coenam** stabis vel passus mille meabis.............. 122
    See dinner.
        Consentire *see* tacere.
Ex habitu **cordia** sonitus depromitus oris 57
Quod in **cordi**, hoc est in ore 57
Mendax **Creta** 99
    Otto 463.
Ubi **crux**, ibi lux.. 149
    Seiler *Sprichwörterkunde* 25.
        Crux *see* demon.
Ubi bona **custodia**, ibi bona pax............................ 149
    Suringar *Bebel* 464.
        Demon *see* evil.
        Deus *see* homo.
Quem **Deus** perdere vult, dementat prius 20
        Diana *see* rana.
Quem **dii** diligunt, adolescens moritur 20
    Plautus *Bacchylides* 816; Sophocles *Antigone* 632;
Apperson 254; Hoyt *New Encyclopedia of practical quota-*
tions pp. 396, 10; 397, 11. *See* Juppiter, pedagogus.
        Deus *see* pedagogus.
        Dies *see* day, vesper.
        Dilectio *see* amor.

Discretio mater virtutis 147
    Seiler *Zeitschrift f. deutsche Philologie* XLVIII (1919
—20) 82 no. 6.
Divide et impera 83
    Winter 52; Büchmann 452.
Qualis **dominus**, talis et servus 149
    See master.
Domus sua cuique est tutissimum refugium 90,   95
Duo sunt exercitus uni 7
    See zwei.
Caveat **emptor** 92
Errare est humanum 25
    See err.
Exceptio probat regulam 78
    See exception.
Exitus actus probat 41
    See end.
Qui **facit** per alium facit per se 96
    Williams *Law Magazine and Review* 4th Ser. XX 292.
Hiberno pulvere verno luto grandia **farra**, Camille, metes 114
    Macrobius *Sat.* V. 20. 18.
Saepe solet similis **filius** esse patri 123
    C. Meaux Saint-Marc 179.
Ubi mala **fortuna**, ibi mala fides 149
    Suringar *Bebel* 364.
Frisia non cantat 100
    Küffner 278.
Parvus pendetur **fur**, magnus abire videtur 138
    Proverbia communia 274; Suringar *Bebel* 428; *see*
Dieb.
Res miranda nova, picae **fur** abstulit ova 138
    Proverbia communia 185; Suringar *Bebel* 400.
Fures clamorem 144
    Erasmus *Adagia* (ed. 1528) p. 86; Wander IV 374
»Schuldiger» 23; cf. Prov. 28: 1.

Furca *see* natura.

»Phi», sonuit **fuscum** ridens ardaria furnum 205
     Gloria *see* invidia.

Qualis **grex**, talis rex 149

Qualis **hera**, tales pedissaeque 149
     Suringar *Erasmus* 182; Polites IV 665—6.
     Hibernus *see* farra.

Quot **homines**, tot sententiae 138, 149, 150
     See many.

Qualis **homo**, talis sermo 149
     Otto 1299; Suringar *Bebel* 117.

Homo proponit, Deus disponit 40, 55, 58, 153
     See man.
        Honos *see* onus.
        Hostis *see* civis.

Ignavis semper feriae 157
     From Theocritus; cf. Erasmus *Adagia* (1520) 443.

Tanto plus calidum, quanto vicinius **igni** 21
     See fire.

»Plus valet il quam nil», pulicem gluciens lupus inquit 205
     Werner P 68.
        Imperare *see* dividere.
        Impossibilium *see* obligatio.
        Impransus *see* civis.

Quolibet in capite viget **ingenium** speciale 138
     Proverbia communia 46.

Quod **initio** vitiosum est non potest tractu temporis con-
     valescere 95
     Volkmar *Paroemia et regula juris* (Berlin 1854) 511;
Williams *Law Magazine and Law Review* 4th Ser. XX
(1895) 289.

Volenti non fit **injuria** 95
     Volkmar 164; Williams *Law Magazine and Law
Review* 4th Ser. XX (1895) 293.

Injuria *see* jus.

Invidia gloriae comes [est] 146
    Otto 871.

Credat **Judaeus** Apelles 131
    Hor. *Sat.* 1. 5. 100. Compare Crealo Judas (Cervantes *Don Quijote* II ch. lxx).

Quem **Juppiter** vult perdere, dementat prius 20
    Chabert »Juppiter dementat» *Revue des études anciennes* XX (1918) 141—63; Polites IV 73 —5.

Summum **jus,** summa injuria 88
    Otto 884; Büchmann 367; Tilley 200; Quitard 485;
Seiler *Lehnsprichwort* V 226.

        Laus *see* vesper.

De minimis non curat **lex** 96
    Volkmar 502; Williams *Law Magazine and Law Review* 4th Ser. XX (1895) 294.

Leges bonae ex malis moribus procreantur 88
    Otto 944.

        Lex *see* ratio.

        Loqui *see* tacere.

In discendo **lupus** nimis affirmans ait »agnus» 205
    See wolf.

        Luscus *see* caecus.

        Lux *see* crux, vesper.

Quod male **lucratur,** male perditur et nihilatur 138
    Proverbia communia 598.

Vespere laudatur **lux,** hospes mane probatur 179
    See day.

Mense malas **Maio** nubere vulgus ait 73
    See May.

Inter **manus** et mentem 50
    Otto 1035; see cup.

Contra vim **mortis** non est medicamen in hortis 123
    C. Meaux Saint-Marc 264; *see* Tod.

        Minerva *see* sus.

Parturiunt **montes**, nascetur ridiculus mus 30, 31
   Otto 1174; Altenkirch 335 —6 no. 39; Büchmann 389;
Apperson 430; Harrebomée III 124; Stoett 206; Harder
Zs. d. Ver. f. Volksk. XXXV—XXXVI (1925 —6)
278 —80.
Quot regiones, tot **mores** 150
   Suringar *Bebel* 28.
      Mos *see* leges.
      Mus *see* montes.
Naturalia non sunt turpia 171
Naturam expellas furca licet usque recurret 38
   Otto 1200; Bohn 74; *see* bone.
Necessitas dat (var.: frangit) legem 152
   See necessity.
Sub **nive**, quod tegitur, dum nix perit, omne videtur ... 47
   Proverbia communia 695.
In **nocte** consilium 147
Impossibilium nulla **obligatio** est 95
   Williams *Law Magazine and Law Review* 4th Ser.
XX (1895) 289, 293. Cf. posse (Latin).
      Obsequium *see* veritas.
Clamat **ocellus**: amat! Dolet hic manus anxia clamat ... 205
Campus habet **oculos**, silva aures 142
   Suringar *Bebel* 102; Haeckel 71; Polites II 655 —6;
Apperson 210; *see* walls.
Onus est honos 62
   Otto 829; Seiler *Zs. f. dt. Phiol.* XLVIII (1919 —20)
83 no. 27.
      Opes *see* amici.
Inter **os** et offam 50
   Otto 1311, 1035; *see* manus
Plus valet in dextra **passer**, quam quattuor extra 23
   Werner P. 69.
Plus valet in manibus **passer** quam sub dubio grus 23
   Werner P. 69.

Passere sub tecto remanente recedit yrundo 46
    Müllenhoff and Scherer II 146 nos. 157—8; Werner
P 11; Fecunda ratis 66; Polites II 388—9.
        Pater familias *see* scurra.
Paupertas omnium artium repertrix 145
    Otto 1358; *see* necessity.
        Pax *see* custodia.
Quem oderint dii, hunc **pedagogem** fecerunt 19, 20
    Margalits (1895) 380.
        Pedissa *see* hera.
P. erectus non habet conscientiam 171
Vir **pilosus** aut fortis aut luxuriosus 128
    Kane *Modern Language Notes* XLV (1930) 104 ff.
Pisces natare oportet 125
    Petronius *Sat.* 39; Otto 1428.
»Nos **poma** natamus» 209
    See apples.
Pons Polonicus, monachus Boemicus, Suevica monialis,
    miles Australis, Italorum devotio et Alemannorum
    iciunia; fabam valent omnia 102
        Suringar *Bebel* 43; Küffner 138 a—g; Walther *Zeit-*
schrift f. deutsches Altertum LXV (1928) 289.
        Pontifex *see* auctoritas.
Ultra **posse** nemo obligatur 95
    Harrebomée III 289. Cf. obligatio.
Praemonitus, praemunitus 144, 154
    See forewarned.
Ius est implere **promissa** decentia vere 138
    Proverbia communia 460; *see* promise.
        Pudor *see* timor.
Sunt **pueri** pueri, vivunt pueriliter illi 138
    Proverbia communia 443.
Qui fuit **rana**, nunc est rex 30
    See the following.
Si quis amat **ranam**, ranam putet esse Dianam 30

Otto 1505; Voigt *Romanische Forschungen* VI (1891)
561 no. 60; Bolte and Polívka *Anmerkungen* I 7; *Modern
Philology* V (1907—8) 507 n. 19; XI (1913—4) 499 n. 6.

Otto 1118; Suringar *Erasmus* 218.

Suum cuique 91

Büchmann 435; Polites IV 438—44; the classical
Latin »Suum cuique pulchrum est» (Otto 1726) has a
different meaning.

Cum loqui nesciant, **tacere** non possunt 39
Otto p. xxi, 1732.

Qui **tacet,** consentire videtur.............................. 93
See silence.

Testis unus, testis nullus 90, 93, 143
Seiler *Lehnsprichwort* V 202; Stoett 675, 1464; Chaisemartin 467—8; H. Rademin *Dissertatio juridica, vulgato
dicto Unus testis, nullus* . . ., Königsberg 1695 (Bernstein catalogue 2925).

Ubi **timor,** ibi pudor 148, 149
Suringar *Erasmus* 233; Altenkirch 352 no. 71.

Sunt **tria** damna domus:

Imber, mala femina, fumus 40, 50
See three.

Inanis **venter** non audit verba libenter.................. 123

Plenus **venter** non studet libenter...................... 123
C. Meaux Saint-Marc *L'école de Salerne* 78.

Utcumque est **ventus,** exin velum vortitur 63
Otto 1855.

Obsequium amicos, **veritas** odium parit 146
Otto 1875.

Veritas odium, prosperitas superbiam, securitas periculum, familiaritas contemptum, id est, parit......... 146
Wesselski *Poliziano* 87 no. 179; *see* familiarity.

Veritas temporis filia 147
Suringar *Bebel* 134; Hulme 22; Harrebomée III 163.
Vernus *see* farra.

Sed vero laus in fine canitur, et **vespere** laudatur dies 178, 179

Vespere laudatur lux, hospes mane probatur 26, 179
See day.

Virtus *see* discretio.
Vicina sunt vitia **virtutibus** 146
  Otto 1920.
  Vitia *see* avaritia.
  Vitrum *see* amici.
  Volens *see* injuria.
Vox populi, vox dei 41
  Apperson 664; Sutphen p. 390; Seiler *Lehnspr.* V
  265; Quitard 597—8; Büchmann 329; *Mod. Lang. Rev.*
  XXII (1927) 75 n. 4; Lean III 375.

NORWEGIAN

April grode er sjelden til gode 115
  Kock and Petersen II 88.
Boner spiser Böner 107

POLISH

Chrązszcz etc. 108

SPANISH

Dar una **calabaza** 197
Al hombre venturero la **hija** le nasce primero 73
  See donna (Italian).
Ingles borracho, Frances gabacho, Hollandes mante-
  quero, Español gran caballero 100
  Reinsberg-Düringsfeld *Internationale Titulaturen* I 7.
Italia para nacer, Francia para vivir, España para morir 102
Dexo la **lache** al vino, »Bien seas venido, amigo» 124
  See milk.
Peor es meneallo 170
  See weed.
Digo la **sarten** a la caldera, »Qui tate alla ojnegra» 158

SWEDISH

Då **Adam** vävde och Eva span, Var fanns då en adelsman? 24
   See Adam.

Man ska **börja** i rätta ändan, sa Rundqvist 214

Dag följer även på vinternatten 165

»**Snart** kommer snön, svenner», sa **finnarna,** hade skidor
   til salu 212
   Cederschiöld 23.

Grisarna skulle grymta om de visste vad galten lider ... 36

Hjälpen vore nog god, ginge bara inte maten åt 212
   Cederschiöld 14.

Ett liv utan **kärlek,** ett år utan sommar..................... 165

Menniskan spår, och Gud rår 154
   See man.

Midsommarnatten är inte lång, men den sätter många
   vaggor i gång 165

Där **odygd** åker fram, sitter i baksätet skam.............. 55
   See pride.

»**Behövs** ingen rulle», sa **räven,** drog musselskalet på isen 212
   Cederschiöld 27.

»**Inte** ett dugg», sa **Settervall** 213
   Cederschiöld 7—8.

Solen skiner også på liten stuga 165

Föra **swin** til Rhin, det blir antå swin 155

»De va fina manchetter», sa **tjuven** om handklovarna 217, 219
   Cederschiöld 29.

»Den här **veckan** börjar trevligt», sa han, som skulle
   hängas på måndagen 217, 219
   Cederschiöld 28.

LIST OF BOOKS CITED.

Adalberg, S.: Księga przysłów, przypowieści i wyrażeń przysłowiowych polskich. Warsaw 1894.

Altenkirch, R.: »Die Beziehungen zwischen Slaven und Griechen in ihren Sprichwörtern» Archiv f. slavische Philologie XXX (1909) 1—47, 321—64.

Apperson, G. L.: English proverbs and proverbial phrases: a historical dictionary. London 1929.

Bartlett, J.: Familiar quotations, [10] rev. by N. H. Dole. Boston, 1924.

Benham, W. G.: Book of quotations, proverbs and household words. London, 1924.

Bohn, H. G.: A hand-book of proverbs, comprising an entire republication of Ray's Collection of English proverbs. London, 1855.

Borchardt, W.: Die sprichwörtlichen Redensarten im deutschen Volksmund nach Sinn und Ursprung erläutert. Leipzig [1] 1889,[6] 1925. The second to the fifth editions were revised by G. Wustmann; the sixth by Schoppe. The work is usually referred to as Borchardt-Wustmann.

Büchmann, G.: Geflügelte Worte; der Citatenschatz des deutschen Volkes. Leipzig [1] 1864, Berlin [25] 1912. The preface to the last edition gives an interesting account of the history of this book.

Burckhardt, J. L.: Arabic Proverbs; or the manners and customs of the ancient Egyptians. London [1] 1830, [2] 1875; German transl. Weimar, 1834.

Cederschiöld, G.: Om ordstäv och andra ämnen. Lund, 1923. The first essay, »Om ordstäv», (pp. 5—34) is reprinted from Letterst. tidskr. (1916) 521 ff.

Chaisemartin, A.: Proverbes et maximes du droit germanique étudiés en eux-mêmes et dans leurs rapports avec le droit français. Paris, 1891.

de Cock, A.: Spreekwoorden en zegswijzen, afkomstig van oude gebruiken. Gent [1] 1905, [2] 1908.

—»— Spreekwoorden, zegswijzen en uitdrukkingen op volksgeloof berustend. II. Antwerp, 1920—22.

—»— Spreekwoorden en zegswijzen over de vrouwen, de liefde en het huwelijk. Gent, 1911.

These three books by de Cock appeared first in the form of articles in Volkskunde (Ghent). All of them contain valuable collectanea and comment.

Dejardin, J.: Dictionnaire des spots ou proverbes wallons . . . précédé d'un étude sur les proverbes par J. Stecher. Liège, 1863.

Dunwoody, H. H. C.: Weather proverbs (Signal Service Notes IX). Washington, 1883.

Fecunda ratis, see Egbert of Liège.

Graf, E. and *M. Dietherr:* Deutsche Rechtssprichwörter. Nördlingen, [1] 1864, [2] 1869.

Haeckel, W.: Das Sprichwort bei Chaucer (Erlanger Beiträge zur englischen Philologie VIII). Erlangen, 1890.

Harrebomée, P. J.: Spreekwoordenboek der nederlandsche taal. III. Utrecht, 1858—70.

Hazlitt, W. C.: English proverbs and proverbial phrases. London [1] 1869, [2] 1882, [3] 1907.

Hellmann, G.: »Über den Ursprung der volkstümlichen Wetterregeln (Bauernregeln)», Sitzungsberichte der preussischen Akademie, physikalisch-mathematische Klasse, 1923, 148—170.

Hulme, F. E.: Proverb Lore. London, 1902, 1906.

Jente, R.: »The Proverbs of Shakespeare with early and contemporary parallels.» Washington University Studies (St Louis) Humanistic series XII (1926) 391—444.

Kock, A. and *Carl af Petersens,* Östnordiska och latinska medeltidsordspråk: Peder Låles ordspråk och en motsvarande svensk samling (Samfund til udgivelse af gammel nordisk litteratur XX), II. Kobenhavn, 1889—94.

Krumbacher, K.: »Mittelgriechische Sprichwörter» Sitzungsberichte der philos.-philol. u. d. hist. Classe d.k. bayer. Akad. (Munich) 1893 II no. 1; ibid., 1900.

Küffner, G. M.: Die Deutschen im Sprichwort. Diss. Heidelberg, 1899.

Lauchert, F.: Sprichwörter und sprichwörtliche Redensarten bei P. Abraham a S. Clara. Bonn, 1893.

Lean, V. S.: Collectanea. IV in 5 vols. Bristol, 1902—4.

Lenschau, M.: Grimmelshausens Sprichwörter. Frankfurt a. M.
1924.

Le Roux de Lincy: Le Livre des proverbes français. II. Paris, [1] 1842,
[2] 1859.

Margalits, E.: Florilegium proverbiorum universae latinitatis.
Budapest, 1895; Supplementum ad Opus Florilegium. 1910.

Martin, P.: Studien auf dem Gebiete des griechischen Sprichworts.
Programm. Plauen i.V. 1889.

Marvin D. E.: The antiquity of proverbs. New York, 1922.

—»— Curiosities in proverbs. New York, 1916.

Mau, E.: Dansk ordsprogs-skat. II. Copenhagen, 1899.

de Morawski, J.: Les Diz et proverbes des sages. Paris, 1924.

Müllenhoff, K. and *W. Scherer,* Denkmäler deutscher Poesie und
Prosa aus dem 8.—12. Jahrhundert.[3] by E. Steinmeyer. Berlin, 1892.

Northall, G. F.: English folk-rhymes. London, 1892.

O'Rahilly, T. F.: A miscellany of Irish proverbs. Dublin, 1922.

Otto, A.: Die Sprichwörter und sprichwörtlichen Redensarten der
Römer. Leipzig, 1890.

Polites, N. G.: Paroimiai (Bibliotheke Marasle 5). IV. Athens,
1899—1902.

Proverbia communia (ed. *H. A. Hoffmann* von Fallersleben),
»Horae Belgicae», XI. Hannover, 1854.

Quitard, P. M.: Dictionnaire étymologique, historique et anec-
dotique des proverbes et des locutions proverbiales de la
langue française. Paris, 1842.

von(Reinsberg)-Düringsfeld, Ida and *O. Freiherr von Reinsberg-
Düringsfeld,* Sprichwörter der germanischen und romanischen
Sprachen vergleichend zusammengestellt. II. Leipzig, 1872.

Freiherr von Reinsberg-Düringsfeld, O.: Internationale Titulaturen.
II. Leipzig, 1863.

Richter, A.: Deutsche Redensarten. Leipzig, [1]1889, [2]1893, [3]1910,
[4]1921.

Schrader, H.: Der Bilderschmuck der deutschen Sprache. Weimar,
[5]1896.

Schulze, C.: Die biblischen Sprichwörter der deutschen Sprache.
Göttingen, 1860.

Seiler, F.: Deutsche Kultur im Spiegel des deutschen Lehnworts.
Pts. 5—8: Das deutsche Lehnsprichwort. Halle, 1921 ff.

—»— Deutsche Sprichwörterkunde (Handbuch des deutschen
Unterrichts IV iii). Munich, 1922.

Singer, S.: »Alte schweizerische Sprichwörter» Schweizerisches
Archiv f. Volkskunde XX (1916) 389—419.

Skeat, W. W.: Early English Proverbs. Oxford, 1910.

Stoett, F. A.: Nederlandsche spreekwoorden, spreekwijzen, uitdrukkingen en gezegden. II. Zutphen, 1924—5.

Ström, F.: Svenskarna i sina ordspråk. Stockholm, 1926.

Suringar, W. H. D.: Erasmus over nederlandsche spreekwoorden
en spreekwoordenlijke uitdrukkingen. Utrecht, 1873.

—»— (ed.) Heinrich Bebel's Proverbia germanica. Leiden, 1879.

Sutphen, M. C.: A collection of Latin proverbs. Baltimore, 1902.

Terner, E.: Die Wortbildung im deutschen Sprichwort. Diss.
(Giessen). Gelsenkirchen, 1908.

Thiele, E.: (ed.) Luthers Sprichwörtersammlung. Weimar, 1900.

Tilley, M. P.: Elizabethan Proverb lore in Lyly's Euphues and
Pettie's Petite Pallace (Univ. of Michigan Publ. in lang.
and lit. II). New York, 1926.

Trench, R. C.: On the lessons in proverbs. London, [1] 1853, many
later reprints. Final edition ed. by A. Smythe Palmer,
London, 1905.

Tuinman, C.: De oorsprong en uitlegging van dagelyks gebruikte
nederduitsche spreekwoorden. II. Middelburg, 1720.

Volkmar, L.: Paroemia et regula juris. Berlin, 1854.

Wander, K. F. W.: Deutsches Sprichwörter-lexikon. V. Leipzig,
1867—80.

Werner, J.: Lateinische Sprichwörter und Sinnsprüche des Mittelalters (Sammlung mittellateinischer Texte III). Heidelberg,
1912.

Wesselski, A.: (ed., tr.) Angelo Polizianos Tagebuch. Leipzig, 1929.

Wesselski, A.: Erlesenes (Gesellschaft deutscher Bücherfreunde in
Böhmen VIII). Prague, 1928.

Winter, G.: Unbeflügelte Worte. Augsburg, 1888.

Zingerle, I. V.: Die deutschen Sprichwörter im Mittelalter. Vienna,
1864.

Reprinted for private circulation from
MODERN PHILOLOGY, Vol. XXX, No. 2, November, 1932
PRINTED IN THE U.S.A.

AN INTRODUCTORY BIBLIOGRAPHY FOR THE STUDY OF PROVERBS

IN SO large a field as the study of proverbs it is altogether desirable
to assemble in convenient form the more useful and important
scholarly aids: the bibliographies of proverb collections, the
standard collections in different languages, and the significant books
and articles about proverbs. Interest in proverbs extends over a very
long period of time, from the writing of the Old Testament to the
present day, and every language of any cultural importance has made
some contribution to the proverbial stock. Historically and linguisti-
cally, then, the study of proverbs is a subject of wide scope. A review
of the available materials will serve a useful purpose in pointing out
an attractive field for investigation. The problems involved are usually not very difficult; and they are often very interesting and attractive because they may deal with important cultural, philological, or
linguistic facts. Until now, a regrettably small number of scholars
have given any attention to them.

BIBLIOGRAPHIES

General bibliographies.—In large measure the works of Nopitsch,
Literatur der Sprichwörter (Nürnberg, 1822; 2d ed. [1833], unchanged),
and Duplessis, *Bibliographie parémiologique* (Paris, 1847), with the useful but not very extensive supplement of Brunet, "Bibliographie des
proverbes," *Bulletin du bibliophile belge*, IX (1852), 233–40, are superseded by W. Bonser and T. A. Stephens, *Proverb Literature* ("Publications of the Folk-Lore Society," Vol. LXXXIX [London, 1930]). Yet
the many excerpts and critical comments in Duplessis are still very
useful. Occasionally, the indications in Nopitsch and Duplessis are
untrustworthy, since they rest only partially on first-hand information; and the same, although perhaps less often, is true of Bonser-
Stephens. In common with all branches of folkloristic studies, the
study of proverbs suffers from the want of a good annual survey of
what has been accomplished.[1] During the past fifteen years, however,

---

[1] For a review of the various annual bibliographies of folk-lore see Taylor, *Modern
Philology*, XXIV (1926), 124–27.

[MODERN PHILOLOGY, November, 1932]   195

we have had Eduard Hoffmann-Krayer's *Volkskundliche Bibliographie* (Strassburg, Berlin, 1919 ff.), which aims to collect the materials in the European languages completely and in Asiatic and savage languages less completely. The works which I have named aim at comprehensiveness, although they do not attain it. In particular, journal articles are likely to fail to find a place in them. The annual bibliographies of folk lore include journal articles with relative completeness. Smaller essays of this sort are especially important because the proverb is so small a bit of popular tradition that it ordinarily needs only a brief study.

Two catalogues of important collections of proverb literature make no pretense whatever to completeness and are yet very useful tools in general paremiological bibliography. Their special importance lies in the fulness and accuracy of the bibliographical descriptions. They list the books in the collections of William Stirling (*An Essay towards a Collection of Books relating to Proverbs, Emblems, Apophthegms, Epitaphs, and Ana* [London, 1860]) and Ignace Bernstein (*Catalogue des livres parémiologiques composant la bibliothèque de Ignace Bernstein* [Warsaw, 1900]). The Stirling catalogue was privately printed in 75 copies and is consequently very difficult to come by. It describes somewhat over 500 items then owned by William Stirling. The collection was later increased to about 1,200. In 1866 William Stirling succeeded to the name, baronetcy, and estates of his uncle, Sir John Maxwell, and thereafter bore the name Stirling-Maxwell. The Bernstein catalogue is a beautiful example of modern book-making. Although issued in a limited edition, copies can still be found with comparative ease. It lists 4,761 items—many of them manuscripts and reprints of magazine articles—and is therefore much the largest existing bibliography of proverbs. The description of the books is extremely complete, and title-pages are often reproduced. Like the Stirling catalogue, it names only the books in Bernstein's possession; the omissions are sometimes surprising. The indexes to the Bernstein catalogue are full and helpful.

At present, one can form a complete general bibliography only by using Bonser-Stephens as a basis and adding the titles in the Stirling and Bernstein catalogues, the national bibliographies (which are next to be mentioned), and the annual bibliographies of folk lore.

National bibliographies.—In general, the standard proverb collections for each country contain a bibliography of the significant books and articles; a list of such standard collections is given below. The indexes of the Bernstein catalogue provide useful lists according to languages. Nopitsch, Duplessis, and Bonser-Stephens are arranged according to separate languages. There are, furthermore, special bibliographical aids for certain languages: CATALAN: A. Bulbena e Tosell, *Assaig de bibliografía paremiológica catalana o sía catálech d'aquelles obres o fragments contenint dites, aforismes, consells, adagis, proverbis, mácsimes e sentencies en llénga catalanesca* (Barcelona, 1915). CZECH: I. J. Hanuš, *Literatura přislovnictví slovanského a německého* (Prague, 1853) and F. Longin, *Slawistische Schulblätter* (Prague), II (1928), 13 ff. ENGLISH: R. Jente, "The Proverbs of Shakespeare with Early and Contemporary Parallels," *Washington University Studies* ("Humanistic Series"), XIII (1926), 391–98; and M. P. Tilley, *Elizabethan Proverb Lore in Lyly's "Euphues" and in Pettie's "Petite Pallace"* ("University of Michigan Publications, Language and Literature," Vol. II [New York, 1926], pp. 53–62. FRENCH: C. Friesland, "Verzeichnis der seit 1847 erschienenen Sammlungen französischer Sprichwörter," *Zeitschrift für französische Sprache und Literatur*, XVIII, Part II (1896), 221–37; XIX, Part II (1897), 122–23; XXVIII, Part I (1905), 260–87. GERMAN: J. Meier, "Deutsche und niederländische Volkspoesie," [Paul's] *Grundriss der germanischen Philologie*[2], II, i (Strassburg, 1909), III, "Sprichwörter," pp. 1258–81 (Zacher, *Die deutschen Sprichwörtersammlungen* [Leipzig, 1852], is superseded); F. Seiler (*Deutsche Sprichwörterkunde* [Munich, 1922], pp. 98–149) gives an admirable critical survey of the more important collections. CLASSICAL GREEK: see the bibliography below. ICELANDIC: H. Hermannsson, *Catalogue of the Icelandic Collection Bequeathed by W. Fiske* (Ithaca, 1914), p. 739. ITALIAN: G. Pitrè, *Bibliografia delle tradizioni popolari d' Italia* (Turin, 1894); a continuation down to 1912 exists in manuscript and its publication has long been promised. LATIN: W. H. D. Suringar, "Lijst van geschriften over de latijnsche spreekwoorden," *Tijdschrift voor de nederlandsche gymnasiën* (Leiden, 1861), pp. 111–34. SCANDINAVIAN: J. A. Lundell, "Skandinavische Volkspoesie in mündlicher Überlieferung," in [Paul's] *Grundriss der germanischen Philologie*[2], II, i (Strassburg, 1909), 1172–75. SLAVIC: G.

Krek, *Einleitung in die slavische Literaturgeschichte*[2] (Graz, 1887), "Sprichwörter, Aberglaube, Zaubersprüche und Rätsel," pp. 786–818. Spanish: M. García Moreno, *Catálogo paremiológico* (Madrid, 1918); J. Haller, *Altspanische Sprichwörter und sprichwörtliche Redensarten* (Regensburg, 1883); and J. M. Sbarbi, *Monografía sobre los refranes, adagios y proverbios castellanos y las obras o fragmentos que expresamente traten de ellos en nuestra lengua* (Madrid, 1891).

G. Meyer ("Zu den mittelgriechischen Sprichwörtern," *Byzantinische Zeitschrift*, III [1894], 396–408, particularly pp. 397–99) gives a good bibliography of Balkan (Albanian, Bulgarian, modern Greek, Rumanian, and Turkish) proverbs, and an even better list may be found in N. G. Polites, Παροιμίαι (Athens, 1899–1902). W. H. D. Suringar (*Erasmus over nederlandsche spreekwoorden en spreekwoordelijke uitdrukkingen* [Utrecht, 1873]) surveys in admirable manner the Renaissance proverb.

Collections

International collections.—Mayreder's bibliography ("Die polyglotte Sprichwörterliteratur," *Rivista di letteratura popolare*, I [1877], 241–65) is, although old, still useful. International collections are of two main types: a thesaurus without particular limitations and a collection according to some principle. Unfortunately, most international collections of either type are worth very little to the scholar, since references to sources are ordinarily lacking. For the most part, such collections appear to be calculated for the general reader.

In international collections of the thesaurus type we can distinguish two varieties according to the arrangement of the proverbs in one or several alphabets. The most useful works which give a general survey of proverb lore in a single alphabet are Ida von [Reinsberg-] Düringsfeld and O. Freiherr von Reinsberg-Düringsfeld, *Sprichwörter der germanischen und romanischen Sprachen vergleichend zusammengestellt* (Leipzig, 1872–75), and G. Strafforello, *La sapienza del mondo ovvero dizionario universale dei proverbi di tutti i popoli* (Turin, [1883]). Strictly speaking, the two volumes of Reinsberg-Düringsfeld do not give a general survey, since they limit themselves to the Germanic and Romance peoples. Notwithstanding the lack of references, which are in a sense provided for by the fact that the authors ordinarily use but a single source for each language or dialect, it is a useful work. It is arranged in a single alphabet according to the German proverbs. Strafforello translates most of the proverbs into Italian and omits references. Although his work is very extensive (three volumes quarto), its value is not in proportion to its size. K. F. W. Wander has translated a considerable number of foreign proverbs in his comprehensive German lexicon (*Deutsches Sprichwörter-Lexikon* [Leipzig, 1867–80]). The epoch-making *Chiliades* of Erasmus might also be mentioned here, although the materials are not arranged in alphabetical order. Erasmus based his work on classical proverbs, but added so many illustrations from the vernacular (ordinarily Dutch in Latin translation) that, in the latest editions with the usual supplements, the work is a huge compendium of proverb lore. The best recent alphabetical index of international proverbs is sufficiently described by its title: A. Arthaber, *Dizionario comparato di proverbi e modi proverbiali italiani, latini, francesi, spagnuoli, tedeschi, inglesi e greci antichi con relativi indici sistematico-alfabetici* (Milan, ca. 1929).

There is an abundance of dictionaries of proverbs which devote a section to each of several languages. One of the first in English, for example, is the admirable ΠΑΡΟΙΜΙΟΓΡΑΦΙΑ, *Proverbs or old Sayed Savves & Adages, in English (or the Saxon Toung), Italian, French and Spanish whereunto the British, for their great Antiquity, and weight are added* (London, 1659) of James Howell, which sometimes appears separately and sometimes as a part of his *Lexicon Tetraglotton*. G. von Gaal (*Sprüchwörterbuch in sechs Sprachen, deutsch, englisch, Latein, italienisch und ungarisch* [Vienna, 1830]) includes six languages. Typical collections of this sort published in English are H. G. Bohn, *A polyglot of Foreign Proverbs, comprising French, Italian, German, Dutch, Spanish, Portuguese, and Danish* (London, 1857), W. K. Kelly, *A Collection of the Proverbs of All Nations* (London, 1st ed., n.d.; ²1859; ³1870), D. W. Marvin, *The Antiquity of Proverbs* (New York, 1922) and *Curiosities in Proverbs* (New York, 1916), E. B. Mawr, *Analogous Proverbs in Ten Languages* (London, 1885), J. Middlemore, *Proverbs, Sayings and Comparisons in Various Languages* (London, 1889). Perhaps none of these is very important to the scholar; most of them may serve some useful purpose in bringing to light chance references or miscellaneous information not otherwise readily accessible.

The value of international collections based on some principle of selection is naturally determined by the merit of the principle and the care in the assembling of materials. Of course, the principle of selection varies in every instance. Collections based on a linguistic principle are unusual: Čelakovsky (*Mudrosloví národu slovanského ve příslovích* [Prague, 1852]), for example, gives a convenient survey of Slavic proverbs in a single volume; and the previously mentioned *Sprichwörter der germanischen und romanischen Sprachen* by Baron von Reinsberg-Düringsfeld and his wife is, in a sense, an analogous work, since it reviews the proverbial stock of a comparatively homogeneous group. For Scandinavia we have an undertaking similar to Čelakovský in K. Stroembaeck, *Nordiskt ordspråkslexikon*, which lists Danish, Icelandic, Norwegian, and Swedish proberbs; but, although the work, a manuscript in the Royal Library (Stockholm), is cited in the usual bibliographies, it was never published. In collections of proverbs according to subject the collector ordinarily illustrates the reactions of the folk to certain classes of people (the trades, women, or children), things (weather or dogs), or ideas (God or humor). The bibliography of such collections—for there are many of them—is best found in Bonser-Stephens, *Proverb Literature* (London, 1930), and in Taylor, *The Proverb* (Cambridge, Massachusetts, 1931). Characteristic examples of such collections are the volumes issued by the Baron and Baroness von Reinsberg-Düringsfeld, independently or in collaboration: *Die Frau im Sprichwort* (Leipzig, 1862); *Internationale Titulaturen* (Leipzig, 1863); *Das Kind im Sprichwort* (Leipzig, 1864); "Das Sprichwort als Gastrosoph," *Magazin für die Literatur des Auslandes*, XXXII (1863), 555–56, 569–71, 603–5; *Das Sprichwort als Kosmopolit: I, Das Sprichwort als Philosoph, II, Das Sprichwort als Praktikus, III, Das Sprichwort als Humorist* (Leipzig, 1863); *Das Wetter im Sprichwort* (Leipzig, 1864). Works of this sort ordinarily translate the proverbs quoted and give no sources. Their purpose is the entertainment of the general reader. An example of a scholarly work which deals with a particular subject is M. Besso, *Roma nei proverbi e nei modi di dire* (Rome, 1889; ²1904).

The classical Greek proverb.—Unfortunately, there is no comprehensive standard collection of classical Greek proverbs. The Greek paremiographers (edited by Leutsch and Schneidewin [Göttingen,

1839–51]) do not provide us with such a collection. We should note, moreover, that there is a complete break between ancient and modern Greek proverbial tradition (see W. von Christ, W. Schmid, and O. Stählin, *Geschichte der griechischen Literatur*, II⁵, 700–702; II⁶, 879–81). In the absence of even a bibliography of what has been accomplished in this direction (see, however, Christ, Schmid, and Stählin, p. 879, n. 1), the following list of collections of proverbs from the various classical Greek authors will prove useful: A. Baar, *Sprichwörter und Sentenzen aus den griechischen Idyllendichtern* (Görz, 1887); L. Bauck, *De proverbiis aliisque locutionibus ex usu vitae communis petitis apud Aristophanem comicum* (Königsberg, 1880); O. Crusius, *Plutarchi de proverbiis Alexandrinorum libellus ineditus* (Tübingen, 1887); "Zu Plutarch [de paroemiis Alexandrinorum]," *Rheinisches Museum*, XLIII (1888), 461–66; "Ad Plutarchi de proverbiis Alexandrinorum libellum nuper repertum," *Jahrbücher für classische Philologie*, CXXXV (1887), 241–57, 657–75; "Ad Plutarchi de proverbiis Alexandrinorum libellum commentarius de proverbiis Alexandrinorum libelli inediti fasciculus alter," *Verzeichnis der Doktoren* (Tübingen, 1895); "Ad Plutarchi de proverbiis Alexandrinorum libellum addendum," *Philologus*, LIV (1895), 746; E. Geisler, *Beiträge zur Geschichte des griechischen Sprichwortes* (Breslau, 1908); M. Goebel, *De graecarum civitatum proprietatibus proverbio notatis* (Breslau, 1915); L. Grasberger, *Die griechischen Stichnamen* (Würzburg, 1877, ²1883); E. Grünwald, *Sprichwörter und sprichwörtliche Redensarten bei Plato* (Berlin, 1893); G. Hoffmann, *Schimpfwörter der Griechen und Römer* (Berlin, 1892); A. Hotop, *De Eustathii proverbiis* (Leipzig, 1888) = *Jahrbücher für classische Philologie*, Supplementheft XVI, 249–313; J. Keim, *Sprichwörter und parömiographische Überlieferung bei Strabo* (Munich, 1909); J. Koch, *Quaestionum de proverbiis apud Aeschylum, Sophoclem, Euripidem*, Vol. I (Königsberg, 1887); Vol. II (Bartenstein, 1892); E. Kurtz, "Die Sprichwörter bei Eustathius," *Philologus*, Supplementheft VI (1891–93), 307–21; C. Linde, *De proverbiorum apud tragicos graecos usu* (Gotha, 1896); J. W. Lingenberg, *Platonische Bilder und Sprichwörter* (Cologne, [1872]); P. Martin, *Studien auf dem Gebiete des griechischen Sprichworts* (Plauen, 1889); E. von Prittwitz-Gaffron, *Das Sprichwort im griechischen Epigramm* (Giessen, 1912); T. W. Rein, *Sprichwörter und sprichwörtliche Redensarten bei Lucian*

(Tübingen, 1894); Rohdewald, *De usu proverbiorum apud Aristophanem* (Burgsteinfurt, 1857); E. Salzmann, *Sprichwörter und sprichwörtliche Redensarten bei Libanios* (Tübingen, 1910); O. Schmidt, *Metapher und Gleichnis in den Schriften Lukians* (Zürich, 1897); T. Schmidt, *Florilegium palatinum sententias continens ex poetis graecis collectas* (Heidelberg Programm, Leipzig, 1890); C. Schwidop, *Observationum Lucianearum specimina*, Vols. I–V (Königsberg, 1848–72), particularly Vol. II (1850); P. Tribukait, *De proverbiis vulgaribus que aliis locutionibus apud bucolicos graecos obviis* (Königsberg, 1899); L. Weber, *Anacreontea* (Göttingen, 1895); M. Wiesenthal, *Quaestiones de nominibus propriis quae graecis hominibus in proverbio fuerunt* (Barmen, 1895); C. Wunderer, *Polybios-Forschungen, I, Sprichwörter und sprichwörtliche Redensarten bei Polybios* (Leipzig, 1898–1909). For the bibliography of Renaissance and later collections of classical Greek proverbs and for the bibliography of the paremiographers, see Bonser-Stephens, *Proverb Literature* (London, 1930), pp. 39–47, Nos. 314–99.

The classical and medieval Latin proverb.—A. Otto (*Die Sprichwörter und sprichwörtlichen Redensarten der Römer* [Leipzig, 1890]) collects the classical Latin proverbs and supplies parallels from classical Greek. The additions are rather abundant (see M. C. Sutphen, *A Collection of Latin proverbs* [Baltimore, 1902] = *American Journal of Philology*, XXII [1901], 1–28, 121–48, 241–60, 361–91; V. Szelinski, *Nachträge und Ergänzungen zu "Otto, Die Sprichwörter und sprichwörtlichen Redensarten der Römer"* [Jena, 1892]) but are concerned often with sententious rather than proverbial matter. The medieval Latin proverbs have never been assembled in a satisfactory collection. A. Novarinus (*Adagia formulaeque proverbiales ex sanctorum patrum, ecclesiasticorumque scriptorum monumentis* [Verona, 1651]) gives the very difficultly accessible patristic and ecclesiastical sources. J. Wegeler enlarged his collection very greatly in the course of its various editions (*Philosophia patrum* [Coblenz, ¹1869; ²1872; ³1874; ⁴1877; Nachträge . . . . und Register, 1879); but, although he gave translations into German, he neglected to tell whence he took the proverbs. Unfortunately, all the editions of Wegeler's privately printed collection, which he finally withdrew entirely from the book trade, are very hard to come by. E. Margalits, whose large collection and its supplement (*Florilegium proverbiorum universae latinitatis* [Budapest, 1895]; *Sup-*

plementum ad opus florilegium [Budapest, 1910]), are undeservedly little known, includes patristic, medieval, and classical proverbs in great abundance, but ordinarily without naming the sources. The most extensive edition of medieval Latin proverb collections from the manuscripts is J. Werner, *Lateinische Sprichwörter und Sinnsprüche des Mittelalters* ("Sammlung mittellateinischer Texte," Vol. III [Heidelberg, 1912]); his notes are very sparse. Several editions of medieval Latin manuscript collections and didactic poems which came out before the end of the last century have admirable comparative notes; see K. Müllenhoff and W. Scherer, *Denkmäler deutscher Poesie und Prosa aus dem 8.–12. Jahrhundert* (3d ed. by E. Steinmeyer [Berlin, 1892]); E. Voigt, *Egberts von Lüttich "Fecunda ratis"* (Halle, 1889; the author's galley proof is in the University of Chicago Library, shelf-mark PA. Eg 17 F); "Florilegium gottingense," *Romanische Forschungen*, III (1887), 281–314 (and "Nachträge," p. 464); "Proverbia rustici," *Romanische Forschungen*, III (1887), 633–41; *Ysengrimus* (Halle, 1884). Perhaps the best general collection is L. DeMauri (i.e., Ernesto Sarasino), *Flores sententiarum. Raccolta di 5,000 sentenze, proverbi e motti latini di uso quotidiano in ordine per materie con le fonti indicate, schiarimenti e la tradizione italiana* (Milan, 1926).

Medieval vernacular proverbs.—Although there is little or no justification for separating the medieval from the modern vernacular proverb, there are, nevertheless, some important and useful collections which restrict themselves to the Middle Ages. The separation is merely for convenience and rests on no logical or necessary basis. W. W. Skeat's English collection (*Early English Proverbs* [Oxford, 1910]) does not pretend to give more than his casual jottings by the way. Morawski's French collections (*Proverbes français antérieurs au XVᵉ siècle* ["Les Classiques français du moyen âge," XLVII (Paris, 1925)]) is excellent. Zingerle's good, but antiquated, German collection (*Die deutschen Sprichwörter im Mittelalter* [Vienna, 1864]) is supplemented by C. Schröder's notes (("Hundert niederdeutsche Sprichwörter," *Archiv für das Studium der neueren Sprachen*, XLIII [1868], 411–20; "Aber hundert niederdeutsche Sprichwörter," *ibid.*, XLIV [1869], 337–44) and S. Singer's admirable Swiss collectanea ("Alte schweizerische Sprichwörter," *Schweizerisches Archiv für Volkskunde*, XX [1916], 389–419).

There are German dissertations dealing with the proverbs in particular medieval authors. Those in the field of English are especially good and merit praise for the generous quotation of parallels: J. Duschl, *Das Sprichwort bei Lydgate* (Weiden, 1912), W. Haeckel, *Das Sprichwort bei Chaucer* ("Erlanger Beiträge zur englischen Philologie," Vol. VIII [Erlangen, 1890]), with the addenda of A. Andrae ("Noch einmal Chaucer's Sprichwörter," *Beiblatt zur Anglia*, III [1893], 276–82; "Sprichwörtliches bei Chaucer," *ibid.*, IV [1894], 330–41) and those in E. Koeppel's review of Haeckel (*ibid.*, II [1892], 169–73); Kissel, *Das Sprichwort bei dem mittelschottischen Dichter Sir David Lyndesay* (Nuremberg, 1892); G. Walz, *Das Sprichwort bei Gower* (Nördlingen, 1907). See the excellent bibliography of R. Jente ("The Proverbs of Shakespeare," *Washington University Studies* ["Humanistic Series"], XIII [1926], 392). Dissertations on French and Provençal writers are equally numerous, although perhaps not so amply annotated: E. Bouchet, "Maximes et proverbes tirés des chansons de geste," *Mémoires de la société d'agriculture ... d'Orléans*, XXXI (1892), 81–130; E. Ebert, *Die Sprichwörter der altfranzösischen Karlsepen* ("Ausgaben und Abhandlungen aus dem Gebiete der romanischen Philologie," Vol. XXVIII [Marburg, 1884]); C. Homann, *Beiträge zur Kenntnis des Wortschatzes des altfranzösischen Wortschatzes* (Greifswald, 1900), a very useful tool in locating proverbs; A. Kadler, *Sprichwörter und Sentenzen der altfranzösischen Artus- und Abenteuerromane* ("Ausgaben und Abhandlungen aus dem Gebiete der romanischen Philologie," Vol. XLIX [Marburg, 1885]); J. Loth, *Die Sprichwörter und Sentenzen der altfranzösischen Fabliaux* (Greifenberg i. P., 1896); F. Schepp, *Altfranzösische Sprichwörter und Sentenzen aus den höfischen Kunstepen über antike Sagenstoffe und aus einigen didaktischen Dichtungen* (Greifswald, 1905); O. Wandelt, *Sprichwörter und Sentenzen des altfranzösischen Dramas* (Marburg, 1887). For medieval Provençal proverbs see E. Cnyrim, *Sprichwörter, sprichwörtliche Redensarten und Sentenzen bei den provenzalischen Lyrikern* ("Ausgaben und Abhandlungen aus dem Gebiete der romanischen Philologie," Vol. LXXI [Marburg, 1871]), and B. Peretz, *Altprovenzalische Sprichwörter mit einem kurzen Hinweis auf den mittelhochdeutschen Freidank* (Göttingen, 1887) = *Romanische Forschungen*, III (1887), 415–57. Strange as it may seem, collections of proverbs from individual Middle High German authors seem not to have been made, except in so far as they may appear in the special vocabularies attached to the editions.

Modern vernacular collections.—In the more important cultural languages—English, French, and German—the standard collections are not particularly meritorious. The English collections are incomplete, badly arranged, and uncritical in details, although the new historical dictionary of G. L. Apperson (*English Proverbs and Proverbial Phrases* [London, 1929]) marks a considerable advance. The French collections are antiquated and especially unsatisfactory. The German collections are comparatively good, but the most important collection (K. F. W. Wander, *Deutsches Sprichwörter-Lexikon* [Leipzig, 1867–80]) is far from critical in its choice of matter and contains many duplications. In less readily accessible languages, the standard collections are often models of completeness, accuracy, neatness, and availability: Bohemian, Danish, Dutch, Greek, Rumanian, and Ukrainian all possess collections of great value. The generosity of such collections with Latin, English, French, and German parallels often provides useful information on matters with which the collections are not directly concerned. Of all these collections, Polites' great thesaurus of modern Greek proverbs, which with its four quarto volumes reaches only into the letter *D*, is the most ambitious in its plan and execution. Zanne's Rumanian collection in ten quarto volumes is an invaluable guide to the Balkan and Near Eastern proverb, and often supplements Polites.

There are a few important collections which record the proverbs current in oral tradition; models for work of this sort are E. T. Kristensen, *Danske ordsprog og mundheld, skjæmtesprog, stedlige talemåder, ordspil och samtaleord* (Copenhagen, 1890), and V. Solstrand, *Ordstäv* ("Finlands svenska folkdiktning," Vol. III = "Skrifter utgivna av svenska litteratursällskapet i Finland," Vol. CLXXII [Helsingfors, 1923]). In these works, and particularly in Kristensen, as the title indicates, we have collections of proverbial and analogous materials of sorts which have rarely been included in proverbial investigations.

In the following list I name the standard collection of proverbs for each of a number of languages. Where it has seemed desirable, a sec-

ond collection or a word of comment is added. ARABIC: J. L. Burck-
hardt, *Arabic Proverbs; or the manners and customs of the ancient
Egyptians* (London, ¹1830, ²1875; German trans., Weimar, 1834);
G. W. Freytag, *Arabum proverbia* (lists the classical Arabic proverb;
Bonn, 1838–43); C. Landberg, *Proverbes et dictons de la province de
Syrie* ("Proverbes et dictons du peuple arabe," Vol. I [Leiden, 1883])
lists the colloquial Levantine Arabic proverb; C. Snouck Hurgronje,
Mekkanische Sprichwörter (The Hague, 1886), reprinted in *Ver-
spreide geschriften*, V (Bonn and Leipzig, 1925), 1–112; A. Socin,
Arabische Sprichwörter und Redensarten (Tübingen, 1878). CATALAN:
J. Musso y Fontes, *Diccionario de las ... refranes de la lengua catalana*
(Barcelona, 1876). CZECH: V. Flajšhans, *Česká přislovi* (2 vols.,
Prague, 1911–13). DANISH: E. T. Kristensen, *Danske ordsprog og
mundheld* (Copenhagen, 1890) lists the modern oral traditional prov-
erb; E. Mau, *Dansk ordsprogs-skat* (2 vols., Copenhagen, 1879).
DUTCH: P. J. Harrebomée, *Spreekwoordenboek der nederlandsche taal*
(Utrecht, 1858–70). ENGLISH: G. L. Apperson, *English Proverbs and
Proverbial Phrases* (London, 1929); W. G. Benham, *Book of Quota-
tions, Proverbs, and Household Words* (London, 1924); H. G. Bohn,
*A Handbook of Proverbs; Comprising an Entire Republication of Ray's
"Collection of English Proverbs"* (an easily available handbook; Lon-
don, 1855); W. C. Hazlitt, *English Proverbs and Proverbial Phrases*
(London, ¹1869, ²1882, ³1907); V. S. Lean, *Collectanea* (Bristol, 1902–
4). In all these collections proverbs are included on insufficient evi-
dence and older collections are excerpted without acknowledgment.
Obvious errors which are perpetuated for centuries occur. Many proverbs are taken from sources which are not English but translations.
The lack of arrangement in Lean is extremely inconvenient. FINNISH:
A. V. Koskimies, *Kokoelma suomen kansan sananlaskuja* ("Suomalaisen kirjallisuuden seuran toimituksia," Vol. CXIII [Helsingfors, 1906]).
FRENCH: Le Roux de Lincy, *Le Livre des proverbes français* (Paris,
¹1842, ²1859). Although antiquated and incomplete, the citation of
sources is excellent. GERMAN: K. F. W. Wander, *Deutsches Sprichwörter-Lexikon* (comprehensive, but includes much translated or un-
supported matter; Leipzig, 1867–80). Smaller collections are: J. Eiselein, *Die Sprichwörter und Sinnreden des deutschen Volkes in alter und
neuer Zeit* (Donauöschingen, 1838, ²[unchanged] Freiburg i. Br., 1840);

W. Körte, *Die Sprichwörter und sprichwörtlichen Redensarten der Deutschen* (Leipzig, [1]1837, [2]1861); K. Simrock, *Die deutschen Sprichwörter* (no sources; Frankfurt a. M., 1846, and many later editions, all unchanged except for the omission of the serial numbers for the proverbs in all editions after the first). MODERN GREEK: N. G. Polites, Παροιμίαι ("Βιβλιοθήκη Μαράσλη," V [Athens, 1899–1902]). ICELANDIC: F. Jónsson, *Íslenskt málsháttasafn* (Copenhagen, 1920). IRISH (in English): T. F. O'Rahilly, *A Miscellany of Irish Proverbs* (Dublin, 1922). NORWEGIAN: J. Aasen, *Norske ordsprog* (Christiania, [1]1856, [2]1881); R. T. Christiansen, *Gamle visdomsord* (Oslo, 1928). POLISH: S. Adalberg, *Księga przysłów, przypowieści i wyrażeń przysłowiowych polskich* (Warsaw, 1894). PORTUGUESE: Carolina Michaëlis de Vasconcellos, *Tausend portugiesische Sprichwörter* (*Festschrift Adolf Tobler zum 70. Geburtstage* [Braunschweig, 1905]), pp. 13–48. RUMANIAN: J. A. Zanne, *Proverbele românilor* (Bucharest, 1895–1901). RUSSIAN: V. Dal, *Poslovitsy russkago naroda* (Moscow, 1862). SCOTCH: GAELIC: A. Nicholson, *A collection of Gaelic proverbs and familiar phrases* (Edinburgh, [1]1881, [2]1882). SLOVAK: A. P. Zaturecký, *Slovenská přísloví, pořekadla a úsloví* (Prague, 1896). SPANISH: G. Correas, *Vocabulario de refranes y frases proverbiales y otras fórmulas comunes de la lengua castellana* (Madrid, [1]1906, [2]1924); F. Rodríguez Marín, *Más de 21,000 refranes castellanos no contenidos en la copiosa colección del maestro Gonzalo Correas* (Madrid, 1926), and *12,600 refranes más* (Madrid, 1931); J. M. Sbarbi and M. García Moreno, *Diccionario de refranes, adagios, proverbios ... de la lengua española* (Madrid, 1922). J. M. Sbarbi (*El refranero general español, parte recopilado, y parte compuesto* [Madrid, 1874–78]) reprints manuscripts and older books of proverbs. SWEDISH: F. Ström, *Svenskarna i sina ordspråk* (Stockholm, 1926). SWEDISH (in Finland): V. Solstrand, *Ordstäv* ("Finlands svenska folkdiktning," Vol. III = "Skrifter utgivna av svenska litteratursällskapet i Finland," Vol. CLXXII [Helsingfors, 1923]). SWISS (German): O. Sutermeister, *Die schweizerischen Sprichwörter der Gegenwart* (Aarau, 1869). See also S. Singer, "Alte schweizerische Sprichwörter," *Schweizerisches Archiv für Volkskunde*, XX (1916), 389–419. UKRAINIAN: I. Franko, "Galits'ko-rus'ki narodni pripovidki," *Etnografični Zbirnik* (Lemberg), Vol. X (1901), and later volumes. YIDDISH: I. Bernstein, *Jüdische Sprichwörter und Redensarten* (Warsaw, [2]1908; the first edition [1888–89] was reprinted from a magazine, *Der Haus-freund*).

Special collections of modern authors.—Since such collections give us first hand information regarding proverbs which are actually in use, they are extremely important aids for the scholar. A number of German writers[2] have been searched for proverbs: Abraham à Santa Clara: F. Lauchert, *Sprichwörter und sprichwörtliche Redensarten bei P. Abraham à S. Clara* (Bonn, 1893); and K. F. Wander, *Abrahamisches Parömiakon* (Breslau, 1838). Bismarck: H. Blümner, *Der bildliche Ausdruck in den Reden des Fürsten Bismarck* (Leipzig, 1891). Goethe: H. Henkel, "Sprichwörtliches bei Goethe," *Goethe-Jahrbuch*, XI (1890), 179–83; and F. Seiler, "Goethe und das deutsche Sprichwort," *Germanisch-romanische Monatsschrift*, X (1922), 328–40. Grimmelshausen: M. Lenschau, *Grimmelshausens Sprichwörter und Redensarten* ("Deutsche Forschungen," Vol. X [Frankfurt a. M., 1924]). Luther: J. A. Heuseler, *Luthers Sprichwörter aus seinen Schriften gesammelt* (Leipzig, 1824). Melanchthon and Burkhard Waldis: F. Sandvoss, *Sprichwörter aus Burkhard Waldis mit . . . . einem Verzeichniss von Melanchthon gebrauchter Sprichwörter* (Friedland, 1866). Moscherosch: A. Stöber, "Sprichwörter und sprichwörtliche Redensarten aus J. M. Moscherosch," *Alsatia*, 1868–72, pp. 319–38. Murner: A. Risse, "Sprichwörter und Redensarten bei Th. Murner," *Zeitschrift für den deutschen Unterricht*, XXXI, 1917, 215–27, 289–303, 359–69, 450–58. Hans Sachs: C. H. Handschin, *Das Sprichwort bei Hans Sachs, I: Verzeichnis der Sprichwörter* (all pub., Madison, 1904); C. Schweitzer, "Sprichwörter und sprichwörtliche Redensarten bei Hans Sachs," *Hans Sachs Forschungen* (ed. A. L. Stiefel; Nürnberg, 1894). Martha Lenschau's collection of Grimmelshausen's proverbs is a model for later workers. In English practically nothing has been done: Lyly: M. P. Tilley, *Elizabethan Proverb Lore in Lyly's "Euphues" and Pettie's "Petite Pallace"* ("University of Michigan Publications in Language and Literature," Vol. II [New York, 1926]). Scott: Anon., *The Waverly Proverbial Birthday Book* (London, 1890). Shakespeare: R. Jente, "The Proverbs of Shakespeare with Early and Contemporary Parallels," *Washington University Studies* ("Humanistic Series"), XIII (1926), 391–444. Scattered through *Notes and Queries*

[2] See a list in F. Seiler, *Deutsche Sprichwörterkunde*, pp. 53–65.

(London) one can find many useful notes on proverbs in different authors. For French the appendixes in Le Roux de Lincy (*Le Livre des proverbes français*[2] [Paris, 1859]) contain proverbs extracted from several authors. In Spanish, the proverbs in *Don Quixote* have been excerpted by U. R. Burke (*Sancho Panza's Proverbs and Others Which Occur in "Don Quixote"* [London, 1892]) and by J. Coll y Vehi (*Los refranes de Quijote* [Barcelona, 1874]).

BOOKS AND ARTICLES ABOUT PROVERBS

General treatises.—Unfortunately, most works on proverbs are written for the "general reader" and are regrettably superficial in treatment and inaccurate in detail. I have endeavored to survey the field in *The Proverb* (Cambridge, Massachusetts, 1931). In this book I have considered the proverb almost solely as it occurs in European tradition and have passed over without mention the problems which African, Asiatic, or American Indian proverbs might raise. F. Seiler's various works, although primarily concerned with German proverbs, have a general usefulness and value and supply a good introduction to many sides of proverb study: see *Deutsche Sprichwörterkunde* ("Handbuch des deutschen Unterrichts," IV, iii [Munich, 1922]), *Das deutsche Sprichwort* ("Grundriss der deutschen Volkskunde," Vol. II = "Trübners Bibliothek," Vol. X [Strassburg, 1917]). Comparable works are the long preface (pp. lxxi–ccxxxiv) to G. Pitrè, *Proverbi siciliani* (Palermo, 1880), and J. M. Sbarbi, *Monografía sobre los refranes, adagios y proverbios castellanos* (Madrid, 1891). R. C. Trench's discussion of the moral values in proverbs (*On the Lessons in Proverbs* [London, 1853; best ed. by A. S. Palmer, 1905) has enjoyed a deserved popularity. F. E. Hulme, *Proverb Lore* (London, 1902, [2][unchanged] 1906) is not so useful as its title might suggest.

Studies of individual proverbs.—The problems in proverb study are so definite and attractive that we might expect to find many brief essays with clearly conceived aims. Yet, such essays are rare; see J. Bolte, "Den Hund vor dem Löwen schlagen," *Zeitschrift des Vereins für Volkskunde*, XVI (1906), 77–81; XXX–XXXXII (1920–22), 145–46; XXXVII (1927), 19; R. Jente, "Morgenstunde hat Gold im Munde," *Publications of the Modern Language Association*, XLII (1927), 865–72, and (forthcoming) "German Proverbs of Eastern

Origin," *ibid.*, XLVII (1932); A. A. Koskenjaakko, *Koira suomalai-sissa ynnä virolaisissa sananlaskuissa* = *The Dog in Finnish and Estho-nian Proverbs* (Helsingfors, 1909) and *Sananlaskututkimuksia I: Laki, oikeus ja oikeudenkäynti suomalaisissa sananlaskuissa* = *Proverb Stu-dies, I: Law, Right, and Legal Procedure in Finnish Proverbs* (Helsing-fors, 1913); B. Salditt, "Der Schneider und die Geiss im deutschen Volksmunde bis zum 17. Jahrhundert," *Hessische Blätter für Volks-kunde*, XXX (1931); Archer Taylor, "In the Evening Praise the Day," *Modern Language Notes*, XXXVI (1921), 115–18, and "Sunt tria damna domus," *Hessische Blätter für Volkskunde*, XXIV (1926), 130–46, and "The Proverbial Formula 'Man soll,'" *Zeitschrift für Volks-kunde*, XL (=neue Folge II; 1930), 152–56. A. Wesselski has a num-ber of altogether admirable essays in *Erlesenes* ("Gesellschaft deut-scher Bücherfreunde in Böhmen," Vol. VIII [Prague, 1928]).

ARCHER TAYLOR

UNIVERSITY OF CHICAGO